# Communication, Marital Dispute, and Divorce Mediation

# COMMUNICATION TEXTBOOK SERIES
Jennings Bryant—Editor

## Organizational Communication
Linda Putnam—Advisor

DONOHUE • Communication, Marital Dispute, and Divorce Mediation

# Communication, Marital Dispute, and Divorce Mediation

William A. Donohue
*Michigan State University*

**LEA** LAWRENCE ERLBAUM ASSOCIATES, PUBLISHERS
1991  Hillsdale, New Jersey          Hove and London

Copyright © 1991, by Lawrence Erlbaum Associates, Inc.
All rights reserved. No part of the book may be reporduced in
any form, by photostat, microform, retrieval system, or any other
means, without the prior written permission of the publisher.

Lawrence Erlbaum Associations, Inc., Publishers
365 Broadway
Hillsdale, New Jersey 07642

**Library of Congress Cataloging in Publication Data**

Donohue, William A., 1957-
    Communication, marital dispute, and divorce mediation / William A.
Donohue.
      p.  cm. — (Communication textbook series)
    Includes bibliographical references and index.
    ISBN 0-8058-0387-4 (cloth). — ISBN 0-8058-0388-2 (pbk.)
    1. Communication in divorce mediation—United States.  I. Title.
  II. Series.
HQ834.D65   1991
306.89—dc20                                                          91-538
                                                                                               CIP

Printed in the United States of America
10  9  8  7  6  5  4  3  2  1

To *Susan* and *Nicholas*

# Contents

| | | |
|---|---|---|
| **1** | The Context of Communication in Divorce Mediation | **1** |
| **2** | Communicating in Divorce Mediation | **33** |
| **3** | Mediator-Interaction Management Model | **67** |
| **4** | Background Features of the Transcripts | **93** |
| **5** | Disputant Communication Patterns | **108** |
| **6** | Mediator-Intervention Strategies | **135** |
| **7** | Lessons from the Data | **161** |
| **8** | The Mediation of Ted and Betty Johnson | **186** |
| | Appendix A: Coding Procedures for Chapter 5 Analyses | **211** |
| | Appendix B: Coding Procedures for Chapter 6 Analyses | **222** |
| | References | **228** |
| | Author Index | **236** |
| | Subject Index | **240** |

# Preface

WHY THIS BOOK?

Divorce touches most people in America, either directly, through their own marital breakup, or indirectly, through the dissolution of marriages of friends and relatives. When I teach courses on conflict, many of my students talk about growing up listening to divorced, warring parents. Their faces grimace with pain when telling stories about attempts to escape the constant fighting and turmoil at home. Perhaps it was their inspiration that directed me toward learning more about the prospect of mediation and its ability to reduce destructive fighting after divorce.

Fortunately, I discovered in writing this book and conducting research in divorce mediation that it does work fairly well under most circumstances. Most parents want to take control of their child custody and visitation arrangements and look forward to participating in that decision making. Certainly, divorce mediation has its critics, and they identify some legitimate concerns about the process. But, overall, mediation offers a good alternative to the strictly adversarial divorce process so prevalent before mediation programs began to emerge. So, I hope that writing this book both supports the mediation process and contributes to its growth.

Another important reason for writing this book deals more with my intellectual interest in the process of communication. Prior to my interest in mediation, I conducted several studies in negotiation, focusing mainly in the area of labor–management bargaining. I chose to focus on negotiation because I believed that conflict offers a unique opportunity to learn about communication processes. Quite simply, conflict places a great deal of stress on the communication system. Our normally cooperative communiction practices involve frequent interruptions, inaccurate information exchanges, and rapid movement from topic to topic. However, in a competitive conflict mode, those habits become quite dysfunctional. In conflict, we need more accurate information to clarify intentions, frequent interruptions disrupt the exposure of divisive issues, and topic stability is important to make progress in decision making. So, studying conflict helps expose those pivotal features of the communication that are associated with effectiveness.

The advantage of studying mediation to learn about communication is that, in this context, more stress is placed on the communication system than labor–management negotiation. In child-custody mediation, couples essentially bargain for their children. Even though couples can choose joint legal custody that theoretically reduces the need to compete for custody, the issue of physical custody, or where the child will live, remains a hot topic. Under such circumstances, conflict can become extremely intense, and, as the chapters in the book reveal, it can quickly escalate out of control. Observing communication under these circumstances reveals many interesting insights about the limits of communication. For example, the research reported in the book indicates that communication focusing exclusively on relational problems quickly becomes destructive by gaining a life of its own, so that mediators experience great difficulty redirecting it.

Finally, I wanted to write this book to show my respect for divorce mediators. I probably study mediation because I lack the courage to step into the ring (and that metaphor is fairly accurate) with warring couples. Mediators seldom receive the kind of recognition they deserve for their work, so I want this book to provide some of that recognition. I wish I could write an advertisement for *The New York Times* and tell the world that mediators do a great job helping couples every day. This book must serve as a more modest attempt to accomplish this goal.

## WHY THIS RESEARCH APPROACH

In addition to revealing something about my motivations for writing this book, I would also like to present some of my research values to provide a rationale for the methods used in approaching these divorce mediation transcripts. First, why focus these analyses on interaction? Why not ask mediators and couples to self-report the kinds of strategies they use and build the analysis around these self-reports? The reason interaction analysis was selected is that I wanted a detailed, microscopic description of the actual strategies and tactics mediators used in coping with fighting couples. The main question this book seeks to address is, what kinds of strategies and tactics do mediators use *in relation to* the comments presented by disputants? Self-reports about strategies gloss over this microscopic, moment-to-moment development of conflict dynamics. They obscure the interaction that determines how issues emerge or fail to get developed. Whereas self-reports of strategies give researchers a feel for what mediators and disputants think are significant strategies, they fail to provide the kind of detailed information necessary to adequately understand the communication dynamics in divorce mediation.

Second, why select actual divorce mediation transcripts for analyses? Analyzing simulated transcripts is certainly more simple because the researcher can control the length of the interactions, topics, and even mediator intervention strategies, if desired. Focusing on actual mediations is more messy in the sense that transcripts vary a great deal from mediator to mediator and situation to situation. On the other hand, it is difficult to simulate parents bargaining for their children. The intensity of that conflict cannot be easily simulated. Couples reveal very intimate details of their lives that simulations simply cannot match. I suspect that a mediator would not give much credibility to analyses of simulated divorce mediation transcripts.

Third, the analyses provided in this book are meant to be descriptive of communication patterns in divorce mediation. The analyses do not intend to make any causal claims about mediation. Making such claims requires controlling the research context and manipulating strategies and other variables. As indicated, simulated transcripts are not useful at this point in our understanding of communication in divorce mediation. Perhaps simulations might be useful at some point to learn whether certain strategies and tactics *cause* certain outcomes. I enthusiastically endorse multiple methodologies in learning about communication patterns.

Finally, one of my most pressing needs for using an interaction-based research methodology is to provide mediators with a language for understanding their own and their disputants' strategies and tactics. All the texts on mediation cited in the following chapters label only mediator behaviors and ignore the disputants. Mediators need to be interaction managers. They need to *see* what disputants are doing and how to match their own strategies to those presented by the disputants. The rationale for this book may lie in the simple objective of giving mediators a language for understanding disputant communication patterns. If mediators find this language useful, I will be satisfied.

## ACKNOWLEDGMENTS

Interaction analyses of actual transcripts is a very time-consuming and messy business requiring the help of many people. I would like to thank Jessica Pearson for her generosity in providing the audio tapes from which transcripts were developed. I would like to thank Deborah Weider-Hatfield for transcribing the audio tapes and stimulating my thinking about how to approach the transcripts. Many thanks must also be extended to the people who coded the transcripts including Mary Diez, Renee Stahle, Becky Stewart, Mike Allen, Nancy Burrell, Judy Lyles, and Randy Rogan.

In addition to those responsible for producing the data, I would like to extend my deepest thanks to Linda Putnam for editing this book. If this project succeeds, she will be mostly responsible because her editing was remarkably useful and insightful. I received comments and reviews on the manuscript from Joe Folger, Allen Sillars, Mary Beth Gersich, and Hugh McIsaac. Their input was invaluable in providing direction for the project.

Finally, I would like to thank Hugh McIsaac and Tim Salius for educating me about divorce mediation. Whenever academics step into the "real world," they need guides that know the territory. These two gentlemen know this province very well and worked with me very patiently in the years I was associated with them. Their lessons about mediation, and more generally communication, still stick with me. Divorce mediation will work because people like Hugh and Tim are there to make it work. Thanks guys.

# 1

# The Context of Communication in Divorce Mediation

Husband: [To mediator] She still has the trash [wife's relatives] in the house and I'm not goin' over there with the trash in the house!
Wife: My brother has his own place. He's only living there temporarily. If I ask him to move out, he will. His girlfriend has a job. . .
Husband: Then get the pig out!

This actual interchange between a husband and wife fighting for the custody of their children during a divorce mediation session illustrates the kinds of communication challenges divorce mediators face every day. With this particular couple, the husband appeared to hold many strong feelings for his wife, whereas she simply wanted to terminate the relationship quickly and get on with her life. The husband was supporting his wife and children in the family home but objected to also supporting his brother-in-law who was also living there. The wife wanted her brother living with her for protection from a potentially physically abusive husband. The mediation ended with no agreement.

In response to this family turmoil the job of the mediator, according to Keltner (1987), is to serve as a neutral third party intervening

> into an already existing process of negotiation in order to facilitate the joint decision making process between two people who are

becoming polarized and are colliding unproductively over differences in goals, methods, values, perceptions, etc. The mediator makes no decisions for the parties, has no authority to direct or control the action of the parties, and can only work effectively when both parties are willing to the mediation. (p.11)

This definition is similar to others offered by Kressel and Pruitt (1985) and Folberg and Taylor (1984).

This book aims at learning how mediators use communication skills to facilitate disputants' joint decision-making processes. What communication patterns typify more or less cooperative mediation sessions? What strategies and tactics do mediators use to encourage integrative communication or to discourage destructive conflict cycles? In short, this book seeks to unravel the complex, microscopic interaction patterns that move mediations down more or less productive roads. This book presents the results of a research program working to discover these patterns in 20 actual divorce mediation transcripts, gathered in various southern California mediation programs.

To establish a foundation for these results, the first three chapters of this book uncover important dimensions of the mediation process that appear to affect disputant-mediation communication patterns. For example, this first chapter begins with a comparison of common mediation types to learn what divorce mediation shares with these other forms. Next, the divorce mediation context is explored in detail to understand how the legal system and issues of divorce and separation affect mediation communication patterns in general, and these transcripts specifically. Finally, the chapter concludes with a discussion of the participants' orientations, goals, and perspectives to see how they cope with these contextual constraints.

Chapter 2 begins by describing the kinds of issues and topics that commonly arise during divorce mediation, and how these concerns affect conflict intensity. Chapter 2 then focuses on communication processes in mediation by first reviewing practitioners' perspectives on communication, and then reviewing research on family communication patterns and literature focusing on verbal aggressiveness. Chapter 3 builds on these reviews by offering a conceptual framework for understanding the communication challenges mediators face in working with distressed couples. Chapters 4–6 present a series of studies exploring mediation and disputant communication variables generated from this conceptual framework. Chapter 7 integrates the results from the studies and interprets them from a crisis-bargaining framework by forwarding the argument that severely distressed couples who experience little success in mediation are actually bargaining in a crisis mode. The final chapter presents a divorce mediation simulation intended to help readers apply the concepts provided in the book, and to assess their own intervention values.

## TYPES OF MEDIATION

Folberg and Taylor (1984), Keltner (1987), Kressel (1985), and Moore (1986) provided excellent overviews of mediation types and critiques of their effectiveness. However, it might be useful to compare these types because divorce mediation makes different assumptions about the mediation process and the mediator's goals in that process.

### Labor Mediation

According to these mediation reviews, the most developed form of mediation is in the labor–management area. The Federal Mediation and Conciliation Service (FMCS), established in 1947, deals with disputes capable of threatening labor stability. Following the FMCS lead, other dispute-management organizations emerged, such as the American Arbitration Association (AAA). This group offers arbitration and conciliation services in addition to mediation to help deal with labor–management and other disputes, as well. The goal of these labor–management mediation services is to resolve these disputes as quickly as possible to avoid any violent escalation in the conflict.

In a typical mediation, both labor and management representatives select a mediator from one of these organizations after face-to-face bargaining has broken down. With strict confidentiality, the mediator caucuses with each side to learn their positions and then decides on a strategy for helping both sides exchange offers and counter-offers. For example, the mediator might carry offers back and forth between the two parties who are physically separate from one another. Or, the mediator might encourage the two sides to meet face to face and exchange proposals and settlement ideas. In general, the mediators remain strictly neutral regarding the proposals because they focus primarily on helping disputants reach agreement rather than on the substance of a settlement. This neutrality encourages each side to remain completely open with the mediators. In addition, the mediators have little vested interest in the outcome other than accomplishing the general goal of avoiding unnecessary conflict escalation. In the event of a deadlock the mediators have no power to impose a settlement on the participants and the dispute may either continue or enter the adjudication arena.

**Community Mediation**

A variety of other mediation programs have also emerged since the 1960s. Community Justice Centers provide free mediation for a wide variety of community problems such as angry neighbors, minor criminal actions, consumer–business problems, and landlord–tenant disputes. Public policy mediation programs have also emerged to deal with civil rights, environmental problems, and other state concerns (Susskind & Cruikshank, 1987). These programs are usually not tied to a court system with binding legal status. As a result, the mediators have no power to arbitrate a settlement, unless the parties agree to some form of arbitration prior to beginning the mediation (see McGillicuddy, Welton, & Pruitt, 1987).

The general model these programs follow involves first assigning disputants to a mediator upon entering the program. Often these mediators are volunteers who have an interest and perhaps some formal training in dispute resolution. Some mediators prefer to begin the process by first caucusing with each disputant separately to learn their perspectives on the issues, whereas other mediators decide to initiate a face-to-face interaction right away. In common with the labor model, the community mediators remain strictly neutral in the dispute, the proceedings are strictly confidential to encourage open communication, and the mediators retain no vested interest in the settlement. They simply desire to improve disputant collaboration and satisfaction.

**Divorce Mediation**

Perhaps the most rapidly growing form of mediation is divorce mediation. Over two thirds of the United States and many foreign countries have passed formal legislation offering divorce mediation programs. These programs began to emerge in 1963 with the founding of the Association of Family and Conciliation Courts, a court-centered organization promoting more cooperative means of resolving divorce-related disputes. Coogler (1978) began the effort to systematize the divorce mediation process with significant subsequent contributions by Haynes (1981), Saposnek (1983), Folberg and Taylor (1984), and Kressel (1985). Generally, divorce mediation programs were established to help soften the blow of divorce on children. Divorces settled through an adversarial system tend to create long-lasting and bitter disputes because couples in such a system typically do not work together to manage their problems. Mediation provides couples with an opportunity to take control of the divorce as a team through cooperative problem solving. This cooperative spirit helps protect children from severe developmental problems that can emerge when their parents fight excessively (Wallerstein & Kelly, 1980).

In their discussions of divorce mediation services, Pearson, Ring, and Milne (1983) and Kressel (1985) provided an overview of private and public divorce mediation programs. Typically, private mediation programs consist of divorce professionals who are hired by couples to help them formulate agreements about whatever issues the couples want to discuss. Because private mediators are restrained only by what the couples want to discuss, many private mediations can last for several sessions, depending on the complexity of the couples' problems. These professionals are generally credentialed as attorneys, family therapists, psychologists, or some other kind of family/divorce specialist. Because they are private, these programs are not connected with any court. The recommended agreements are presented to the courts by the couple, and the court may or may not choose to go along with them. In contrast, public mediators are court connected. That is, the mediators serve the court, and receive referrals from within the court system. For example, when a couple files for divorce, certain courts would direct the couple to seek mediation to resolve particular issues. Because courts often restrict the kinds of topics couples can discuss, public mediations consume fewer sessions than private mediations. Any agreements worked out through this system are then presented to the judge for official legal action. The public mediators generally hold credentials similar to the private mediators.

Although no specific figures are available on the ratio of private to public mediations, it seems clear that most divorce mediation activity is court connected. After all, couples directly pay for private mediation services, whereas most public programs are free, or much less expensive. Also, the couples seeking private mediation must agree to meet with the mediator. In many court programs, divorce policies may not provide couples with any choice in seeking mediation. Thus, the public programs are much more common.

Because the transcripts studied in this volume emerged from public, court-connected mediation programs, it might be useful to discuss in more detail how such programs work. Typically, courts activate mediation when parents have a dispute about child custody, visitation, support, or property resolution (mediation issues are discussed in chapter 2). Like the community justice centers, the court assigns a mediator to the case. The mediator then conducts one or more face-to-face meetings. The mediator's goal is to promote cooperative relations between the couple so they can build their own agreement. This process helps them take control of their future family structure. Generally, these negotiations are confidential, in the sense that the mediator may not testify about the case (some important differences in confidentiality are discussed later in this chapter). In the event of a deadlock, the mediator refers the case back to the court for resolution.

Publically mandated divorce mediation differs from these other mediation contexts in two important ways. First, divorce mediators in most states are mandated to help couples create an agreement "in the best interests of the child." In practice, this requirement means that the mediators are no longer neutral, but they actually represent, or become advocates for the child. As a result, divorce mediators find themselves serving as advocates for a secondary party in the dispute. This advocacy position requires the divorce mediators to assume an interventionist role in the mediation (Folger & Bernard, 1985). In this role, mediators direct the couple toward positions and issues in the best interests of the child. For example, if the couple begins negotiating a visitation arrangement that the mediator feels is harmful to the child, the mediator's job is to direct the couple away from that agreement and toward one that is less harmful. In other forms of mediation mentioned previously the mediators assume a more neutralist position simply facilitating whatever agreements disputants select.

Second, public divorce mediators are court connected. If the couple fails to reach an agreement through mediation, the judge handles the case and makes a final judgment. If the couple reaches agreement the judge typically approves the arrangement to make it legally enforceable. This "official," court-connected status gives mediators considerable power because they are inside the system that will ultimately decide the couple's fate. Although mediators may use this power differently across the various court systems, it provides them with a resource to increase the couple's motivation to bargain in good faith. Most labor mediation programs and some community mediation programs are not connected to any court that can create a legally binding agreement in the event that the couples cannot formulate their own agreement. When mediation programs are not connected to some legal system, disputants are not subject to any specific consequences for refusing to bargain in good faith. As a result, disputants can use mediation to stall for time, abuse the other person verbally, or for other illegitimate purposes. The implications of these differences are discussed later in this chapter when the specific models of divorce mediation are presented.

## THE DIVORCE MEDIATION CONTEXT

Parents considering the mediation option to help deal with their family problems face very different options from court to court. Although no comprehensive description of these options exists, several studies have provided in-depth detail of various court systems (e.g., Little, Thoennes, Pearson, & Appleford, 1985; Payne, 1986; Pearson & Thoennes, 1985). Understanding the specific options facing the disputants studied in this book sheds important light on the results of the studies reported here.

### Voluntary/Mandatory

First, laws in different states vary according to whether court-connected mediation is voluntary or mandatory. When it is mandatory, couples with certain kinds of disputes (e.g., child custody or visitation) must try mediation before their case can be heard by the court. Mediation is mandatory in the California court system. In voluntary programs, such as Michigan, the court must inform couples of the mediation option and let them decide whether or not to pursue the option. In practice, some courts in voluntary states "strongly suggest" that couples pursue mediation because those courts strongly support mediation.

The key advantage of mandatory mediation is that people must become exposed to it. Research by Pearson and Thoennes (1985) indicates that once people try it, they find that it works to improve cooperative parental practices. Although mediation laws in some voluntary states require courts to inform parties of mediation, many are not very aggressive in their information efforts. As a result, many are never exposed adequately to the mediation option. A key disadvantage of mandatory mediation is that some couples may intensify their disputes through mediation. For example, some couples forced into mediation might use it to verbally abuse or punish the other person, or to stall for time. Although few studies have sought direct comparisons between the effectiveness of mandatory or voluntary programs, Pearson and Thoennes (1985) compared two mandatory systems (California and Connecticut) with one voluntary system (Minnesota) and found few differences in effectiveness across the three systems.

**Confidentiality**

The second dimension along which mediation contexts differ surrounds the issue of confidentiality. In the confidential context, the mediator is neither permitted to testify about the mediation in court, nor allowed to turn into an arbitrator and decide the outcome in the event of deadlock. When the mediation is not confidential, the disputants can be made accountable in court for everything they say during the mediation process. The advantages and disadvantages of confidentiality appear later in this chapter. The California court involved in our studies is a strong advocate of confidentiality.

**Topics**

The third important contextual constraint on mediation surrounds the kinds of topics and individuals involved in the mediation process. Most public, court-affiliated programs restrict mediation topics to child custody and visitation issues. In these courts, child support and property issues are handled through the traditional court system. Some courts mediate all of these disputes through various kinds of programs because they are strongly committed to cooperative dispute resolution methods. For example, Michigan is currently pilot testing a conciliation program in which the court is mediating custody, visitation, and support disputes (Staffeld, 1987). Private divorce mediators hired by the couple themselves can mediate any issue their clients wish to discuss. Regardless of their public or private status, most mediators would probably prefer few topical restrictions so they would be free to disclose any issue that might interfere with cooperative parental interaction. California programs generally restrict their mediators to child custody and visitation disputes.

Regarding restrictions on individuals, most courts discourage attorneys from participating in the mediation process along with the parents to encourage the parents to communicate with one another in a less restricted context. Many California programs frown on attorneys sitting in on the mediation process. However, the attorneys can review the agreements with the mediators and the couple following the mediation sessions.

## Outcome Options

Fourth, interaction is often affected by the types of child custody and visitation options offered legally in a state. Most states are turning to a joint custody arrangement in which each parent retains equal legal custody of the minor child. The evidence on the effectiveness of pursuing the joint custody option appears quite promising. In a recent Michigan study, Stahl (1986) found that

> nearly all the family members who had joint custody were pleased with their joint custodial, co-parenting arrangement. The major advantages of joint custody were found in the continued relationship of the children to both parents, the opportunity for easy and equal access to both parents by the children, the freedom from the burden of single parenting for the parents, especially the mothers, and the opportunity for the fathers to continue a stable relationship with their children after the divorce. (p. 42)

The cooperation of the parents is key in joint custody because the physical custody arrangements of the child may not be equal. For example, parents might decide in mediation to have the child live with the mother during the week and the father on the weekend and during a month in the summer. According to Stahl, cooperation is needed between parents to facilitate these logistical arrangements. The California mediators encourage joint custody in mediation because it offers an opportunity for both parents to win on this issue as opposed to setting up custody in which only one parent can win.

## Logistics

Finally, a variety of logistical considerations appear to affect the mediation context. For example, court mediation programs differ widely on the amount of time they offer disputants to reach agreement. Some programs are limited to 1 hour, whereas others, like the California program in this research, offer as many sessions as disputants need. Usually sessions last between 1 and 2 hours and are scheduled 2–4 weeks apart, depending on disputants' needs.

In addition to time, the physical surroundings in which mediation occurs can impact the mediation process. In most court systems the couple comes to the court building and sessions are held in the mediator's office or in a conference room. This location may be problematic for some disputants, particularly when the court has "sided" with one of the other disputants. For example, if the court gives legal and physical custody to the mother, and the father consents to mediate some current visitation dispute, that father might perceive that the court is biased toward the mother. Regarding seating arrangements, many mediators prefer to seat the couple side by side to reinforce the court's desire to have the parties work together in their conflict. However, mediators generally place sufficient distance between the seats so neither party appears uncomfortable or threatened.

## THE EFFECTIVENESS OF DIVORCE MEDIATION

Given these structural properties, it seems relevant to assess the extent to which divorce mediation programs have lived up to their claims. Do these programs help people more than the traditional adversarial system? The effectiveness of divorce mediation programs has received considerable attention among researchers and practitioners. In a critique of several studies assessing mediation's general effectiveness, Kressel (1985) found that divorce mediation appears to be generally satisfying to the majority of persons using such programs. The most recent research conducted by Pearson and Thoennes (1985) evaluates several programs across the country. These authors found that between 79% and 91% of those who tried mediation in these various programs expressed satisfaction with the process. They were glad they tried mediation, they would recommend it to others, and they believed it should be mandatory. According to Pearson and Thoennes (1985), three factors appear to stimulate this satisfaction: Mediation helps focus on the needs of the children, it provides an opportunity to air grievances, and it helps couples focus on the important issues. Pearson and Thoennes (1985) also learned that across the various programs, between 50% and 70% of those using mediation expressed dissatisfaction with the adversarial legal system that affords no opportunity for parents to participate in divorce decision making.

Other measures of effectiveness are less clear, but they generally reflect positively on mediation. For example, Kressel (1985) concluded that settlement rates appear quite variable across most studies. Between 22% and 97% of respondents in the studies reviewed report reaching an agreement. A study focusing on the Santa Cruz, California court system (Saposnek, Hamburg, Delano, & Michaelsen, 1984) found 75% settlement rates in all mediation cases since 1981. Of those respondents settling in mediation, 54% reported that their agreements were working satisfactorily after 1 year. In the most recent data (McIsaac, 1987), 62% of all cases entering mediation in California achieved full or partial agreement. In addition, Kressel (1985) noted that legal fees for those pursuing mediation are about one third as much as those not pursuing mediation on the average ($1,630 vs. $2,360). Also, courts with active mediation programs save many thousands of dollars annually by not having to become extensively involved in successfully mediated cases.

Although these estimates of mediation's effectiveness are encouraging, Kressel (1985) noted that they may be inflated by a variety of research method problems in the supporting studies. He also concluded that the research is not definitive regarding mediation's superiority over "adversarial" means of divorce settlement. Nevertheless, the research appears to conclude that mediation is at least no worse than adversarial methods of divorcing and may be very beneficial for certain kinds of couples under certain conditions.

## THE NATURE OF DIVORCE AND SEPARATION

Couples enter this mediation context in the face of very significant family restructuring. They are going through a divorce or they were divorced recently and perhaps they are romantically involved with another person. Children may suffer emotional problems because their daily living arrangements have changed, and their parents may be fighting about them. Generally, both parties come to rely on attorneys for advice about the divorce, their family problems, and financial protection. The extended family often finds itself in the middle of bitter disputes resulting from this family restructuring. These significant life changes must be addressed to better understand the frame of mind typically confronting couples when they enter mediation.

## Levels of Divorce

To describe the kinds of changes parents and children experience during this significant life change, psychological divorce, McIsaac (1986) identified three levels of the divorce process.

***Psychological Divorce.*** The first stage, psychological divorce, involves severing the affectional bonds in the relationship. The relationship suddenly becomes a burden and not an opportunity (Lederer & Jackson, 1968). Generally, one person initiates the psychological divorce without discussing it with the other spouse. Couples who fail to complete the psychological divorce but still complete the divorce legally can become enmeshed, or still bonded to one another. Such bonds, according to McIsaac, can be the source of intense conflict.

***Social Divorce.*** This second level of divorce is the point at which one or both parties begin taking the overt steps necessary to implement the psychological divorce. Communication breaks down, attorneys are counseled, and physical separation is initiated. Finally, two new homes are created during the final phases of this social divorce phase. Under ideal conditions parents feel satisfied with the new lives. They form different but productive new parenting roles and the children make the necessary adjustments. These adjustments are particularly successful when the children are well informed about the divorce and the noncustodial parent is involved in frequent and consistent visitation (Luepnitz, 1978). Unfortunately, many families do not make this transition smoothly and experience significant trauma.

***Legal Divorce.*** In this final level of divorce, the court steps in to define the legal rights and obligations of the parents and their responsibilities to the children. In addition, the financial assets are distributed by the court. After the legal divorce the nuclear family structure is dissolved and new structures emerge. If the couple experiences successful social and psychological divorce the legal divorce will simply legalize those arrangements. Couples unable to achieve these objectives experience significant consequences that are detailed next.

## The Causes and Consequences of Divorce

In their review of the causes and consequences of divorce, Kitson and Raschke (1981) indicated that specifying exact causes why two out of five couples divorce is very difficult due to variability across families. However, several factors appear highly related to divorcing couples. For example, high-status occupational groups have lower divorce rates than do low, whereas households with periodically unemployed husbands witness significantly higher divorce rates. Blacks are more likely to get divorced and stay divorced than Whites. Couples who marry in their teens are twice as likely to divorce as those who marry in their 20s, but marriages are less stable for women who marry in their 30s. Children of divorced parents are slightly more likely to get divorced themselves.

However, in a review of marital interaction, Fitzpatrick (1987) indicated that marital stability appears not so much related to these individual differences, but it is more a product of the degree of happiness or contentment experienced by couples. This happiness appears to be a function of each spouses's ability to tolerate conflict and to negotiate differences. Couples communicating more extensively about their differences exhibit greater marital satisfaction and contentment toward their marriage. Gottman's (1979) work on marital interaction identifies some key differences between happy and unhappy marriages that are discussed in chapter 2. Nevertheless, it is probably safe to conclude that couples who cannot communicate productively about their differences stand a good chance of experiencing marital strife.

The consequences of divorce remain most significant to mediators. As indicated in the definition of mediation cited earlier, the real goal of mediation is to help families make their divorce-induced transitions more cooperatively. Certainly, the consequences of divorce are sufficiently severe that families need as much help as possible. In their review of divorce consequences,

Kitson and Raschke (1981) reported that divorced adults are less well adjusted (able to develop a self-identity) than married or widowed people. They are more likely to demonstrate symptoms of physical and psychological stress. Also, divorced adults develop more restricted relationships with others due to ambiguous societal norms about how divorced people should act in their social surroundings.

Children also suffer serious consequences from divorce. In her review of research exploring this topic, Kelly (1980, in press) found that children develop an intense loyalty to their family structure. When the divorce comes, they experience a painful disruption of their lives. The affection of the parents typically decreases because they concentrate on fighting one another and not on interacting with the children. As a result, divorce can decrease a child's attachment to the parent, which is crucial for the child to develop a strong self-concept and a sense of independence. Emotionally, children become very sad and vulnerable because of their sense of loss and need for continuity in relationships with both parents. Unfortunately, Kelly and Wallerstein (1977) found that few parents tell their children about divorce and the changes it will bring to the family. The resulting confusion intensifies the vulnerability and pain suffered from the sense of family loss.

This kind of psychological turmoil demands a heavy toll. For example, children find it difficult to concentrate at school and experience lower academic performance during this period of depressed feelings (Hetherington, Cox, & Cox, 1982; Kelly & Wallerstein, 1979). However, Luepnitz (1978) pointed out that the children suffer most when the parents continue to fight after the divorce. She concluded that "the stress on the child of divorce is not primarily in response to the one-parent home, but rather to the turmoil involved in parental conflict" (p. 176). As conflict increases, the child's ability to adjust to the new family structure decreases.

According to another review by Kelly (1981), children adjust most effectively to divorce when the noncustodial parent maintains a frequent visitation pattern with the child. She cited research indicating that children develop a profound yearning for the noncustodial parent even when their predivorce relationship was not especially gratifying. Unfortunately, only 40% of the children and adolescents see the noncustodial parent (usually the father) at least once a week. Many fathers become angry at the mother and use the children to punish the mother by threatening custody suits. Kelly found that the more angry these men became the less likely they were to visit with their children.

However, according to Luepnitz (1978), evidence seems to be growing that parental conflict is a greater stressor for children than parental absence. Children adjust more effectively when they see the parents cooperating. When parents conflict heavily, children tend to act more aggressively toward others because they are simply modeling the aggression displayed by their parents (Grossman & Burton, 1978). It is this observation that serves as the main driving force behind mediation. By removing custody and visitation disputes from the adversarial arena of the court, couples take greater control of their lives and demonstrate cooperativeness to the children. Mediation provides the opportunity to successfully complete the psychological and social divorce referred to earlier because mediators often find themselves dealing with important relational issues separating the couple.

A third consequence of divorce relates to the economic conditions individuals experience after divorce. After a 7-year project researching court records in California, Weitzman (1985) found that divorce has radically different economic consequences for men and women. By comparing income to needs, Weitzman (1985) found that "divorced men experience an average 42 percent rise in their standard of living in the first year after the divorce, while divorced women (and their children) experience a 73 percent decline" (p. 323). She argued that women experience significant downward mobility, inferior housing, diminished recreation and leisure, social dislocation, loss of familiar networks, and intense psychological stress due to a loss in self-esteem. She indicted the present legal system because it provides neither economic justice nor economic equality.

The present legal system in California includes the divorce mediation programs. Weitzman would argue that mediation may have a problem protecting women's economic rights because the women submitting to mediation are not represented by an attorney during the mediation itself. Under such conditions, women might give in to some of their husbands' demands that could ultimately create an economic disadvantage for them. This tendency might be particularly problematic if the mediation involves any economic issues. Weitzman's critics (McIsaac, 1987) contend that focusing on the economic plight of women diminishes the focus on the family's psychological and social welfare that is a product of increased cooperation. Although the premediation, adversarial divorce system cushioned the economic problem for women by awarding them alimony, it burdened couples with intense conflict that, as just noted, creates serious negative consequences for children. This debate is certain to continue for some time.

## PARTICIPANTS' ROLES

According to McIsaac's (1986) data, between 11% and 15% of all divorce filings involve child custody disputes. When parents bring these custody and visitation disputes into the court mediation program, each participant has an important role to play. The parents are negotiators with a deep relational history; the mediator is a professional dedicated to helping the couple form an agreement; the young children helplessly await the decisions of their parents (adolescents often participate in mediation sessions); the attorneys are counselors who play many different kinds of roles. This section is intended to sort out the various roles the participants play in the divorce mediation process.

### The Mediator

Professionally, divorce mediators come from a variety of backgrounds. According to a review of court programs by Pearson et al. (1983), the majority of court-based mediators have social work or marriage and family therapy backgrounds. Also, nearly 80% of the mediators boast graduate-level degrees, whereas 20% have an undergraduate degree only. In addition, more than 70% of mediators receive training in divorce mediation that generally consists of role playing and lecturing from scholars and practitioners in the field. These data suggest that court-based mediators are fairly well trained as a group. The California mediators are highly professional and well educated, because nearly all mediators have masters degrees with some doctoral degrees, as well.

Regardless of their educational background, divorce mediators are charged with the responsibility of helping couples to achieve an agreement through cooperative decision making. However, mediators employ many different approaches in achieving this goal. In a recent paper, Donohue, Allen, and Burrell (1989) identified four models of mediation, each of which reflects a different set of goals about the purposes of mediation. It might be useful to review these different varieties of mediation to provide a feel for the range of philosophies mediators can pursue.

### The Mediator-Control Model

***Definition.*** In this model the mediator assumes the facilitator role as long as both parties continue making progress toward a settlement. When the mediator feels that progress has broken down, the mediator assumes an arbitration position and makes the decision for the parents. For example, in a child-custody dispute, if a couple refuses to compromise regarding the holiday time their child should spend with each parent, the mediator turns arbitrator and decides with whom the child spends the holidays. Under this model, the mediator's role shifts from active facilitator to actual decision maker. It must be noted that this shift is typically not simply the mediator's choice. Generally, selecting the arbitration option is typically sanctioned or even prescribed by the court or other organization sponsoring the mediation. These organizations make this option available to take advantage of some of the strengths of this model described here.

This mediator-control model has also been termed the *med-arb* model by Pruitt and Rubin (1986). The first role of the third party is to serve as a neutral mediator who performs a good-faith effort to allow the disputants to control the outcome of the dispute. However, if the mediator believes at some point that the parties are hopelessly deadlocked, then the arbitration option can be invoked.

***Strengths.*** Laboratory research examining this model finds that more concession making occurs in straight mediation in which the mediator has no control over the outcome (Carnevale & Leatherwood, 1985). However, a recent field study reports that when mediators retain control in this mixed med-arb context, disputants tend to increase their cooperativeness and focus more on the issues (McGillicuddy et al., 1987). The authors argued that this superior performance probably stems from the disputants' realization that the same person can turn against them as an arbitrator if they act too contentiously. The resulting increase in peaceful communication allows the disputants to focus on the substantive issues in dispute.

***Weaknesses.*** However, McGillicuddy et al. (1987) warned that the power available in a potential shift to decision maker can be abused by mediators if they ignore mediation and turn initially to arbitration. Opponents of this model (McIsaac, 1985) contend that any process resulting in the decrease of disputant power may create suspicion and diminish cooperation in the long run. Unfortunately, long-term data evaluating this model are limited.

Finally, the reader should not be left with the impression that mediators can choose the arbitration option as part of their style of mediation. This option is a fundamental switch away from mediation and involves removing the couples' power to work out an agreement themselves. Thus, having the arbitration option makes the mediator-control model structurally different than the remaining models that do not contain the option of moving to something other than mediation.

### The Disputant-Control Model

***Definition.*** This model holds that disputants must retain total control over the outcome of the mediation session. McIsaac (1985) said that if the mediator retains any control over outcome, disputants are less likely to openly discuss feelings and key issues. Or, under such mediator-control conditions, disputants might attempt to persuade the mediator that their position is superior, thus reducing possible negotiation and compromise. Attorneys may even caution their clients to carefully monitor the information given at a mediation session because it may be used against them at subsequent proceedings.

***Strengths.*** The disputant-control model exhibits three main advantages when compared with the mediator-control model. First is the issue of which model secures the most cooperation and satisfaction. Some studies indicate that disputant-controlled mediation obtains high levels of cooperation and outcome satisfaction (Carnevale & Leatherwood, 1985; Welton & Pruitt, 1987). These researchers attribute those desirable outcomes to the perceived fairness of the mediator, an attribute that may be missing when mediators can control outcome. When disputants control the outcome, they are more likely to accept the mediator's role and to comply with mediator requests.

A second advantage of the disputant-controlled model is that it relieves the mediator of the burden of "double processing" information.That is, when the arbitration responsibility is added, the mediator must make two contrasting judgments about the incoming information: (a) how it can help the couple work more closely together, and (b) how it might favor one disputant over the other in the event of deadlock. This potential role conflict (i.e., confidential assistant/confessor vs. judge) places an exceptional burden on mediators such that they may begin to favor one role over the other.

A third criticism of the mediator-control model from the disputant-control perspective is that a bad decision is worse than no decision. This is especially true for the mediator-control model. McIsaac (1985) pointed out that the "mediation conferences are not a proper forum for developing accurate information about the family because they are too short in duration, limited in scope, and not checked out against other equally important sources of data" (p. 64). Mediators using information gained mostly during mediation may make decisions that are fundamentally not in the best interests of the child or the parents.

**Weaknesses.** The primary weakness of the disputant-control model relates to its value when couples are unable to control themselves. When couples enter mediation with very complex relational difficulties or with histories of spouse or drug abuse, they are not in a very good position to bargain effectively. The relational problems can cloud the desire to listen despite the mediator's best efforts to help the couple hear one another. The spouse and drug problems create very large power imbalances such that one party may be too afraid of further abuse by communicating with the abusive party. Should mediators simply avoid cases in which couples cannot control themselves despite the mediator's efforts? This is a controversial question that mediators must consider.

### The Relational-Development Model

**Definition.** The next two models focus on the approach mediators should pursue in structuring the process of mediation. This third model holds that the mediator's primary function is to help both divorcing parties renegotiate their relationship so they can resolve their own problems in the future. The mediator's first priority is to develop a sense of cooperation and trust between the individuals. If this sense of trust is created, a satisfactory agreement will naturally follow. A critical assumption of this relational development model is that any agreement resulting from mediator pressure will not last; good agreements are reached voluntarily and based on a new definition of the relationship clarified during mediation.

**Strengths.** The primary strength of this model is that it forces the mediator to make a distinction between reaching an agreement and establishing a new relationship. If the real goal of mediation is to train couples to handle their own disputes more effectively, then establishing a new relationship should really be the primary goal of mediation. To accomplish this "relationship first, agreement second" objective, Wallerstein (1986) argued that mediators need a clinical understanding of relationships and communication because the outcome skill mediators seek to achieve focuses on relationship building and communication training. Mediators do not teach disputants to focus their disagreement on the issue of who is right or wrong. Rather, they encourage couples to look at the underlying relational issues separating couples (Kiely & Crary, 1986). For example, is trust, respect, or equity a concern? In these kinds of almost therapy-like sessions, the mediator tries not to force agreement or even expect to achieve agreement necessarily on all issues. Rather, the mediator hopes to reframe personal attacks into disagreements they may have on issues.

If the couple fails to both recognize these relational problems and to work out a process for addressing them on their own, the mediation process has failed according to this relational-development model. The model holds that disagreements between parents over the children are inevitable. The mediator has an obligation not to resolve all the issues, but to create methods the couple can use to resolve future conflict.

**Weaknesses.** The major drawbacks to this model include time and resources. Research remains inconclusive about the amount of time couples need to create new relationships that will allow them to more constructively deal with their conflicts. However, it seems safe to conclude that altering long-standing, dysfunctional conflict patterns might take a long time and might outstrip the resource base supporting such an ambitious objective. Without a firm basis in research, the promise of achieving this relational restructuring remains an ideal and "wishful thinking" (Weaver, 1986). Given the extensive time and monetary resources required to implement this model, it seems unlikely that courts will turn exclusively to it.

## The Interventionist Model

**Definition.** Mediators using this model pursue a more directive path by actively creating a process consistent with the mediator's own ideology and sense of morality (Bernard, Folger, Weingarten, & Zumeta, 1984; Folger & Bernard, 1985). Mediators take this course because they want to represent the interests of an absent, important third party (e.g., the children). Most state laws demand that agreements must focus on the best interests of the children. If a mediator believes that an agreement strays from this criterion, he or she will direct it toward the third party's interests. Second, mediators might believe, based on their professional training and neutral position, that their own knowledge and values should gain precedence over stands the disputants might take in the negotiations. For example, disputants might retain a value for punishing one another for alleged wrong-doing. The mediator might wish to challenge this value and to provide another that is more forward-looking.

Philosophically, mediators pursuing an interventionist stance might also feel comfortable functioning with mediator control of outcome. Both models advocate strong control over the process and outcome of mediation. Such a highly controlling model is often called *muscle mediation*. Ferrick (1986) has specified three operations for muscle mediators: experiencing, understanding, and judging. Mediators begin by experiencing the circumstances of the dispute and proceed by asking questions about possible options for solving the problems. Finally, the mediator reflects on the options and passes judgment about their viability regarding the children. This directive process embodies the priorities established by the interventionist and the mediator-control models.

**Strengths.** The primary strength of this model is its focus on the best interests of the child. Mediators using this model direct couples toward issues and proposals that most benefit the child. This advocacy position is missing in the other models and is most important in divorce mediation given that the child's interests are not represented by attorneys. Because couples coming to mediation focus so heavily on their problems with one another, the focus on the child might be lost without mediator assistance.

Some research has explored the value of assuming this more directive, evaluative orientation in mediation. For example, Jones (1988) compared a series of agreement and no-agreement divorce mediations regarding the phases of interaction used in these sessions. She found that mediators achieving more cooperative interaction and agreements followed a more directive, involved course of action. They spent the first part of the sessions relying on process and information-exchange behaviors, followed by a focus on solutions, agreements, and process behaviors. The mediators achieving less integrative behavior waited until later phases to focus on process and information-exchange behaviors.

***Weaknesses.*** Although these results tend to support an interventionist model, other studies suggest that mediators adopting this model should be careful about how they evaluate couples' comments. Jones (1987) found that mediators achieving more cooperation used more neutral nonverbal affect in their voice; those achieving less cooperation relied more heavily on negative nonverbal affect. She concluded that the evaluative affect sent in a negative tone by the mediator was reciprocated by the couple. In another study, Donohue, Allen, and Burrell (1986) found that reinforcing agreement and giving positive affect is more closely associated with integrative disputant behavior. What these studies suggest is that the positive judgmental interventions may prove more powerful in creating integrative agreements than negative judgments.

A second concern about this model, as suggested earlier, is its general inattention to underlying relational concerns. The interventionist model focuses almost exclusively on legal issues and devotes little time to improving the couple's relationship. Certainly, an improved parental relationship and less fighting would serve the best interest of the child. However, the directive, task-oriented nature of an interventionist role often precludes time to explore complex, underlying relational issues. An interventionist might be interested in helping couples understand their emotions, but only in the context of how those emotions are likely to affect their agreements related to the child.

### *Model Comparisons*

Clearly, the two most incompatible models are the relational-development and mediator-control models. Each contrasts sharply with one another on basic philosophical grounds. The relational-development model maintains that building a new, fragile relationship is probably very difficult if the mediator retains outcome control. The relational-development model concentrates not on reaching a settlement as quickly as possible; the goal is to empower the couple to resolve their own conflicts. Letting the mediator arbitrate a deadlocked session formally announces to the couple that they still communicate unproductively even after receiving assistance from a third party. The system, in effect, is "giving up" on the couple and telling them not to bother working it out between themselves. They must reenter the system whenever a conflict occurs in the future. Functionally, nothing prevents a mediator empowered with the arbitration option from using a facilitation model during the mediation part of the session. However, the mentality associated with the mediator's arbitration option stresses quick settlements that flies in the face of the relational-development model.

The two most compatible models include the relational development and disputant-control models. The neutrality built into the disputant-control model confirms the mediator's goal of helping both parties work together. Thus, the goals of each model are compatible and easily permit their integration. In fact, one can argue that the two may be complementary to one another (i.e., the knowledge of disputant control provides a secure framework within which to facilitate relational restructuring).

The interventionist model reflects elements of both the mediator-control and the disputant-control models. The interventionist wants and needs to direct couples, but not through the arbitration approach. The mediator wants to persuade the couple to do the right thing. In that sense, the interventionist still wants the couple to make the final decision. So, disputant control is still the interventionist's top priority, after having gained the mediator's insights on the issue. The interventionist still views the outcome as the top priority and demonstrates less concern for the therapeutic goal of helping the couple forge a better relationship.

These four models reflect the range of roles mediators pursue in the divorce mediation context. Aside from the mediator-control model in which the mediator has the right to turn arbitrator, mediators often mix models from time to time, depending on their case loads and the needs of the couples. For example, if a mediator encounters a couple with severe relational problems and has the time to help the couple, the mediator may begin with a session aimed at relational development. At later sessions with an improved relationship, the mediator may try to pursue an interventionist model that is more task centered. Mixing models in many courts is quite common.

As indicated previously, the court from which tapes for this book are derived endorses the disputant control model from an outcome perspective, and an interventionist model from a process perspective. The court is interested in having people open up, but the crush of case loads demands that the mediators keep fairly focused on the task with both eyes fixed firmly on the best interests of the child. Even if the couple comes to mediation with severe relational problems, the mediators are trained to stick fairly closely to the task.

To help clarify further sections of the book, it must be noted that this book develops largely from the disputant-control/interventionist model's perspective for two reasons. First, as just mentioned, the court from which the tapes for this book were gathered used this model combination. Second, most court-oriented divorce mediation organizations would probably contend that they work from this same model combination, as well. Few courts are mediator controlled, and few really spend the time needed for relational development. As a result, this book concentrates on the disputant-control/interventionist models.

## The Disputants

Although the disputants can play many roles in mediation (e.g., the wounded husband or the estranged wife), the mediator would prefer they assume the role of negotiators exchanging information, forwarding proposals and counter proposals, and offering concessions from rigid positions. Of course, the extent to which they are prepared to assume this negotiation posture upon entering mediation rests on a variety of factors. Certainly, the extent to which the couple has achieved psychological and social divorce impacts their ability to come to mediation and to bargain in good faith. However, a variety of other factors also influence the parent's negotiation stance.

### *Reconstituted Family Structure*

McIsaac (1986) indicated that families appearing in the Los Angeles Conciliation Court appear to demonstrate some unifying characteristics. He identified seven family types that routinely appear in his court. The first family is called the *Kramer versus Kramer* type after the early 1980s movie with Dustin Hoffman that involved a story about divorcing parents. In this type, the parents have decided to end their relationship and have not become involved in relationships with any third parties. The parents are competent, involved in the child's life, yet they need help in developing a sensible parenting plan. As a result, these parents are good candidates for mediation.

The second type of family is termed the *Triangle*. In this family, both parties have remarried, and the new spouse is competing inappropriately with the unmarried natural parent. The triangle created by this threesome produces an unstable relationship in which the unremarried spouse can feel outnumbered by the other side. Although the parents are competent, the competition created by the triangle produces unsatisfactory outcomes. These families are good candidates for mediation because they are competent, involved in the child's life, and generally capable of working out the inappropriate role behavior.

In the third type of family that McIsaac (1986) described, the *Child Preference*, one child in this triangle identifies with one of the parents and has stated a preference to live with that parent. As in the triangle, the family is a good candidate for mediation, except that mediators should probably include the child stating the preference in the process, particularly when the preference is not in the child's best interest.

The fourth family type, *Parent with Deficit*, is a second variation of the triangle theme. In this family, one of the parents has severe deficits (e.g., personality disorders) that limit his or her parenting skills. Although these families can be mediated, McIsaac (1986) contended that the court should evaluate them first to determine whether the deficits can present problems for the children. McIsaac said that these families are not good candidates for joint custody because the disturbed parent may not make a good model for the child.

In the fifth type of family, the *Enmeshed Parents*, both original parents remarry or couple in some way with another person, and become involved in an ongoing emotional morass, unable to work through the divorce process. These families live to fight and generally consume great quantities of mediator and court time. They often need court evaluation to determine their functioning regarding the best interests of the child. These families are not good mediation candidates because they are not particularly motivated to negotiate in good faith. Such couples need extensive therapy, or perhaps a highly facilitation-oriented mediator to help them work through these emotional problems.

The sixth type, the *Trigenerational Family*, is a variation of the enmeshed families in which the grandparents become involved in raising the children because of parental death or abandonment. These grandparents often experience intergenerational conflicts with the other natural parent who has developed a new family structure. In the seventh type of family, the *Change of Circumstance* type, one of the parents moves out of town. Both of these family types provide difficult challenges for mediators because the generational or circumstance problems are difficult to resolve. Focusing on the child's needs is generally the mediator's best strategy in trying to help these two complex family types.

### *Power Orientations and Conflict Styles*

According to McIsaac (1986), these family orientations have significant impact on the motivations and abilities of the parents to mediate. However, other orientations also appear to impact couples when entering mediation. For example, disputant's power relations are important for mediators to understand. Deutsch (1973) defined a person as powerful when that person has the resources to act and to influence others and the skills to do this effectively. When the parties differ in access to such resources as money, information, and the ability to tolerate prolonged conflict, the prospects for constructive, cooperative decision making are limited (Kressel, 1985). According to Kressel, most divorce mediation cases tend to show wives in a disadvantaged power position. Often, wives sacrifice college for their husbands, give up a career outside the home, and hold less financial expertise than their husbands.

Clearly, power differences affect negotiation behavior. Specifically, the high-power person is less motivated to negotiate in good faith and the low-power person is oriented toward giving in on key demands (Kressel, 1985). High-power persons do not need to negotiate to achieve their goals; they simply exert their power. In contrast, lower power parties concede often out of fear that they may achieve nothing at all. This kind of imbalance compromises the mediation process because the high-power person does not need to negotiate, whereas the low-power person may try desperate tactics to gain some control over the other party. When mediators sense power imbalances they can rely on a number of strategies and tactics to balance power, which are described in chapter 2.

A very significant influence on the extent to which parties in a divorce choose to work together cooperatively is the attorney for each party. This influence stems from the fact that most people turn first to an attorney when seeking divorce. The parties are very vulnerable at this emotional time and become very dependent on the attorney's advice. However, attorneys take many different approaches to serving divorcing couples, which are detailed in the next section of this chapter.

## The Attorneys

Consider a husband who has just decided to file for divorce after an emotional exchange with his wife. He selects an attorney who fails to deal with the husband's emotional state, and further holds little respect for divorcing people. The attorney may even feel that the children's interests are of little concern in the divorcing process. When these less sensitive attorneys are combined with heavily controlling mediators who are also less sensitive to the clients' emotional needs, how well can these professionals serve the best interests of their clients?

On the other hand, some attorneys may give their clients more than they need. If the couple is basically competent and capable of negotiating key issues (e.g., the Kramer vs. Kramer family model proposed by McIsaac, 1986), a heavily therapy-oriented attorney may prolong the divorce process unnecessarily to make sure that the couple is therapeutically sound. Although Kressel's (1985) research dealing with attorneys does not extend itself to such issues, the possibilities of mismatch are certainly there, particularly because couples coming to attorneys are very vulnerable. At this point, it might be useful to identify the different roles attorneys pursue in divorce to better understand their influence in the divorce and mediation process.

In his book on divorce, Kressel (1985) presented a typology of the "divorce lawyer elite" to describe the roles attorneys play in the divorce process. He identified three key areas in which opinions of divorce lawyers differ: attitudes toward the client, the objectives of legal intervention, and the nature and value of collaboration with mental health professionals. Although the typology derived from these three dimensions has not been empirically validated, it provides a useful means of understanding the divorce attorney's orientation toward divorce and mediation.

### The Undertaker

This first type of attorney assumes that the job of being a divorce attorney is a thankless, messy business. Clients are emotionally deranged such that positive outcomes are rarely possible. They also believe that psychological counseling or more therapeutic approaches to divorce settlements are of little benefit to the client. These views generally evolve from the attorney's very pragmatic approach to the world. The job is to win and all the psychology stuff is simply part of the theater necessary to win. Undertaker attorneys cannot be expected to advise disputants to seek therapy, counseling, or more cooperative approaches to problem solving.

### The Mechanic

These attorneys are also very pragmatic and technically oriented. They assume that clients are capable of knowing what they want. As a result, the lawyer's job is to ascertain the legal feasibility of doing the client's bidding. Unlike the undertaker, the mechanic does not believe that clients are poorly adjusted, incompetent people with little hope of achieving positive results from divorce. The mechanic believes that positive outcomes are possible.

### The Mediator

Attorneys with this orientation believe in negotiated compromise and rational problem solving with an emphasis on cooperation, particularly with the other attorney. The client's wants should be tempered by "what's fair." Yet, the mediator remains emotionally neutral and uninvolved in the disputants' conflicts. Unlike the undertaker and the mechanic, the mediator downplays the need to win, but will fight if pushed by the other side. Nevertheless, the mediator prefers negotiated compromise and often refuses the aggressive, conflict-oriented demands of his or her clients.

### The Social Worker

These individuals focus on their clients' postdivorce adjustment and general social welfare needs. They are concerned about their clients' (particularly women) ability to pursue a proper profession after the divorce. They keep the entire family in mind when counseling the client by attending to the long-range plans of the children, for example. They sell the view that divorce is not necessarily a remedy for marital unhappiness. Although undertakers maintain a similar view, the social workers sell this perspective to aid the clients' postdivorce adjustment. These individuals are open to reconciliation, but they do not push it aggressively. However, they will facilitate it if the opportunity arises. Finally, the social workers are enthusiastic about psychotherapy, and believe that clients, with work, can achieve social re-integration into society.

## The Therapist

Therapist-oriented attorneys actively accept the client's state of emotional strain and turmoil, and it is the lawyer's responsibility to ease this strain before the legal aspects of the case can be addressed. These attorneys look for opportunities to reconcile the couple's marriage. However, the main job of therapist attorneys is to protect their clients by making sure that their emotional stability is in tact before the legal divorce process is initiated. They assume this position because they believe that the legal system meets neither the people's psychological needs nor their conflict management needs. Therapist-oriented attorneys assume those two responsibilities.

## The Moral Agent

Finally, the moral agent attorneys reject neutrality in favor of what they believe is "right" and "wrong" about their client or the system. This stance appears to be invoked most frequently as a means of protecting the children. These attorneys will oppose clients' wishes if those wishes are contrary to the attorney's moral order. They permit themselves extensive latitude in making these judgments, according to Kressel's (1985) research.

Clearly, many different professionals with many different approaches combine to intervene in a couple's divorce. How can couples know when they are being well served by these professionals? To address this question, this chapter now turns to a discussion of what constitutes a successful divorce settlement negotiation.

## CRITERIA FOR A SUCCESSFUL DIVORCE SETTLEMENT NEGOTIATION

When most couples enter the divorce mediation arena burdened with concerns about family, children, and attorneys, they seek a successful divorce settlement. What does such a settlement look like? What are the disputants and the courts trying to achieve? To some extent the answers to these questions rest on the perspectives of those passing judgment on the settlement. However, Kressel (1985) presented a list of criteria for constructive settlements that seem sufficiently broad to cover a variety of perspectives. The first criterion addresses the resolution of issues. Have all relevant issues been resolved through the divorce process? Has the couple achieved a psychological and social divorce so they can move into the legal divorce with a newly reconstituted family structure? When issues remain unresolved, the remaining tension and conflict can severely undermine postdivorce adjustment (Johnson, 1985).

The second criterion of a constructive settlement focuses on financial and emotional costs. Are the spouses financially and emotionally depleted after the legal divorce, or does the family still retain sufficient resources to get back on their feet? In light of Weitzman's (1985) revelation that women suffer dramatic economic and emotional consequences of divorce, it is essential that mediators and courts take a long-term perspective in helping couples structure agreements.

The next four criteria offered by Kressel (1985) deal with the technical features of the agreements themselves. Are the agreements technically correct? Are they perceived as fair and equitable by the parties involved? Do they protect the rights, interests, and welfare of affected third parties, especially children? Finally, are they creative in the sense of innovative, imaginative, and flexible so they offer a constructive framework for managing future problems? In her feminist critique of mediation, Leitch (1986) contended that the court system inherently builds unfairness into agreements. She argued that mediators, courts, attorneys, and couples enter the divorce process with built-in biases that often result in unfair agreements. For example, a recent study (Beer & Stief, 1985) found that women enter mediation to avoid hostility whereas men consent to mediation because they can get a better deal. Given these initial motivations, creating fair agreements is a difficult and challenging task.

Kressel's (1985) remaining four criteria deal with the effects of the agreements. Were the parties satisfied with the overall results? Did they experience a sense of "ownership" with the agreement? Did the couple comply with the terms of the agreement? Finally, were the spouses better able to cooperate as a result of the agreement? Parties responding positively to these questions are likely to adjust well to divorce and move on to new family structures. Parties responding negatively may find themselves using the court system frequently to carry forth their individual concerns in a competitive, destructive manner. Clearly, mediation is viewed as an important step in creating more effective agreements by encouraging couples to get more involved in their divorce agreements, experience ownership and satisfaction with the agreements, and learn to cooperate on future parenting challenges.

Understanding these criteria is useful for this book because mediators view these criteria as goals they try to pursue. For example, the first criterion tells the mediator that couples are better served when all the relevant issues surrounding custody and visitation have been resolved. Because some or all of these criteria provide direct input to mediator goals, they also provide a guide for what kinds of analyses should be performed in looking at disputant–mediator communication. Certainly, this book should address how mediators: (a) process issues, (b) deal with a couple's emotional difficulties, (c) construct agreements, and (d) help couples cooperate with one another. Of course, this book provides information about these mediator behaviors and a variety of others, as well.

## CONCLUSION

This chapter establishes the context and the challenges couples confront when coming to mediation. Couples face court systems with different philosophies and approaches to mediation. They must learn how to work within the court's time constraints, legal constraints on topics, and their different approaches to mediation.

Moreover, couples must confront these concerns in the face of very traumatic consequences of their divorce. Spouses, their children, and their reconstituted families face psychological and social pressures creating problems with stress and depression. Economically, couples confront other changes that may disadvantage them tremendously.

When couples arrive in mediation they face mediators and courts with very different goals and orientations toward mediation. Some mediators prefer more controlling strategies, whereas others prefer more therapeutic approaches. In addition, attorneys vary considerably regarding their goals and orientations toward their clients. Some attorneys remain very insensitive to clients' needs and are more concerned with winning. Others focus on the social and psychological well-being of their clients. Hopefully, the mediation process can be conducted in a manner that helps couples develop insights that provide breakthroughs in negotiating the psychological, social, and legal terms of their marital separation. In chapter 2 the communication problems couples and mediators face to achieve this successful outcome are discussed in detail.

# 2

# Communicating in Divorce Mediation

Before entering divorce mediation, all the parties bring various perspectives with them that can influence communication. Chapter 1 described those various perspectives. Now the issue turns to reviewing prior research concerned with the process of mediation itself. The goal of this chapter is to lay the research groundwork for the studies presented in chapters 5 and 6.

This chapter begins by specifying the kinds of issues typically discussed during divorce mediation, with a particular emphasis on how these issues might affect the mediation process. From that point, chapter 2 reviews prior research exploring the variety of strategies and tactics mediators use to increase disputant cooperation and to improve the chances for long-term agreement. The chapter then turns to research on marital interaction and verbal aggression to learn what is known about how marital couples are likely to communicate in this highly intense conflict setting. This research is reviewed critically as a means of exposing its strengths and weaknesses as they relate to the research in this book. Finally, the chapter concludes with a series of research questions that integrate these three bodies of research.

## ISSUES IN DIVORCE MEDIATION

### The Legal Issues

When disputants enter mediation, they understand that the purpose of the session is to address certain key legal issues that brought them into the court system. The types of legal issues discussed in divorce mediation depend upon whether the mediator functions in a public or private context. Typically, private mediators can discuss any topic of interest to the disputants because they are not subjected to state laws limiting the range of topics they may discuss. The five broad categories of legal issues typically discussed in any divorce involve child custody, child financial support, child visitation, spousal support, and property dissolution (Elkin, 1985). However, most states limit court-based mediators to discuss only child custody and visitation issues. However, some states permit the mediation of both support issues. Few states permit the discussion of property dissolution in the context of disputant-controlled, public mediations. Some states, like Michigan, offer nonbinding arbitration options they term *mediation* for property dissolution. Such arbitration options are not disputant controlled in the sense that the couple interacts freely about the issues and then formulates their own decision.

In states that restrict discussions to child custody, support, and visitation, the mediator works with the couple to create an agreement that specifies, in detail, how those responsibilities will be shared. Folberg and Taylor (1984) provided a sample agreement form for mediators to use as a guide in conducting their sessions. This guide provides an excellent example of the kinds of substantive issues that must be decided in mediation. The categories contained in their parenting plan include:

*Custody.* Who will be responsible for the physical and legal custody of the minor children? Most states offer joint custody plans in which both parents can share equally in these responsibilities.
*Alternating Residences.* Where will the children live, and for how much time during the week, weekends, and vacations?
*Visitation, Holidays, and Vacations.* How frequently will the children visit the parent with whom they are not living, and at what exact hours will the visitation begin and terminate? What exact holiday schedule is appropriate for visitation?
*Parental Responsibility.* What are the exact responsibilities of the parent who has physical care of the children, including medical, educational, and cultural activities?
*Modification and Review.* At what interval (e.g., yearly) should the agreement be reviewed, and if problems arise, what should be the procedure for modifying the agreement?
*Change of Circumstance or Death of Parents.* How can the parents minimize disruption in the child's life in the event that one parent

moves away from the area, dies, or in other ways cannot meet the obligations specified in the agreement? Provisions for such events should be established.

*Financial Considerations.* What procedures should be used for paying child support, what exact amounts should be paid and by whom, and what are the ways in which this money can be spent by the recipient of the funds? How long will the payments last? What financial provisions will be made in the event of the parent's death?

*Future Conflict Resolution.* What procedures will the couple follow in the event of future disputes about the agreement?

Pearson and Thoennes (1985) indicated that individuals may need counseling before they can meaningfully discuss these legal issues. Such counseling may be needed if, for example, one person is less psychologically divorced from the relationship than the other. If one party is desperate to save the marriage, that person can severely impede any progress in mediation. Or, if the couple's children appear to be experiencing problems that prevent the couple from discussing the issues, then the counseling option might be appropriate.

According to Pearson and Thoennes' (1985) research exploring couples' responses to mediation, the custody issue creates the greatest controversy during mediation. Clearly, bargaining over the division of parental responsibilities is very emotionally demanding on the couple. When arguing for custody, each side feels compelled to make the case that the other parent is unfit to raise the children properly. Such attacks can lead to sustained, bitter arguments unless the mediator channels that energy in a more productive direction. The visitation and support issues also create serious controversies because these two issues define access and monetary commitment to the children. As access decreases, potential influence in the children's lives decreases. Also, the person receiving support becomes very dependent on that support. Thus, influence and dependency become very powerful issues in mediation.

To deal with these custody problems, courts have created a variety of custody options (Allen, 1984). These options are reviewed in detail to gain a sense of the resources mediators have available to them in assisting couples.

**Sole Custody.** In this most traditional form of custody, one parent is awarded total custody of the child with the other parent being awarded only visiting rights. The custodial parent retains all decision-making rights regarding the children. According to Allen (1984), about 90% of the sole custody awards are given to the mother.

***Split Custody.*** In families with more than one child, the judge may decide to split the children between the two parents. This arrangement may be used in circumstances when children are not bonded significantly to one another, they are old enough to handle separation, and they specify a definite preference to live with one parent over the other.

***Divided or Alternating Custody.*** In this arrangement, one spouse has sole custody for a predetermined period and the other parent has sole custody for the remaining period of time. Each parent becomes the noncustodial parent when the other parent is with the child. This arrangement may emerge when parents live long distances apart.

***Joint Custody.*** In this option, both parents retain legal custody and responsibility for the children. However, the physical custody of the child, or where the child lives most of the time, may not be evenly split. For example, one child may live with one parent during the week and the other parent on weekends. However, the key feature of this arrangement is that both parents must share the legal decision-making control of the children's lives.

Although fewer than 20 states have the joint custody option (Allen, 1984), most mediators push parents to adopt this option when appropriate because of its advantages over the other options. According to Allen and Strouse and McPhee (1985), joint custody has the following advantages: continued contact with both parents, parental participation in child rearing is encouraged, relief from some decision-making responsibilities for the custodial parent, improved overall cooperation and communication, and a decrease in postdivorce litigation. According to the Strouse and McPhee (1985) study in Michigan, fathers like joint custody better than mothers because sole custody arrangements have traditionally given very little decision-making power to the fathers.

## The Parenting Issues

Although custody, visitation, and possibly support define the legal issues disputants address during mediation, the course of these issues is often shaped by how disputants stand on a variety of parenting issues. For example, most state laws specify that custody and visitation arrangements must be in the best interests of the children. These best interests are typically based on the following parenting issues: bonding (who can best provide love and affection to the children), parental competence (who can provide the most secure home with the best environment for raising the children), and family development (what are the disputants' personal and professional goals and how might these impact the children's intellectual and spiritual growth). As a result of these criteria, the mediator must encourage the parents to discuss these issues as a basis for formulating the best custody and/or visitation option.

**Bonding.** Perhaps the most critical criterion on which custody decisions are made relates to the attachment of the children to the parents. Is one parent more psychologically bonded with the children than the other? How do they manifest this bonding in their day-to-day interaction with the children? The reason why this criterion is so critical is that, according to Pesikoff and Pesikoff (1985), "The development of effective functioning and feeling responses (for children) are closely dependent on adequate bonding between children and these attached adults during childhood" (p.53). Attachment is critical, according to these authors, because the children's identity is formed through these attachments. Feelings of self-esteem and emotional development are heavily influenced by the attachment process. A premature loss of a significantly attached adult in infancy or childhood increases emotional difficulty later on. In custody disputes, one parent may claim greater attachment to the children than the other. Parents may cite evidence about who the child runs to in times of pain or emergency. In particularly bitter disputes, a parent might even claim that the children have told that parent that they dislike the other parent.

**Parental Competence.** A second parenting issue that relates to the children's best interests speaks to the parents' general child-rearing competence. Parents may claim differential levels of competence in meeting the children's needs in addition to the love and affection associated with the bonding subissue. Who can provide the best home and the most secure environment for the children? One parent may claim that the other parent has alcohol or drug abuse problems that disqualify that person as a competent parent. Or, the parent might claim that the other party sustains affairs with multiple partners, and that such an environment is not conducive to raising children.

In very bitter mediations, two particularly troubling parental-competency issues may arise that pose special problems for mediators. First, one parent may make allegations of sexual abuse by the other parent. This sexual allegations in divorce (SAID) syndrome (Blush & Ross, 1987) appears to be increasing dramatically. Research cited by Blush and Ross indicate that children rarely lie about sexual abuse. Whether the parent is accurately reporting the children's comments is another matter, however.

The second critical issue relating to competency is physical or psychological abuse of the children. One parent may allege that the other parent beats the children, has hurt them significantly in the past, or torments the children causing psychological damage. If mediators hear allegations related to sexual, physical, or psychological abuse they are faced with a difficult decision. Should these allegations be explored as legitimate problems, or are they simply an attempt to anger the other parent or to make them look bad in front of the mediator? If the mediator judges that the allegations may contain some merit, the mediator may wish to discontinue the process and have these allegations investigated. If they appear to have no merit, the mediator may wish to continue the session, but the session may prove particularly difficult given the intense acrimony developed by discussing these topics.

**Family Development.** In addition to the kind of affection the parents share with the children and the kind of home they can provide for them, the mediator may also wish to explore a third parenting issue that might impact the child. Specifically, what are each parent's personal and professional goals? Folberg and Taylor (1984) indicated that parents must come to grips with their individual and family development in facing their divorce. How will the divorce change their personal and professional goals? The answer to this question is critical because it impacts how the children fit into these goals. For example, if the mother wishes to improve her education and professional standing in life, the amount of time she can spend with the children may be affected. Such arrangements might also affect where the children should live. Thus, individual and family development remain as an important subissue relating to the best interests of the children.

## The Individual Perspective Issues

Although the legal and parenting issues constitute the substantive focus of the couple's interaction, the mediator must also try to access the kinds of individual perspectives disputants bring to the mediation session. What are disputants' values and feelings about conflict, their spouse, divorce, the children, and so forth. Disputants' perspectives on these problems serve as their foundation for judging how to generally address these problems. For example, suppose a mother held rigidly to the value that children can be raised properly only if their mother controls their lives. Sharing this responsibility with the father is simply inappropriate. Failing to expose and discuss this value would severely limit the kinds of custody options the mother might be willing to entertain. As a result, it seems important to discuss the kinds of values and feelings disputants bring with them to the mediation session.

***Values.*** Littlejohn and Shailor (1986) conducted a study related to values of several community mediation sessions to learn about the perspectives that disputants use as foundations for their stands on the substantive issues. They found that disputants based their issue positions on three sets of values. First, disputants maintain very strong values about morality, or the proper conduct of human life. Should people be able to decide their moral standards themselves (an expressionist view of morality), or should people's standards depend on civic judgment (a republican morality)? Second, disputants rely on strong values about conflict and how it should be handled. Should outside parties handle disputes or should individuals be free to decide outcomes themselves? Should conflicts be avoided, or is there some value in sustaining conflict?

The third set of values underlying disputants' positions on issues relates to their sense of justice. Some individuals might feel that justice must make a distinction between right and wrong, and that justice is done when wrongdoers are punished. Others might argue that justice must be viewed in terms of equality, without any sense of blame, or a clear-cut sense of right and wrong. Still others might view justice as a distributive problem in which resources should be distributed not necessarily equally, but in the interests of the society as a whole. Some inequality might persist within this distribution, but the inequality is a temporary necessity to reach the larger goal.

As suggested earlier, understanding disputants' values is essential for building cooperative interaction because such understanding leads to exposing incompatible values that can sabotage an agreement. For example, if one party sustains a punishment perspective of justice, that person will only entertain options that build in some form of retribution for wrongdoing. Or, if one disputant holds an expressionist view of morality whereas the other holds a republican view of morality, then these disputants will have a difficult time coordinating options. The expressionist wants to control which moral criteria apply to the options, whereas the republican seeks to use moral criteria established by society. Exposing and then addressing such values seems critical when they get in the way of coordinating perspectives.

**Emotions.** Although these three values lie at the core of an individual's perspective on a given issue, there are other powerful influences motivating disputants' positions on issues. Folberg and Taylor (1984) and Moore (1986) indicated that individual emotions (i.e., highly complex physiological and psychological responses to external stimuli) can have a significant impact on the disputant perspectives on issues. For example, Moore (1986) cited Kessler (1978) and Ricci (1980) as scholars attempting to identify the central emotions that disputants experience during mediation. Kessler and Ricci argued that at the beginning of the negotiations, disputants often feel:

1. angry because of some immediate problem that brought them to mediation. The father may have just sued for custody because of some perceived visitation problem with the children, or one party may have recently attacked the other in some particularly vicious manner;
2. hurt because of a failed marriage and the knowledge that the family is breaking up and will never be the same;
3. frustrated because the legal system is taking them through a long process of family dissolution;
4. distrustful because the former partner has used extreme measures (i.e., the courts, to manipulate the family structure). As a result, the other cannot be trusted to be cooperative;
5. alienated and hopeless that the system and the other spouse are working against them and they seem to be powerless in changing events; and
6. fearful of possible outcomes because either party may feel that the other seeks to replace that party as a parent with another

relationship, that the children may dislike that parent because of the family breakup, or that the children will be taken away from that person and access will be significantly reduced.

Moore (1986) concluded that such emotional energy must find a release in the mediation process. Couples with intense feelings must find a way to vent these emotions to allow them to focus on the substantive issues. If the feelings remain unexpressed, they can undermine individual interests or discussions of fact. For example, a woman who is fearful that she will be replaced as a mother by the father's girlfriend and has not had a chance to express that feeling, is very likely to sabotage any agreement that gives the father more time with the children.

Also, Moore (1986) indicated that these emotions must emerge so the parties can educate one another about the intensity of their views on an issue. Typically, couples coming to mediation may not have spoken for several months or even years. As a result, their access to one another's feelings underlying certain critical issues is limited. In addition, expressing emotions helps the parent to educate him or herself on the legitimacy of their feelings. Prior to mediation, the parent may be experiencing a complex web of emotions about the divorce and may perceive that these feelings are unique or unjustified. Bringing them out in the mediation context helps the parent to better understand the emotions by putting them into words and sorting out their complexity. This process legitimizes the feelings as real and natural responses to the situation, thereby bolstering the parent's self-esteem and confidence. Such confidence will help that parent become a more powerful advocate for his or her position, which should help create a better agreement for the children.

Although disputants need to express feelings for educational and ventilation purposes, mediators must structure such expression to avoid letting it escalate out of control. Interventionist-oriented mediators, like those in the Los Angeles Family and Conciliation Court, allow the brief expression of emotion, but then ask the disputants to understand those emotions and how they might impact the mediation process and the children. A more relational-development-oriented mediator would probably focus on the emotion for much longer periods of time in a more therapeutic format. Regardless of the mediator's approach, the disputants certainly know how to get mad, but they probably cannot label the nature of their anger and understand its implications. So, mediators try to control or process the release of emotion by talking about it, labeling it, and then discussing what it means for the mediation. This process is discussed in greater detail in the next section. Nevertheless, mediators who allow couples to express emotion and then fail to deal with it, turn control over to the disputants. Unfortunately, these disputants have already demonstrated an inability to convert their crisis into constructive outcomes.

## Links Between the Legal, Relational, and Individual Perspective Issues

During a session, mediators typically try to link all three of these issue types together. For example, most topics will naturally combine the legal and relational in dispute. When discussing custody, parents often present evidence about their own or their ex-spouse's parenting competencies, or their perceptions about bonding and attachment. In visitation disputes, parents may present relational issues about spending time with the children or adjusting their professional responsibilities to include the children in specific events.

Although the links between the legal and relational issues seem fairly straightforward, the links between these and the individual perspective issues are much less clear. As suggested earlier, couples rarely retain ready access to their values and emotions. Certainly, few people receive training to label and release their values and emotions in the proper context, particularly in states of arousal accompanied by irrational thinking skills. As a result, the mediator must assume the responsibility of identifying those links for the disputants.

Moore (1986) described several strategies that mediators can use to identify such complex links. He suggested that mediators proceed in three steps: recognizing that the party has a strong emotion, diagnosing the emotion, and selecting an appropriate intervention strategy to help the party manage the emotion. For example, mediators can use *restimulation* as an intervention strategy. It involves helping the parent to surface feelings similar to those generated by some other person or event in the past. Old feelings with clear labels may help the person make sense of current feelings with no labels. Moore also advocated *active listening* that involves feeding back emotional information that may underlie a particular comment. When emotion becomes verbally aggressive (i.e., aimed at belittling the other's self-concept), Moore (1986) suggested the termination of such interactions. He indicated that verbal aggression leads only to more destructive interaction. Mediators might use many of the same techniques for exposing core values underlying disputant issues as they use to reveal key emotions. As indicated earlier, this need is particularly acute when disputants use different values in approaching their dispute.

This section identified the kinds of issues mediators must be prepared to confront in a typical divorce mediation. At this point, it is important to learn how these issues are likely to affect the process of communication that emerges during mediation. To make this link, this chapter turns first to review research examining communication processes in three conflict contexts.

## COMMUNICATION RESEARCH IN FOUR CONFLICT CONTEXTS

Preparing a review of communication research relevant to the mediation context is an ambitious task, given that much has been written about this topic and about other areas of conflict that are directly relevant to mediation (see Roloff, 1987). The review presented here draws on four areas of research: (a) works that speak directly to the kinds of strategies and tactics mediators use to help couples build durable agreements, (b) research in the area of family and marital interaction that identifies patterns of conflict couples may experience during mediation, (c) research in verbal aggression that explores patterns of interaction intended to harm the other party, and (d) research exploring communication issues in divorce mediation. Each area is critiqued at the conclusion of the chapter.

### Mediator Strategies and Tactics

Moore (1986) made an important distinction between strategies and tactics. *Strategies* define the general goal to be pursued, whereas *tactics* define the procedures that can be used to accomplish the general goal. To review research related to mediator strategies and tactics it might be productive to use Kolb's (1983) taxonomy of mediator activities. Based on Simkin's (1971) work, Kolb categorized mediator activities into three groups: (a) commu nication activities intended to facilitate information exchange between the parties, (b) procedural activities that facilitate the mediation process, and (c) substantive activities that refer to mediator-initiated input concerning the issues in dispute.

***Communication Activities.*** Recently, many authors writing about mediation have emphasized the need to facilitate communication between disputants. For example, Moore (1986) stressed the value of several active listening tactics including feeding information back to the parties about their emotions, positions on issues, or the relationship between complex issues. Such information helps the couple adopt a language or set of terms to label their feelings. These labels allow couples to exchange ideas about their emotions and the issues separating them. Saposnek (1983) also suggested pulling out critical comments that reflect important issues and emotions and labeling them. This adopted language helps the parties gain some positive control over the interaction and refrain from using terms used in past disputes that inflame one another.

Walton (1969) moved in a different direction regarding feedback. He suggested that mediators ask the parties to feed back information to one another so important perceptions on emotions and issues can be exchanged. This strategy is important because it gives the couple practice communicating positively with one another. In order to expose emotional issues, Johnson (1971) suggested using reverse role playing in which each party takes the other's perspective.

In addition to facilitating feedback, other authors emphasized the importance of various probing or questioning tactics. Moore (1986) and Walton (1969) indicated that probing is necessary to help disputants elaborate ideas and clarify their positions. Folberg and Taylor (1984) also indicated that various questioning forms are necessary for mediators to gain information from disputants. They suggested organizing this information on paper to help make links between critical ideas, and to show the parties how they are progressing through the issues. Saposnek (1983) suggested that such techniques might also deflect very hurtful or verbally aggressive comments because they would not be eligible to be written down. Mediators might wish to track on paper the legal, relational, and individual perspective issues reflected in such comments but only after they have reframed them into appropriate language.

***Procedural Activities.*** Strategically, most authors writing books about mediation emphasize the need to develop a structure for proceeding in an orderly fashion (e.g., Folberg & Taylor, 1984; Moore, 1986; Saposnek, 1983). Osgood (1962), and more recently Wehr (1979), emphasized the need for structure in conflict. These authors contend that structuring how the conflict should develop provides rules for fighting. Rules regulate individual behavior so the fighting does not get out of control. What productivity would a football game develop if most of the penalties for unsportsman-like conduct were removed? The game would very quickly degenerate into a bloody free-for-all.

Mediators establish a number of rules during mediation. One set of rules deals with the agenda of the meeting. Generally, mediators try to establish an agenda that moves disputants through a set of phases so that information builds on itself and creates the foundation for an agreement. Although phase structures in mediation are reviewed and researched extensively in chapter 6, a review of Kessler's (1972) phases of mediation gives a brief understanding of why phases are valuable.

Kessler (1972) contended that mediators should begin their session by orienting disputants to the mediation process. Explaining the purpose of mediation, the rules for interacting, and goals of the session give the parties a better understanding of what is expected of them. Next, the mediator tries to gain some background information about the children, parental bonding with the children, and information about work schedules and time allocations to the children. Using this background information, the mediator is prepared to begin the third phase, which involves discussing the various issues of relevance to disputants. Generally, mediators address one legal or relational issue at a time until it is clear that other, more significant individual perspective issues are blocking progress on the other issues. Finally, if the mediator makes progress in processing the issues, the disputants can move to the fourth phase, which involves creating and bargaining the various options generated by disputants and the mediator for resolving the issues.

In addition to this agenda, many mediators impose a variety of rules to structure the interaction. For example, Walton (1969) advocated equal air time for participants to avoid allowing one person to dominate the interaction. Moore (1986) asked disputants not to interrupt one another. He said that disputants should be told that each will have a chance to respond to the other after his or her preliminary statements. Moore also recommended setting both specific time limits for the sessions and the schedule of sessions to be conducted. He indicated that these procedures help parties assess the cost and benefits of mediated negotiations.

As the sessions move past the orientation phase, mediators may face the need to initiate other procedures to keep the discussions on track. For example, Moore recommended summarizing and grouping key issues or bits of information into less complex units. These units can then be ordered into some sequence to facilitate their discussion. Moving from simple issues to very complex, controversial issues is one kind of sequence that might help the parties learn how to interact cooperatively with one another (Pruitt, 1981; Rubin, 1981). When couples begin with less controversial issues that have a high probability of agreement, they develop a method of working together. This method can then be transferred to more complex issues.

Another procedural strategy mediators may adopt to facilitate cooperative interaction is to caucus with the parties individually before the mediation begins. Moore (1987) recommended using caucuses to improve one party's attitudes and perceptions toward the other, to generate information that one party may be unwilling to discuss during mediation, and to regulate the expression of destructive, verbally aggressive comments. He also advocated using caucuses during comediation (i.e., when two mediators work with a couple). Both mediators can use the caucuses to coordinate perspectives about the couple.

However, Markowitz and Engram (1983) and Pruitt (1981) contended that caucusing produces four problems. First, working with parties individually might bias the mediator if one party is more persuasive than the other in a dyadic situation. Second, one disputant might perceive that the other disputant biased the mediator during a caucus, thereby decreasing the mediator's potential effectiveness. Third, the mediator might exert undue influence on one party, making it easier to push unwise settlements onto the disputants. Fourth, and perhaps most important, caucuses reduce the opportunity for disputants to talk face to face. This communication practice is necessary to learn how to handle future conflicts.

Despite these drawbacks, Pruitt et al. (1987) found in a recent field study in a community mediation context that caucuses helped mediators get to know disputants better psychologically by learning their needs, motivations, and emotions. Second, caucuses allowed mediators to explain the other party's positions to a disputant to improve understanding of the issues. Third, using caucuses allowed mediators to challenge individual disputants to generate new ideas, a process that is more difficult to do under the supervision of the other disputant. New ideas might be viewed as giving in to the other party. Fourth, caucuses appeared useful in helping mediators criticize a disputant's position more readily because the other party is not present to hear such criticism. Finally, Pruitt et al. found that mediator ideas for solutions were more likely to emerge from a caucus than from joint sessions. Mediators generate ideas better in this context because they are more likely to get a positive and honest reaction to suggestions for compromise if the other party is not present.

**Substantive Activities.** Within the rules and procedures that mediators establish for discussing the issues, they use several strategies and tactics to develop the substance of the interaction. For example, Erickson, Holmes, Frey, Walter, and Thibaut (1974) suggested that mediators take a direct hand in helping disputants identify the key issues in dispute. Shaw and Phear (1987) supported this strategy and recommended a variety of tactics for generating options to solving key problems. The heart of their system involves making connections between key issues that lead toward viable options for the parties. Rubin (1981) and Pruitt (1981) recommended that mediators not only help to identify key issues and options, but work to pull out the superordinate goals affecting the importance of these issues. Without understanding disputant goals, the issues become unnecessarily complex.

In addition to helping parties pull out key issues, options, and goals, others emphasize the need to provide substantive information about the nature of their dispute. Folberg and Taylor (1984) and Moore (1986) recommended giving disputants extensive orientation information, not only about the procedures for discussion, but about conflict, children, and other uncertainties that might inhibit progress. Saposnek (1983) suggested giving information and hope to disputants so they know that others have faced similar situations and that they can succeed if they commit themselves to the process. He also recommended telling anecdotes as a means of conveying information in a more understandable fashion.

A third group of substantive strategies relates to evaluating the validity of information presented by disputants. Pruitt et al. (1987) made it clear that mediators can use caucuses very effectively to assess the reasonableness of parties' positions. Kolb (1983) indicated that such tactics as calculating the option costs and giving opinions about options are very valuable in encouraging cooperation. Indeed, the interventionist model presented in chapter 1 makes a strong case for positively reinforcing progress at every opportunity, and directing parties away from positions not in the best interests of the children. Evaluation is a key component of the interventionist perspective.

### Research in Family and Marital Interaction

Unfortunately, discussions about communication in the mediation literature presented here focus almost exclusively on the mediator, to the exclusion of the disputants. Because mediators must adjust their strategies and tactics to the disputants' communication patterns, more attention should be given to understanding these patterns. Fortunately, a great deal of research outside the mediation area has emerged to learn how marital couples communicate, particularly in conflict contexts. The purpose of this section is to identify those research trends.

***Marital Conflict and Decision Making.*** The research in this section compares the communication patterns of happily and unhappily married couples in managing conflict. For the most part, the studies in this section report that unhappily married couples exhibit few productive negotiation skills. These couples expend most of their energy attacking one another personally and responding to attacks with various defensive behaviors. The net effect of this attack–defend cycle is that the unhappily married couples listen less. They tune out statements about important issues. As a result, they rarely progress to discussing options or proposals designed to address the source of the conflict.

This review begins with some of the pioneering work in this area by Gottman and his colleagues. In his book, *Marital Interaction*, Gottman (1979) provided an excellent history of research that seeks to learn how married couples interact. Although that research stems from a number of perspectives, research addressing how married couples interact from a systems perspective appears to be most relevant to divorce mediation. The systems perspective focuses on the various communicative acts couples exchange in the course of conflict, and then explores the interrelationships among these acts. For example, when a husband expresses disagreement and negative affect, what response from the wife is likely to follow? What sequence of acts constitute healthy and unhealthy marital conflict?

To address these issues, Gottman and his colleagues examined videotaped interaction patterns comparing couples who reported living in unsatisfactory and satisfactory marriages (termed *clinic* and *nonclinic* couples) (Gottman, 1979, 1982; Gottman, Markman, & Notarius, 1977; Mettetal & Gottman, 1980). The general approach used in these studies consists of analyzing the verbal and nonverbal interaction of several samples of clinic and nonclinic couples performing a task in an interaction laboratory. The couples were asked to discuss and attempt to resolve one significant marital problem that both identified in a preinteraction interview.

Because divorcing couples could be easily viewed as clinic in their relationship, the results of Gottman's work focuses on the interaction patterns of clinic couples. As one might expect, clinic couples are not very mutually supportive, or very skilled at negotiating differences when discussing their marital problems. For example, Gottman et al. (1977) found that the clinic couples were less likely to actively listen to one another's positions on issues. Rather, couples were more interested in repeating their own position and in mindreading or labeling the other person's feelings and intentions. How do you feel when others tell you what you are thinking? Most become offended.

In addition, clinic couples were more likely to enter a complaining loop at the beginning of their discussion. This loop involves one party complaining, whereas the other is ignoring the issue surrounding the complaint. These couples were also less likely to make proposals and counterproposals to resolve specific issues at the end of the discussion. The nonclinic couples demonstrated much more effective negotiation skills by providing mutual support and agreement at the beginning of the interaction, avoiding negative affect during the middle part of the discussion, and ending with specific options for resolving their differences.

In his book focusing on more elaborate verbal and nonverbal patterns of interaction using the same data set, Gottman (1979) found very similar results. He learned that the clinic couples were much more likely to reciprocate negative feelings about one another and much less likely to reciprocate positive feelings. They dwell on the negative and rarely share any positive experiences. In addition, they seldom approached the point of proposing solutions to problems. Instead, they focused more on making accusations about past problems. Listening and sharing useful information were not important goals for clinic couples.

Another interesting feature of clinic couples relates to the husbands. They tended to control their wives' affective expressions while remaining less emotionally responsive to them. That is, the wives sent the emotional expressions they were expected to give and not necessarily the ones they wanted to give. Honest, open communication in such one-sided circumstances becomes very difficult. In contrast, the nonclinic couples demonstrated a more equal communication style with neither party dominating the other or controlling one another's communication patterns.

In the Mettetal and Gottman (1980) study, the clinic couples were more likely to reciprocate defensive verbal codes and negative affect nonverbal codes. When such defensive patterns persist, couples are distracted from the substance of the interaction, making progress very difficult. This situation is frustrated by the observation that the clinic couples tended to show little reciprocal support for one another in their interactions. Basically, the clinic couples never created a cooperative interaction context within which to carry out their mission.

Notarius and Johnson (1982) set out to identify the relationship between couples' interaction patterns and their emotional arousal during the interaction. To measure emotional arousal, they attached couples to a machine measuring skin potential, or the amount of perspiration on the skin. Greater perspiration means greater arousal. In this research they recruited six happily married couples to learn about emotional arousal in constructive decision-making contexts, and asked them to discuss a salient relational issue.

After recording, coding the interaction, and analyzing the skin potential, the authors observed that the wives' speech was less neutral and more negative compared to the husbands' speech. The husbands tended to be more neutral in their speech than their wives. The wives also reciprocated their husbands' positive and negative speech, whereas the husbands did not demonstrate this tendency. The husbands tended to be much less expressive than their wives. Yet, the husbands became more emotionally aroused in response to their wives' negative speech than did the wives in response to the husbands' negative speech.

The authors hypothesized that these patterns could explain the escalation of destructive conflict for dissatisfied couples. They contended that such escalations might evolve into identifiable stages of interaction. In Stage 1, the wives perceive more emotional response from their husbands due to their more advanced ability to decode nonverbal information. In Stage 2, the wives confront the husband with more emotion that the husband does not reciprocate, perhaps because he has difficulty understanding such messages. In Stage 3 the wives escalate their emotional response to solicit an emotional reaction from the partner. At Stage 4, the husband finally catches on to the wife's emotion and tries to control it, but is not very successful. This emotion tends to both limit problem-solving strategies and yield more negative affect. This set of patterns appears consistent with the Gottman research reviewed earlier.

Noller's (1988) review of research exploring this conflict-avoidance pattern contends that marriages ultimately succeed or fail based on how couples handle negative affect. She found compelling evidence that, in unhappy marriages, "demands for attention or communication by the wife are typically met with either physical or emotional withdrawal of the husband being met by increasing demands from the wife which are met by increased withdrawal" (p. 324). In the happy marriages, the negative affect is reciprocated. Couples confront it, and ultimately find their way toward discussing the issues associated with the negative affect.

In another examination of couples' marital conflict and decision-making styles, Burggraf and Sillars (1987) coded Fitzpatrick's (1984) 40 transcripts of marital interaction using a modified version of the Sillars, Pike, Jones, and Murphy (1984) categories. Burggraf and Sillars found an exceptionally strong tendency for couples to mirror one another's behaviors as opposed to giving contrasting responses. As a result, conciliatory behavior tended to stimulate conciliatory responses, as opposed to more offensive reactions. This finding is important for mediators because it suggests that when mediators allow couples to start attacking one another, they are unlikely to break away from such attacks on their own. Mediators need to intervene to redirect the attacks into more cooperative behavior. Similarly, when couples begin cooperative behaviors, mediators can step away with some confidence that couples will continue these patterns on their own.

The second important finding is that the sex of the party had no predictive value for the kinds of conflict strategies and tactics parties selected. Men and women used similar strategies in conflict. That is, the reciprocity feature of interaction clearly dominated the results of the study. Although mediators probably should remain sensitive to power differences between disputants, they may not find husbands and wives using radically different conflict strategies.

On the surface, these results are inconsistent with the research reported previously by Noller (1988) indicating that men and women demonstrate very different orientations toward conflict. The studies reported by Noller focused on how unhappily married couples avoid conflict. Men tend to withdraw, whereas women try to involve them unsuccessfully. In contrast, the Sillars, Weisberg, Burggraf, and Wilson (1987) study focused on the strategies couples use when engaging in conflict. In such cases, they found no gender-linked differences once couples chose to engage in conflict. In addition, the Sillars et al. (1987) study found that unhappily married couples reciprocate conflict tactics as opposed to using different tactics (men withdraw–women confront).

In a study of 34 married couples, Ting-Toomey (1982) supported the Sillars et al. position on reciprocation by comparing the conflict styles of these couples with their self-reports of marital satisfaction. Their interaction in a conflict task was coded with a three-part scheme: integrative acts (e.g., confirming, coaxing, compromising), descriptive acts (e.g., descriptions and questions of feelings), and disintegrative acts (e.g., confronting, complaining). Ting-Toomey found that the interaction of satisfied couples evolves integratively in a highly reciprocated manner. Happy couples flatter or humor one another while also asking for feeling information. In contrast, the low-satisfied couples, who are most likely to find their way into divorce mediation, exhibited the more disintegrative cycle of defend–confront–defend–confront. These couples seem to get locked into this cycle of verbal aggression in which they seek to destroy one another's self-image.

These findings are supported in a study by Yelsma (1981) in which he asked couples to assess their marital satisfaction and to identify their conflict-management preferences. He found that the clinic couples selected aggressive conflict preferences. Clearly, mediators who remain insensitive to this aggressive cycle and refrain from helping couples escape it are less likely to build an effective, cooperative discussion context.

In a related set of studies, Krueger and Smith (1982) and Krueger (1983) were interested in learning about the constructive patterns of marital decision making. How do satisfied married couples make decisions? To answer this question, a variety of happily married couples were audiotaped and their interaction was coded using a modified version of the scheme developed by Raush, Barry, Hertel, and Swain (1974). This scheme defines three types of acts: those intended to (a) facilitate task completion, (b) develop the relationship, and (c) control the interaction.

The Krueger and Smith study found that these satisfied couples tend to avoid conflict by responding to rejection messages with support messages. The conflict never escalated to cutting off decision making or constructive negotiation. Couples validated one another's perceptions of issues and showed a great deal of agreement toward one another's positions. These authors concluded that satisfied couples tend to maintain an extensive repertory of responses to negative remarks that serves to inhibit the escalation of conflict. Such deflective responses keep the focus on the issues instead of personalities, and build a cooperative context with extensive support. The second Krueger (1983) study, a case study of one happily married couple's interaction style, supported these findings. The couple in that study used a wide range of supportive responses to a variety of stimuli, including messages that might stimulate conflict. Escalation of conflict rarely occurred with this couple as the wife continuously agreed with her husband, changed the subject, or withheld information to avoid conflict.

**Marital Patterns and Psychological Orientations.** A second set of studies seeks to link the interaction patterns identified here with couples' psychological orientations, including preferences for conflict patterns and communication styles. Two excellent reviews of this research appear in two works on marital interaction by Fitzpatrick (1987, 1988). A recent research program by Sillars and his colleagues (Sillars et al.,1984; Sillars et al., 1987) asked how couples with different marital types use communication to develop relational understanding. The 1984 study focused on how couples' understanding of their own and one another's feelings were related to their verbal and nonverbal communication patterns. The 48 couples used in the study completed questionnaires about feelings toward conflict and their marriage, in addition to completing a task requiring discussion about conflict issues. These interactions were coded using Gottman's (1979) nonverbal affect scheme and Sillars' (1980) verbal conflict tactics coding scheme. Sillars' scheme codes utterances as: (a) avoidance acts (denial, topic avoidance, and shifting levels of abstraction), (b) distributive acts (direct faulting and rejection and indirect questioning and joking), and (c) integrative acts (informational and supportive comments).

This study found that couples overestimated the similarity between their own feelings about conflict and their partner's feelings. Those couples with the most accurate estimates were the couples with less well-adjusted marriages. These couples used more negative nonverbal affect that gave them more accurate and reliable information about one another's feelings. The satisfied couples who understood one another had more negative statements, fewer neutral and noncontinuity statements, and more direct and indirect distributive statements. The most important message from this study is that understanding is often elusive; it does not always follow from direct discussion of the issues, particularly where abstract, emotionally laden and relational cognitions are concerned. It seems more related to the expression of negative nonverbal affect, which is more immediately available for couples.

The implication for mediation is that distressed couples are frequently unable to understand complex issues on their own due to disagreements about how to code or interpret messages. They distort the true intent of one another's messages by focusing on nonverbal affect and ignoring substance. One important function of mediation is to counteract the distortion of messages that naturally takes place in intense conflicts. Mediators need to help couples focus on the substantive features of the interaction through reframing, questioning interpretations, exposing underlying issues, regulating discussion, and so on.

The Sillars et al. (1987) study sought to learn how each of Fitzpatrick's (1984) marital types (i.e., traditionals: maintaining traditional beliefs about marriage in a very stable relational context; separates: emphasizing autonomy, emotional distance, and conflict avoidance; and independents: balancing togetherness and autonomy in a highly expressive, change-oriented relationship) talk about conflict. Forty married couples were asked to complete a questionnaire to assess marital type and satisfaction, after which they discussed a variety of conflict-generating topics. The content themes of these interactions were coded, that is, communal themes (e.g., togetherness and cooperation), individual themes (e.g., separateness, personality) and impersonal themes (e.g., stoic ideas about marriage and environmental influences on their marriage).

This study revealed two important findings. First, couples in general, and dissatisfied couples in particular, tend to focus heavily on personality themes rather than on interaction themes. For example, the dissatisfied couples tend to fight by attributing personality traits to the other such as, "You're an uncaring, aggressive person that is extremely dogmatic about everything." Interaction themes address couples' communication patterns and their impact on the couple's relationship. Focusing on personality themes leads to fault-finding and addressing problems over which people have little control. We really cannot change our personalities. It suggests a preoccupation with "keeping score" of who did what to whom, and probably represents both a cause and a symptom of relational dissatisfaction. However, interaction themes focus on the communication behaviors people can change. These discussions address issues under individuals' personal control. These results suggest that mediators must separate issues from accusations to focus individuals away from personality traits and toward interaction behaviors that they can change.

Second, different couple types emphasize different themes in conflict. In concert with Fitzpatrick's (1988) review of research in this area, the traditional couples avoid power struggles. Their relationship is governed by established conventions and norms that dictate appropriate husband and wife behavior. As a result, they tend to emphasize communal themes that stress collaboration and shared identity. The separate couple types focus on very individualistic, personality themes that can quickly degenerate into destructive conflict spirals, largely because they are emotionally divorced from one another. The relationship is secondary to their own personal needs. When possible, these couples try to avoid openly discussing conflicts and retreat immediately from negative issues and stressful topics.

***Compliance Gaining, Power, and Control.*** Research focusing on the conflict strategies selected by different marital types also addresses the question of how couples seek to control or gain compliance from one another. Three recent studies focus specifically on that question. First, Witteman and Fitzpatrick (1986) sought to differentiate the three marital types described previously (traditionals, separates, and independents) of 51 married couples, according to the types of compliance-gaining strategies they might use in a role-playing simulation. The simulation also contained a payoff feature that favored either the wife, husband, both equally, or a deadlocked outcome.

The verbal interaction results appear consistent with previous research on marital types. Of most interest to mediators, Witteman and Fitzpatrick found that separates focused on the negative consequences of noncompliance. Their messages sought to constrain the behavior and often the psychological states of their spouses. These types did not focus on relationally based or value-based approaches to compliance gaining. They simply tried to persuade the other to adjust their expectations about their goals. In addition, these strategies most often resulted in a deadlocked outcome. Witteman and Fitzpatrick characterized separates as using "gorillalike" strategies. That is, they demand acquiescence from the spouse without verbally staying to fight the whole battle.

This hit-and-run approach to compliance gaining suggests that separates, who are most likely to experience divorce problems, experience difficulty negotiating systematically about their problems. They appear more interested in simply taking shots at one another. This result is consistent with the second study exploring control and power in marital interaction. Using a similar design to the Witteman and Fitzpatrick (1986) study, Williamson and Fitzpatrick (1985) asked 80 couples to complete questionnaires assessing their relational type, and to participate in a discussion task involving both neutral and conflict topics. They coded each utterance as an attempt to gain control, yield control, or neutralize the other's control.

The authors discovered that, once again, separates refused to assert and sustain control over the definition of the relationship in their marriage. Yet, the independent and mixed (different definitions of the marriage) couples chose to compete on asserting the definition of the relationship. These types engage in conflict whether or not the issue is a serious one and carry it toward some kind of conclusion, whereas the separates are not very skilled at productive conflict interactions.

In another study analyzing the same data as Witteman and Fitzpatrick (1986), Dillard and Fitzpatrick (1985) presented many findings of interest to mediators. In particular, they discovered that husbands used more direct and explicit compliance-gaining requests than wives. The wives used more indirect approaches, choosing not to pursue the more straightforward path to achieving their goals. However, these more indirect approaches appeared to succeed more frequently as the wives actually achieved compliance twice as frequently as their husbands. Mediators might try to remain sensitive to the wives' more indirect approaches to getting their way.

The results of the studies on marital interaction point toward significant challenges for mediators. Clearly, mediators most often confront dissatisfied clinic couples. Although research has not established which marital types are associated with clinic couples, it seems clear that the couples who come to mediation are caught in the throws of social, legal, and perhaps psychological separation. Technically, such couples could be traditionals, independents, or separates. However, it might be wise for mediators to prepare for those couple types with the least proficient negotiation skills.

In that regard, the research seems fairly clear that separate couple types, whether their marriage is intact or in the process of divorce, show the fewest negotiation skills. They tend to avoid listening to one another; they remain insensitive to the other partner's needs and feelings. These couples struggle with the definition of their relationship because it is less important than their individual needs. When these couple types engage in conflict after much avoidance, they focus on personality themes that distract them from the substantive issues. This hit-and-run approach suggests an avoidance of real problem solving. Consistent with this pattern, they are more likely to reciprocate negative affect. Moreover, they appear more willing to threaten or obligate one another when seeking compliance, which suggests that they may be more verbally aggressive toward one another in a conflict situation.

Understanding marital communication patterns can help mediators develop interventions capable of enhancing productive and redirecting unproductive patterns. However, another body of literature can also inform mediators about how couples are likely to communicate during this very stressful period. Specifically, the literature on verbal aggression can be very useful because it explores behaviors that both trigger and suppress verbally aggressive actions. This chapter now turns to this very important part of the marital couple interaction puzzle.

## Verbal Aggression

***Interaction Patterns.*** In a particularly well-developed line of research, Felson (1978, 1984) proposed an impression management explanation of verbal aggression. He defined verbal aggression as interaction-based attacks on one's situational identity. An individual's identity consists of those values that remain central to that person's identity (e.g., honesty, integrity, or commitment). A distinction must be made here between verbal aggression and other forms of conflict interaction such as argument. Verbal aggression focuses on person-centered acts intended to harm the other person and the relationship. Arguing for a position is focused on the issues, and keeps away from personal accusation. Given the potential for verbal aggression due to the sensitivity of the topic in mediation and the potential threat caused by this form of behavior, it is important to examine how it functions.

Felson explained why offensive comments might escalate conflict and, ultimately, violence. He limited his focus to verbal aggression used as an outlet for emotional arousal and not for material gain. In general, Felson argued that individuals become verbally aggressive as a means of managing their personal identity in the face of attack. In contrast, the frustration–aggression explanation holds that verbal aggression is a response to frustration from task failure. In support of the impression management theory, he cited research concluding that the perception of the other's intention triggers verbal aggression. When another's hostile act is perceived as intentional, and directed at harming the individual's identity, the individual counters with verbal aggression to protect and maintain the identity. An intentional attack that is not countered can make the target appear weak, incompetent, and cowardly. A successful counterattack is one means of nullifying the imputed negative identity by showing strength, competence, and courage. Honor is restored.

Felson (1978, 1981) argued that verbally aggressive counterattacks will not follow attacks when: (a) the attacker lacks credibility due to that person's capabilities in that situation, (b) the other apologizes for the slight, (c) a third party intervenes to retaliate against the other, and (d) a third party intervenes to de-escalate the conflict. When these conditions are not in place, verbal aggression is quite likely as a counterattack.

This emphasis on third parties is particularly relevant for mediators. Felson's theory maintains that when third parties are present, but they do not actively intervene to move the discussion away from personalities and identities, then the conflict will escalate. The individual sees a greater need to defend the ego because the slight is more public. However, he argued that when the third party assumes a role of active intervention to improve harmony, the third party is no longer seen as a public figure who might judge the offended party's strength and courage. Felson concluded that bigger egos generally resort to greater aggression to stabilize that ego. In addition, males are more likely to maintain bigger egos, and thus, are more likely to retaliate aggressively to an insult.

In two studies designed to test this theory, Felson (1982) and Felson, Ribner, and Siegel (1985) interviewed a sample of former mental patients and former criminal offenders. These subjects were interviewed about their participation in conflicts in which they: (a) did nothing about the conflict, (b) responded verbally, (c) resorted to physical violence with no weapon, and (d) resorted to physical violence with a weapon. The results supported the impression management theory. Subjects, particularly males, were more likely to express anger in response to an insult. The probability of physical violence was lower when participants in the disputes gave accounts of their intentions. Also, conflicts involving same-sex dyads were generally more severe when an audience was present, or a third party instigated the aggression. Finally, active, third-party mediation resulted in less subsequent aggression.

This approach to aggression stresses the interactional, sequential nature of aggression. Aggressive behaviors appear to evolve in the following fashion: (a) a norm violation occurs and is targeted toward a specific person (e.g., an attacked identity), (b) situational factors are immediately assessed (e.g., is there an audience and what is its role; is the person same or other sex, and what is his or her relative age), (c) the attacked person searches for an account of the violation (e.g., a discussion of the intention of the perceived attack), (d) if no acceptable account is given, a passive audience is present and the other person is a same-sex peer, then aggression is likely to follow the original attack.

In a series of studies, Mummenedy set out to test Felson's (1978) impression management theory of aggression. In the first study, Linneweber, Mummenedy, Bornewasser, and Loschper (1984) surveyed more than 600 school children about reactions to aggressive attacks. This study supported Felson's sequential model of aggression. Judgments of intent in response to norm violations emerged as significant predictors of aggressive responsiveness. In an experimental probe of this judgment process, Mummendey, Linneweber, and Loschper (1984) sought to learn how these judgments of intent function over time. They found that parties in aggressive situations diverge significantly in their evaluations of the appropriateness of the others' acts as the number of acts escalate. In other words, each party thinks he or she is more right and less aggressive and that the other person is more wrong and more aggressive.

In another study, Linneweber, Mummendy, Bornewasser, and Loschper (1984) examined the kinds of judgments parties make that are associated with breaking off an aggressive interaction or with escalating the level of aggression. They found that parties are more willing to break off the aggression sequence when the offended party does not feel offended, fears negative consequences from increased aggression, or is compensated by the other party for the offense. On the other hand, parties are more willing to escalate when the offended party feels intensely offended, regards the hostile behavior as meaningful, and has no fear of negative consequences.

The Felson and Mummendey research provides mediators with useful information about how offended parents are likely to react to aggressive behaviors. First, the research suggests rather strongly that when mediators allow couples to attack one another's identity by calling them names or slandering their parental skills, verbal aggression is close behind. We live very closely with our identities. When attacked, it triggers a defensive reaction. Intercepting such attacks by focusing on the issues takes the emphasis away from identities and places it on the problem. Second, once the aggression sequence begins, it runs very quickly toward self-perpetuation. Couples continue to attack one another verbally until someone either fights or flees. Thus, mediators should not be timid about intercepting identity attacks. Clearly, the mediator should concentrate on managing the interaction to reduce the chances of couples blasting one another's identities. This remains a difficult task because emotions often run hot in mediation. The point for mediators is to process the emotions as issues while avoiding couple's reliance on identity attacks.

***Verbal Aggression Predispositions.*** The basic thrust of the work by Felson and his colleagues focuses on identity as an explanation for why verbal aggression escalates to physical aggression. However, another group of scholars adds an important dimension to this research by explaining what kinds of communication skills can short-circuit the connection between verbal aggression and physical violence. These scholars believe that people lacking the argumentative skills needed to save face turn to aggression. In this research, *argumentativeness* is defined as an individual's perceived desire and ability to present and defend positions on controversial issues and attack the other's positions. The basic argument of the research is that when people believe they can address the substance of the problem in a reasoned fashion, they can use words, rather than violence, to save face.

This research began with an early study by Infante, Trebing, Shepherd, and Seeds (1984). The study found that subjects reporting more arguing skills were least likely to be provoked by an obstinate opponent into using verbal aggression. This finding supported the basic idea that when individuals have difficulty articulating arguments to attack the other's position, they turn away from substance and toward the individual. The authors concluded that one of the main factors stimulanting verbal aggression is a lack of argumentation skill. In a further development of this finding, Infante and Wigley (1986) and Infante (1987) proposed that verbal aggressiveness is really a personality trait that is related to an individual's hostility and assertiveness. They argued that verbally aggressive people prefer attacking others' self-concepts instead of their positions on issues. If this contention is upheld in further research, it suggests that individuals with verbally aggressive personalities will have more trouble working toward agreements in mediation.

What does this research tell us about conflict and mediation? First, it tells us that mediators should look closely for signs of verbal aggression because they can escalate destructive conflict quickly. This energy needs to be regulated more to center on the issues and away from personal attacks. Second, this research tells us that people with rich argumentation skills whose personalities are not aggressive in nature want to rely more on solving problems with communication. Communication has worked for them in the past, they are comfortable using it, so they will go a long way with communication before resorting to other options. So, mediators might encourage parties possessing these skills to use them and to turn away from verbal aggression. The research suggests that when they use these skills, problem solving increases considerably.

But, what about people who have trouble arguing? Should mediators train these people to improve their arguing skills? As suggested in chapter 1, some mediation models emphasize improving disputant communication skills, particularly the relational development model. Regardless of the model that mediators decide to use, they can certainly try some minimal argumentation training by asking parties to give reasons for their proposals and to listen to others' reasons, as well. Mediators can also reinforce positive arguing skills by drawing attention to them, and by complementing couples on using them. Should mediators be real explicit with couples and give them a list of appropriate argumentation skills? Perhaps this idea is not too far afield. Simply encouraging people to be self-conscious about these skills might trigger a desire to improve them. Whatever methods are used, mediators might think about devoting some training or orientation time to the process of argumentation. It seems to deter or delay aggressive reactions.

## Communication Research in Mediation

This research in verbal aggression firmly establishes the central role communication plays in managing conflict. When parties bolster their communication skills, productive problem solving appears more likely to succeed. Recognizing the need to learn more about communication and conflict, a group of scholars has begun exploring communication issues in mediation. For example, in a study using the same transcripts used for this book, Jones (1989) identified a variety of mediator strategies that appeared to elicit more cooperative interaction. In her research, Jones coded mediator and disputant statements into seven categories: process (establishing agenda), information (providing objective, observable information), summarize other (paraphrasing the other), self-disclosure (information about one's own feelings and attitudes), attribution (statements about the other's attitudes), solutions (offering and evaluating options), and agreements (past and future agreements).

Jones (1989) found that mediators whose parties reached agreement made extensive use of the following communication behaviors. For example, they worked hard on gathering information about the circumstances of the dispute while keeping the focus of discussion away from personality problems. When parties started making personality complaints (e.g., "You are just too aggressive to listen to me") the interaction degenerated quickly into a shouting match. This result is consistent with the research on marital interaction cited previously. Specifically, couples who focus on the other's personality traits get caught in an attack-defend cycle that leads to highly distributive interaction. By guiding disputants to talk about themselves, mediators can generate insights into the sources of conflict that will facilitate integrative decision making.

Second, Jones (1989) revealed that these agreement mediations used extensive summarizing behaviors. She indicated that these summaries tend to promote supportive communication by identifying points of agreement. They create momentum for a progress-oriented interaction context. Most people are eager to learn if they are making progress in the discussion. When mediators inform couples about this progress, the focus is kept on the future, and people get some reinforcement for doing the mediation.

Finally, Jones' research found that mediators securing agreements stimulated reciprocal problem-solving behaviors. They encouraged offers and facilitated discussions about options for agreement. This result is not surprising, particularly given the prior research on verbal aggression. The offer–counter-offer process is a basic part of negotiation. When couples possess the communication skills to negotiate, they rely more on communication to problem solve. They also get reinforcement for using communication to solve their problems. When mediators facilitate this process, they stand a greater chance of moving toward agreement.

Moving in a little different direction, Jones (1988) also conducted some research on mediation phases and how parties move through them. Using the same coding scheme, Jones (1988) observed significant differences between mediations ending in agreement and those ending in no agreement. She found that in the agreement mediations, couples moved through an identifiable series of phases. Initial stages consisted of process and information-exchange behaviors; middle stages dealt with solutions, agreements, and process behaviors; and later stages focused on agreements. In contrast, the no-agreement mediations emphasized competitive information exchanges in the form of attribution statements, and they failed to develop into cooperative decision making. Mediators in the no-agreement sessions failed to control the interaction process.

Jones' work stresses the need for mediators to assert control over the interaction process. Allowing couples to engage in aggressive interaction can quickly sabotage decision making. Failing to set an agenda in which the interactants can make progress ultimately leads to increased competitiveness. Parties need some kind of regulation to succeed. Left to their own devices, their unregulated behavior becomes a fertile ground for verbal aggression and a difficult mediation experience.

## INTEGRATIONS AND CONCLUSIONS

A full understanding of communication processes in divorce mediation requires integrating the following four areas of research: mediator strategies and tactics, family and marital interaction, verbal aggression, and communication research in mediation. Perhaps the best way to integrate these four areas of research is to analyze a short transcript of a divorce mediation segment of interaction focusing on results derived from research areas. Although this segment is fabricated, its structure closely mirrors an actual divorce mediation interaction. The segment reflects the first few minutes of a child-custody mediation in which the mediator "lets the couple go" to see how they fight.

Mediator: So, what kind of arrangement are you looking for?
Wife: [angry tone] He wants custody because he thinks I stink as a mother. But you should see the way he takes care of the kids. Plus, his girlfriend tells the kids all kinds of stuff about me. Now, he drags me through this court thing.
Husband: [calmly] Look, she has my kids doing lots of weird stuff and the court has to do something about this.
Wife: [very angry tone] Why don't you tell him about what that trashy girlfriend has the kids doing. Huh? Go ahead and tell him.
Husband: [voice rising] Leave her out of this! She's none of your damn business!
Wife: She's in it as long as you continue to see her!
Mediator: Whoa, wait a minute. Let's stick with specific proposals about how we can work out some kind of custody...
Husband: [yelling] It's my life, and it's a hell of a lot better than the one you gave me.

This sample interaction illustrates the kinds of challenges mediators face in helping couples develop cooperative agreements. Clearly, both parents address a variety of parenting issues in discussing the legal custody problem. Both parents express concerns about parental competency. However, the wife seems concerned about the influence of the girlfriend on the children. Perhaps she fears being replaced as a mother. On the other hand, the husband resents his wife's invasion of his privacy and independence. Intense conflict is also evident in the individual perspective issues. The wife appears to believe individuals should be free to handle conflict themselves, whereas the husband may feel that outside parties should handle disputes. If these parenting and individual perspective issues remain unexplored, couples risk bargaining in a confused, emotionally charged context. This confusion and emotion are likely to foster a highly competitive communication context.

The question is, what strategies and tactics should the mediator have pursued to remove this confusion and to reduce the emotional tension? The mediator begins the session with the substantive strategy of trying to identify disputant goals and proposals. Tactically, this strategy becomes a request for proposals and a decision to not interfere in the husband–wife exchange. Near the end of the segment the mediator makes a procedural move to ask couples to forget their problems and focus on developing specific proposals. Would it have been more appropriate to intervene in the discussion more quickly and to change the focus to the parenting and the individual perspective issues?

To answer this question it might be useful to focus on the patterns of marital conflict and verbal aggression in the interaction because these patterns reveal important information about the need to expose these issues. It should be clear that the couple in this interaction is not very skilled at negotiating. They summarize their own positions, read the other person's mind with negative affect, and complain about the same topic over and over. Not listening to the other's position, failing to support the other's positions or interactional rights, and attributing intentions and personality traits to the other keeps the focus on the past problems at the expense of constructive proposal making.

In addition, this interaction segment is typical of destructive conflict patterns among unsatisfied couples. The wife confronts the husband at an elevated emotional level to solicit an emotional reaction from him. The husband takes the bait and starts lashing out at the wife in an unsuccessful attempt to control her emotions. This exchange promotes intense verbal aggression in which each party looks to manage his or her impression to the mediator. This impression management is particularly important because the mediator has done little to establish control of the process. The mediator could gain control, as suggested here, by addressing the relational issues. Such attention might encourage the couple to invest more in the process and to rely more on the mediator's directives. However, as it stands, the mediator's passive role forces the couple to see the mediator as a judge, or as someone who needs to be impressed, as opposed to someone capable of lending insight into the dispute.

The ripple effect of this verbal aggression is that it decreases the couple's ability to argue effectively for their own positions. They appear more interested in hurting the other person than in serving as articulate spokespersons for their positions. Again, the mediator fails to promote argument by not separating and addressing the important issues in dispute. In fact, the mediator fails to perform any of the four recommendations proposed by Jones (1989). The mediator's information gathering does not encourage the disputants to talk about themselves, it does not summarize behaviors, it does not avoid the disputants' distributive behaviors, and it does not stimulate reciprocal problem solving.

For example, the wife's first utterance surfaces her fear that the husband might be looking to replace her as a mother. This fear results in an attack on the husband and an escalating conflict cycle of attack–defend–attack. The mediator fails to encourage the woman to talk about herself by pulling out this fear issue to help her deal with it. As a result, an issue focus is lost to verbal aggression.

Jones' (1988) communication research focusing on mediation phases supports the need for mediators to process issues blocking progress. Not addressing these critical issues encourages the kind of competitive information exchange Jones found in her no agreement transcripts. This kind of information exchange is characterized by the kind of attribution statements evident in the sample transcript. Beginning with this type of interaction makes it difficult to evolve into the more cooperative phases of decision making, including information exchange, a focus on options, and finally, agreements.

Thus, when issues get hot, couples appear to adopt very dysfunctional conflict management procedures. They lapse into verbal aggression, particularly with passive mediators. Chapter 3 develops a model of mediator-interaction management that focuses on disputant communication patterns in relation to mediator strategies and tactics leading to cooperative decision making.

# 3

# Mediator-Interaction Management Model

The first two chapters place the focus of this book squarely on communication, particularly from the mediator's perspective. For example, both chapters emphasize the mediator's need to manage the couple's communication. Often couples regress into communication habits that work against making agreements in the child's best interests. They struggle with the pain and anger of divorce by showing one another hostility and aggression. The most simple decision-making tasks turn into full-scale wars.

In addition, the first two chapters emphasize the importance of examining communication patterns. For example, mediators can get trapped into communicating differently with each party. By consistently evaluating one party negatively, that party may find it difficult to work cooperatively with the mediator. Or, one party may try to side with a mediator's recommendations to create a coalition against the other party. Such manipulation attempts require the mediator's attention to help prevent the focus of the session from turning to verbal aggression. The first two chapters also emphasize the importance of selecting strategies and tactics capable of promoting cooperative interaction. Maintaining an extensive repertory of such intervention skills allows mediators to adapt to many different kinds of mediation needs.

Given the importance of monitoring disputant communication patterns and maintaining a broad range of strategies and tactics to manage these patterns, a conceptual framework is needed that integrates these two important skills. The framework developed here is termed *interaction management*, and is meant to provide insight into the communication context in which a third party seeks to accomplish specific goals with the other two interactants by means of communicating with other parties. In this case the third party is a mediator who uses various communication strategies to assist divorcing couples with their custody/visitation problems.

Managing interaction is defined as directing the communication patterns of the primary communicators toward specific outcomes. However, it must be noted that "managing" means more than just working with the information given by the other parties. Mediators do much more than that. Rather, the term *managing* means both working with what the primary parties give and providing new information that might help the parties. As a result, managing means "directing" or "guiding" the primary communicators' patterns toward specific outcomes by both taking what they give and restructuring it, and by providing additional resources for problem solving.

Managing interaction consists of two basic activities: (a) discriminating between the productive and unproductive communication patterns of the primary parties relative to their goals, and (b) directing the primary parties toward the more productive patterns through various interaction strategies. For the divorce mediator, success in managing interaction is judged by the extent to which the mediator can select the appropriate intervention tactics at the appropriate time to facilitate disputant cooperation. Timing relates to the discrimination dimension of interaction management. Failure to discriminate between constructive and destructive communication patterns can destroy trust, or ruin opportunities for productive decision making.

This model of interaction management is meant only to serve as a descriptive template to place over actual divorce mediation sessions representing both agreement and no-agreement outcomes. The question of interest in the book is how do the mediators differ across the agreement session in their interaction management choices. The model is not intended to tell mediators that if they manage interaction in a particular way they will achieve one outcome or the other. This research is simply descriptive. There are no causal claims made about the variables specified in the model. If the model succeeds in identifying different interaction management patterns across the agreement outcomes, then perhaps future research can manipulate these behaviors in some kind of experiment to see if they actually influence outcome.

Actually, what this model provides is a template for better understanding the interventionist model as practiced by the divorce mediators in the Los Angeles Family and Conciliation Court. What kinds of interaction management choices does this model make? What kinds of disputant communication patterns do mediators in both groups face? How do they manage these patterns? Hopefully, answers to these questions will provide more insight into how the interventionist model functions in that court.

The description of the model begins by focusing first on disputant communication patterns. Following this discussion, the model next considers the range of mediator-interaction management skills in coping with these various disputant communication patterns. The chapter concludes with an evaluation of the model's ability to integrate the various literatures and perspectives on mediation discussed in chapter 2.

## DISPUTANT COMMUNICATION PATTERNS

### Research Review

Divorce mediators face a very perplexing task in discriminating between productive and unproductive disputant communication patterns. Functionally, the task really comes down to deciding when to intervene, because the location of the intervention is the first step in deciding if the primary parties' communicate in productive or unproductive ways. For example, as the conflict intensifies, the interaction pace quickens and issues become very confused and intertwined. Mediators face the problem of deciding whether to allow venting of emotion as a release of hostility, or whether to intervene in such a discussion and begin separating the issues.

Several types of disruptive communication patterns were discussed in chapter 2. For example, when negotiating, couples who enter a complaining loop when beginning their interaction are less likely to negotiate constructively later on. They get caught in the differentiation phase that involves dwelling on past problems instead of considering future needs (Walton, 1969). Or, couples might fail to follow up on one another's or the mediator's proposals with their own ideas about future needs. These kinds of communication patterns result in lost problem-solving opportunities.

Other disruptive patterns relate to a relationship definition. A spouse who consistently downgrades the other's points, interrupts or tries to "mind read" the other presents a domination problem. This domination struggle consumes the interaction time, builds animosity, and moves the couple further away from problem solving. Chapter 2 also describes a pattern in which spouses use outrageous attacks to elicit an emotional reaction from the other spouse. These "button-pressing" attacks escalate the conflict into verbal aggression and the continuous attack–confront–attack–confront cycle of conflict. Couples exchange only negative affect, focus on the past, and generally try to harm the other's self image.

The model proposed here contends that the first step toward managing interaction effectively means interrupting such patterns before they damage the potential for cooperative interaction. This model proposes that three kinds of patterns warrant mediator attention: relational, content, and strategic. This chapter defines each of these types by the kinds of language choices parties make in the course of their conflict. The manner in which disputants sequence these choices is reviewed in detail.

**Relational Patterns**

The model begins with the assumption that disputants define relational parameters in a tacit fashion (Watzlawick, Beavin, & Jackson, 1967). That is, participants generally avoid direct discussions of specific relational rights and obligations. It is not common for people to talk about what the other is obliged to do or has the right to do, unless a conflict arises in which those expectations have been violated. The more common way to define rights and obligations is through a subtle negotiation process. As Scherer and Giles (1979) noted, communicators always mark or label their actions so that others will know how to judge the intention of the action, and subsequently, how to respond to it. The other person responds to that tacit proposal giving the communicator information on whether or not the proposal was accepted. For example, politeness markers (Brown & Levinson, 1978) propose equality or deference because communicators send the indirect message, "I do not have the relational right to threaten your face with my form of address or request." The other can accept that relational definition by matching the marked strategy or by not specifically pursing that strategy as a topic of conversation.

To illustrate, consider these two ways of asking for a cup of coffee: "Dear, if you are up, would you please get me a cup of coffee?" and "Get me a cup of coffee." The first, more polite request acknowledges that the speaker may not have the right to impose on the hearer's good will. The second, less polite request seems to assume that the speaker has the right to impose. If the hearer gets the coffee without comment in response to both requests, then the hearer tacitly accepts the relational definition proposed by the speaker. Thus, redefining relational rights and obligations is a subtle form of negotiation. Communicators propose and counterpropose particular relational states by marking their language (both verbal and nonverbal) with various politeness and other features.

The use of language in negotiating relationships continues to receive considerable attention from communication scholars. Much of this research centers around how speakers use language to establish relational rights and obligations. One of the more promising ways to view the negotiation of relational rights and obligations is to focus on the ways in which disputants signal distance. Distance is defined as the manner in which individuals integrate into one another's personal space. For example, people often comment about how they are developing a very close interpersonal relationship with another person. Or, have you ever heard someone say that another person was distant in a particular situation? The terms *close* and *distant* reflect a conclusion about how people are perceiving their integration into the other's personal space. Saying that I am getting close to someone could mean that I feel intimate with that other person. I am becoming more integrated into that individual's personal space.

One interesting feature of communication is that we signal distance, or reveal our relational views and desires, through various features in our language. For example, in chapter 2, Gottman's (1979) work on marital conflict revealed how couples used various visual cues to express their feelings toward one another. Folded arms, tense hands and neck, and inattention reveal a speaker's desire to retain a distant, or uninvolved relational definition with the other person. Smiling, showing attention with head nodding, and giving empathic facial expressions reveals a desire to move closer to the individual.

It follows that individuals also taylor the structure of their verbal output to reflect or signal their relational aims and assumptions. Certainly, people might be very overt in their relational messages by simply saying how they feel (e.g., "I love you"). But communicators can also drop more subtle cues about their relational thoughts through the way they structure their language. For example, a father might try to sound authoritative with his young child by saying, "Don't eat so fast." However, he might try to downplay his authority with an older child by saying, "Are you sure it's a good idea to eat so fast?" The first statement establishes a firm "one-up, one-down" relationship, whereas the second tries to communicate more equality.

In an attempt to better understand the ways in which communicators send relational messages to one another, Diez (1983) argued that people use three forms of distance to communicate relational aims and assumptions: psychological distance dealing with how attracted people are to one another; social distance, or the level of formality in an interaction; and role distance, which deals with power issues. Each of these three forms of distance are important because couples continuously negotiate them simultaneously during mediation. As a result, all three are described in detail.

***Psychological Distance.*** This type of relational distance is signaled by what Weiner and Mehrabian (1968) called "immediacy," or the degree of directness and intensity of the interaction between communicators and referents. This type of immediacy generally signals attraction for the other person, or the desire to become closer or more distant from that person. For example, when individuals seek to increase distance, they may signal it nonverbally by looking away, folding arms and legs, and appearing generally unapproachable. Verbally, the individuals might use vague language, qualify remarks carefully, or talk in the past to avoid revealing present intentions. When couples come to mediation they typically reveal very nonimmediate or hostile displays to one another. Mediators typically try to reduce this distance by exploring "safe" topics such as facts about the home or the children.

In other cases, mediators may encounter couples with inconsistent levels of commitment to the relationship. As the example in chapter 1 illustrated, the husband remained committed to the marriage, whereas the wife wanted out badly. In such cases, one party may use very immediate verbal and nonverbal language, whereas the other uses very distant forms of communication. For example, one party might refer to the children as "our children," whereas the other might say "my children." This divergence signals the continued negotiation of rights and obligations. Neither party accepts the other's definition of immediacy. Relationally, it also signals a struggle for the right to control the relationship's direction and intensity. When parties use consistent forms of immediacy they tacitly signal that the competition is over, and some stable communication arrangement has been established. They are willing to respect one another's relational rights without imposing excessive obligations on the other.

***Social Distance.*** This form of distance is marked by the overall sense of relative formality/informality conveyed. Brown and Fraser (1979) indicated that formal situations allow fewer stylistic variations than informal situations. Individual differences in communication are more apparent when the situation is more informal. More formal contexts exhibit more restrictions over individual behaviors. For example, in a formal "business meeting," a variety of restrictions in the form of conventions or rituals are commonly in force. Members are expected to direct their comments only toward the chair, ask for permission to speak or to deviate from the current topic, and use language that is to the point, polite, and relatively neutral (i.e., not particularly demonstrative or intense).

On the other hand, informal, social gatherings appear less regulated and planned. Following Labov's (1972) view that formality is a function of the extent to which individuals monitor their speech, Keenan (1978) termed such interaction *unplanned discourse*. Unplanned discourse lacks fore-thought and organizational preparation due to the cognitive demands on the participants. When individuals have little guidance for planning their discourse (e.g., an impromptu fight with a spouse), they have little time to prepare a series of thoughts to accomplish specific goals. Rather, such talk is more contextually driven. Turn-taking violations are common and the language might contain some profanity or colorful metaphors to make a point.

Assessing social distance is important for mediators because of the role it plays in developing working relationships. Conflict situations play funny tricks on the way in which disputants negotiate social distance. Mediators typically begin the session with a relatively formal orientation lecture. However, once the parties begin interacting, the planned nature of the event can change very quickly. If individuals begin an attack–defend verbal aggression loop, the interaction becomes very spontaneous and thus, informal, as individuals use whatever rules they feel useful in gaining an advantage for them. For the mediator, managing social distance means striking a balance between allowing no spontaneity and individual variation and allowing disputants to perform a free-for-all conflict. This kind of balance creates a level of social distance that allows problem solving while limiting verbal aggression.

***Role Distance.*** Role distance is defined in terms of social power development. It seeks to describe how individuals use power to establish their roles in the relationship. Roles are defined as expectations of appropriate and inappropriate behavior. Role distance refers to the relative power of dominance associated with different roles. For example, the husband might try to dominate the wife by using many different power strategies, from interruptions and topic changes to threats and promises. If the husband achieves this objective, then he expands his power to control the outcome. When these kinds of power gaps develop, role distance increases. When gaps are minimal and individuals maintain equal power and status in the relationship, role distance is minimized.

According to Brown and Fraser (1979), role distance is defined relative to settings and purposes. Individuals with formally defined roles assume a communicative style consistent with that particular role setting. Doctors speak like doctors to reinforce their ability to perform the duties of that role. When these same individuals enter other settings, they generally speak in a manner more in line with those new settings. Brown and Fraser suggested that this variability in communication style is found more with occupational roles than with friendship roles. Friends are expected to "act like friends" despite the different tasks they perform.

For mediators, role distance often becomes a problem when couples begin the mediation process. In general, couples may believe when they enter mediation that dominating the other and controlling the agenda lead toward more favorable outcomes. Couples holding this belief might then begin competing with the mediator for the right to direct the interaction. Mediators allowing such struggles to continue have two problems. First, they jeopardize their ability to do their job. Mediators certainly cannot forward particular topics, give disputants insights, or help create agreement options if their role is compromised. Second, giving disputants control of the interaction encourages them to rely on their most frequently used approaches to communication and problem solving. If these habits have not served them well in the past, they are not likely to be productive in mediation. Once the mediator achieves the right to perform the mediation role, the mediator can begin implementing the necessary professional interventions.

## Content Patterns

As the relational discussion indicates, building appropriate levels of psychological, social, and role distance helps achieve a stable set of relational rights and obligations. This stability removes much of the relational negotiation that can get in the way of processing through the issues. Similarly, couples need to build some stability into the content or substantive features of the dispute. Three dimensions of the dispute's content that are most likely to impact decision making include: the substantive topics of discussion, the issues in dispute within those topics, and the basic assumptions disputants use when coming to mediation.

*Topics of Discussion.* Managing topics is one of the more difficult tasks for mediators. As just indicated, one of the resources people use to gain control is manipulating topics. A *topic* is defined as the subject matter of the interaction. Topics are distinct from issues because an *issue* is defined as a point of controversy within a specific subject. To illustrate, the topic of conversation might be the the mother's social life, and an issue within that topic might be whether the mother is conducting herself socially in the best interests of the child.

During periods of competition for control, mediators might try to control the topic to move the interaction in a productive direction and to equalize the disputants' power. If the parties persist in detailing their own emotional concerns and refuse to discuss mediator-directed topics, or focus on the same topic together, then progress toward agreement may prove difficult. For example, in heated arguments one parent may wish to discuss the topic of support, whereas the other may push to discuss past relational problems. All this time the mediator might be asking the couple to discuss the children's living arrangements. In such cases, the mediator might benefit from recognizing this discrepancy and promoting his or her topic more vigorously.

*Issues Within Topics.* If keeping disputants focused on the same topic is difficult, then certainly encouraging issue consistency must be even more difficult. Because mediation issues tend to evoke considerable controversy, mediators are faced with a number of problems in developing consistency. First, multiple issues are often contained in one statement. The mediator must first separate the issues and then prioritize their discussion. Consider this statement: "The reason you're always bringing the kids back after their bedtime is that your new girlfriend is so unorganized and is always trying to play up to the kids with letting them get away with murder." Lingering within this accusation are possibly three issues: (a) the husband's reliability in meeting his visitation arrangements, (b) the wife might be hurt over the new relationship, and (c) the wife's fear of being replaced as a mother. Pulling these issues out and deciding which ones to discuss first are very difficult problems.

Second, if the mediator allows the husband to respond immediately to these accusations, issue proliferation is likely to occur. That is, the husband may respond to such attacks by activating a variety of problems he perceives with his wife's behavior. These problems expose other issues that may not be related to the wife's three issues. Such proliferations create confusion, reduce confidence in the mediation process, and certainly increase competition among disputants.

***Processing Individual Perspective Issues.*** The beginning of chapter 2 described a variety of individual perspective issues that often emerge in mediation. Values about morality, conflict, and justice appear in every mediation. Emotions and feelings run very deep and fast during discussions of important topics. What happens to the process if disputants approach their topics and issues with very different values and emotions? For example, the mother might base her positions on issues on the assumption that people must be punished for their wrong doing. In contrast, the husband might view justice differently. He might believe that there is no clear-cut sense of right and wrong, and that working toward equity is important, not punishment. If such inconsistencies are left unexposed, they could undermine the interaction even though the mediator has succeeded in getting the couple to talk about the same topic and the same issue. Coordinating perspectives is also needed to reduce confusion toward the substance of the interaction.

### Strategic Patterns

The final set of communication patterns that require the mediator's attention deals with the strategic dimension of the interaction. This dimension focuses on how disputants try to achieve their objectives. What strategies and tactics do they use to persuade one another to make concessions, move to other issues, or stop engaging in some behavior? The strategic patterns of interest here include position adjustment, compliance gaining, and proposal development. Each is discussed in detail.

**Position Adjustment Strategies.** A disputant's "position" is conceptualized as a party's opinion or "stand" on a particular issue. As couples negotiate in divorce mediation, each party tries to establish a strong position that accomplishes his or her desired final arrangement. There are four primary strategies that parties might use to accomplish this position objective. First, each party might try to bolster, or strengthen, his or her own position with lists of supporting evidence and persuasive arguments. Second, parties can attempt to weaken the other's position by attacking that person's facts or assertions to show that they are false or misleading. Third, a negotiator might try to defend against such attacks by showing that they are false or misleading. Finally, a disputant might strengthen his or her own position by showing how it is consistent with what the other ultimately desires. Couples often mix these four general strategies in the course of a mediation, using whatever approach seems warranted at the time.

Many factors can contribute to the strength of a negotiator's stand or position on an issue. In divorce mediation in which couples negotiate parental responsibilities, the credibility of a parent's position is often based on his or her identity as a "good parent." Recall from chapter 1 that most of the legal issues in divorce mediation focus on disputants' roles as husbands and wives and mothers and fathers. As a result, disputants' identities or self-concepts about these roles play an important part in the substantive divorce mediation issues. If disputants can enhance or protect their identities as parents, they indirectly strengthen their power to influence outcome favorably for themselves. Conversely, a parent may try to attack the other parent's identity to weaken his or her power to influence outcomes. This identity attack-and-defend process can become a very difficult obstacle for building a cooperative interaction that focuses on building a parenting plan that serves the best interests of the child.

For example, a father might adopt the position that he is the parent who has consistently maintained the best relationship with the daughter. Sustaining that position will depend a great deal on his ability to sustain the image of a loving, caring, available parent. If the mother tarnishes that image in a major way, the father's ability to sustain his position will be weakened a great deal. So, the father will try to show evidence of his parenting ability, deny any parenting weaknesses, and perhaps attack the mother's parenting skills so his look better by comparison. Unfortunately, when this identity negotiation gains momentum, it can degenerate quickly into a difficult attack–defend cycle of interaction.

**Compliance Gaining.** In addition to strengthening their position, disputants also strive to accomplish their goals by using a variety of compliance-gaining strategies. Two questions emerge here: What kinds of strategies do they use to both gain and resist compliance? and What contextual factors influence this message selection (Boster & Stiff, 1984; McLaughlin, Cody, & Robey, 1980; Miller, Boster, Roloff, & Seibold, 1977)? Of most interest to divorce mediators is a study by Fitzpatrick and Winke (1979). They used a five-category classification scheme of interpersonal conflict tactics. These categories include:

1. manipulation (using ingratiation),
2. non-negotiation (refusing to discuss or listen unless the other gives in),
3. emotional appeal (appealing to the other's love and affection),
4. personal rejection (making the other feel stupid and worthless), and
5. empathetic understanding (holding mutual talks without argument).

These authors found that married couples rely more on harsh verbal strategies to achieve their ends through the use of emotional appeals and personal rejection strategies. Intimate couples tend to "bottom line" one another in conflict. That is, they rely on information that is most capable of eliciting the most intense emotional reaction, either positive or negative. Because the parties share an intimate history, they have ready access to such information.

In addition to these compliance-gaining strategies, McLaughlin et al. (1980) identified several strategies individuals use to resist others' compliance-gaining attempts. Their five broad categories include:

1. non-negotiation (straightforward, unapologetic strategies in which the target overtly declines to comply with the agent's request),

2. identity managing (indirect resistance strategies in which the image of the agent, the target, or both, are manipulated,
3. justifying (strategies in which the target justifies his or her unwillingness to comply on the basis of potential outcomes, positive or negative, to self or to others, of compliance or noncompliance),
4. negotiation (exchange strategies in which the target proposes to engage in an alternative behavior to that proposed by the agent and/or empathic understanding strategies in which the target solicits discussion conducive to mutual accommodation), and
5. emotional appeals (direct resistance strategies based on the use of affect, such as a "plea" or "appeal to the other's affection").

They found that couples tend to exploit their relational commitment in conflict situations by using identity-managing strategies, including comparing the other unfavorably to oneself, acting hurt and pretending astonishment to make the other feel guilty. These kinds of compliance-resisting strategies would not work in a context other than an intimate personal relationship.

Although intimacy appears to influence strategy selection, Dillard and Burgoon (1985) provide an excellent overview and analysis of all the situational constraints that are reported to impact compliance-gaining message selection. Their review yields six situational dimensions of compliance gaining:

1. intimacy (amount and quality of information known about one another),
2. self-benefit (the extent to which the situation offers personal rewards),
3. other benefit (the extent to which the other can be advantaged in the situation),
4. consequences (the implications of the outcomes),
5. dominance (the amount of power the persuader sustains over the target), and
6. rights and resistance (the source's perceptions of his or her rights and the anticipated resistance from the target).

In contrast to the studies just reported, the Dillard and Burgoon (1985) study found that intimacy is not a strong predictor of message selection. Rather, the other situational dimensions appear to impact message selection. For example, compliance-gaining attempts are generally motivated by self-interest when the relationship with the target is not important. In contrast, when the relationship is important, individuals pursue more integrative compliance-gaining messages.

These studies suggest that mediators probably should look for these compliance-gaining and compliance-resisting tendencies during a divorce mediation session. Some evidence suggests that conflict encourages couples to exploit their intimacy by using information that elicits the most intense emotional reaction when seeking compliance, or acting hurt and pretending astonishment to make the other feel guilty when resisting compliance-gaining attempts. As indicated earlier, when mediators allow couples to use these competitive, manipulative strategies the couples' best interests are not served. Rather, the Dillard and Burgoon (1985) study points mediators in another direction. Their research suggests that mediators should concentrate on the mutually rewarding aspects of a couple's relationship, like their parenting roles, to encourage integrative decision making. The difference in approach is significant. Instead of allowing couples to turn inward on their relationship, they turn outward toward their children and the future.

***Proposal Development.*** Individuals in mediation use various strategies to adjust their positions and to gain compliance from the other as a means of gaining relative advantage. Disputants try to translate that advantage into an enhanced ability to shape proposals all through the mediation session. In a sense, then, the proposal development process provides some information concerning how well those compliance-gaining strategies work. If the husband gains a relative advantage over the wife, then his proposals should receive more attention. However, if the mediator develops an integrative interaction context that balances mutual advantage, then each person's proposals should carry equal weight.

Moore (1986) identified a specific set of priorities for proposal development based on these principles. He indicated that effective proposal development occurs through a process of incremental convergence. This process adheres to the principle that the most effective means of reaching a mutually satisfying position involves gradual concession making by both parties. Too many concessions too quickly signal a lack of commitment to exploring mutually agreeable options. Or, frequent concessioning can also signal that the giver no longer feels motivated to negotiate and simply wants to avoid the conflict. Too few concessions at later points in the negotiation signal greater competition. Sticking with proposals in the face of the other person making concessions indicates a desire to develop a relative advantage. Both extremes indicate a reluctance to cooperate, endless avoidance behavior, and a lack of commitment to bargaining.

These three sets of patterns should provide mediators with a firm understanding of how disputant communication patterns evolve into more or less mutually satisfying disputant agreements. An ability to discriminate those patterns that promote cooperation from those promoting competition defines mediator timing. That is, mediator interventions "frame" disputant communication patterns. Between each intervention exists a series of communication patterns. If the mediator understands the strengths and weaknesses of those patterns and how to build on them, then the chances of success are increased. Having discussed the important disputant communication patterns influencing outcome, this chapter now moves to specifying those mediator strategies that respond most effectively to those patterns.

## MEDIATOR-INTERVENTION SKILLS

Detecting disrupting and productive disputant-interaction patterns informs mediators when to intervene. The intervention dimension of interaction management focuses on those actions that direct couples toward more productive communication patterns. What are the range of intervention choices capable of stabilizing control and disputant–mediator role relationships? Which choices aim at an improved discussion of the issues and a chance for disputants to develop a more productive relationship?

To answer these questions, this section draws on Kolb's (1983) taxonomy of mediator strategies and tactics discussed in chapter 2 and Diez's (1983) taxonomy of interaction strategies negotiators use to build both competitive and cooperative group settings. Specifically, this chapter focuses on three intervention forms that aim to improve disputant problem solving: (a) substantive coherence (connecting key issues and elements in conflict to improve disputant insight), (b) procedural structuring (organizing the dispute resolution process), and (c) interpersonal distance (managing the disputants' relationships). Each of these forms and their corresponding strategies is described in detail.

## Substantive Coherence

***Overview.*** Recall from chapter 2 that Kolb's (1983) third dimension of mediator strategies and tactics focuses on the substance of the interaction. These strategies clarify and connect key issues in dispute. Diez (1983) began her taxonomy by labeling such functions as *coherence work*. Coherence work refers to the clarifying or sense-making function of language in interaction. Diez described it as making connections, both within the flow of interaction and between the interaction and elements outside of it. The former concerns the clarity of any part of the interaction; the latter is the means of specifying what is given and what is new.

Focusing on the internal features of the interaction, many elements challenge the mediator's ability to manage meaning within the flow of the discourse. In initial stages of mediation, conflict intensity can escalate quite quickly. Under such emotionally laden conditions, parties often take short cuts to conclusions, thereby glossing over important ideas that could contribute to reasoned negotiation. This glossing process may cause couples to miss possible connections that might lead to a settlement. For example, consider the husband's comment, "I don't care about the legal custody problem, I just want to see my son more often!". Deciding to probe this comment, the mediator might discover that the husband is open to a joint custody arrangement as long as he receives liberal visitation rights.

Mediators that help couples synthesize or structure the information can assist couples in deleting the "hidden" principles clouding the assessment of potential solutions. The interaction at the end of chapter 2 illustrates this need very well. In that interaction, several legal issues, including parenting competence and relational concerns, appear in one talking turn. Unfortunately, the speaker has little ability or inclination to sort through them. As a result, such intense conflict often produces a great deal of confusion and ambiguity, some of which may be intentional on either disputant's part to sabotage the negotiations or vent feelings.

On the other hand, less intense conflict involves more reflection and consideration of complex issues. However, mediators must still manage the interaction to clarify how disputants will integrate solutions into their lives. For example, how will the parties' living arrangements affect the child's schooling? How will the custody arrangement affect each individual's career plans and financial status? In both competitive and cooperative interaction, the mediator works with a continuum of explicit/ implicit information. He or she often draws out the implicit elements in the contributions of the parties and carefully constructs relationships among the varied aspects of the situation. By its very nature, the settlement in both conflict extremes needs to be spelled out clearly as a legal document in the end.

Directing couples toward coherent solutions also involves providing them with extensive orientation information about their dispute. The emotional nature of their problem may prevent the couple from understanding its impact on the children. What are the children experiencing psychologically at their ages? How does this dispute and its potential outcomes affect future plans with their lives? Bringing these issues into the dispute both educates couples about the implications of their problems and establishes a more cooperative context for decision making by broadening the focus of the dispute to add elements capable of increasing rationality.

What strategies can mediators use to increase coherence? Based on the review presented in chapter 2, managing interaction to become more coherent requires three basic strategies: framing, reframing, and information control. Each of these is defined and reviewed.

***Framing Strategies.*** Framing involves educating parties and adding elements to the dispute capable of broadening the interaction focus. The "picture frame" metaphor is useful here because picture frames provide a foundation for stabilizing the fragile artwork. Mediators can frame complex issues by providing a more complete informational foundation for the dispute. For example, mediators may provide couples with child development information to aid in understanding how children face divorce. Or, mediators might add financial considerations to the dispute as a means of shedding new light on a particular issue. Mediators might also identify points of agreement or disagreement to reinforce progress and identify areas that need more work.

***Reframing.*** In contrast to framing, reframing works with the elements provided by the disputants and attempts to restructure them to add coherence. Three basic levels of reframing can be identified. At the least abstract level, mediators can simply repeat a disputant's comment to reflect that comment back to the speaker and increase its clarity (e.g., "Are you saying that you don't like your former husband's girlfriend?"). At a second level of abstraction the mediator can repeat the comment and pull out an issue associated with the comment (e.g., "You seem angry about the girlfriend situation and that you might be feeling displaced as a mother"). At the third level of abstraction the mediator might add features to disputants' options that may help deal with the issues. More complete, well-developed options contribute to coherence by encouraging parties to see beyond their own narrow goals and by creating opportunities they may not have considered previously.

***Information Control.*** This type of coherence strategy involves accessing and developing the information resource in mediation (Donohue & Diez, 1985). Information is the key resource necessary in building options. Without information, options cannot develop very broadly. Controlling information means using questions and other directives to access couples' perceptions of the child's circumstances, living arrangements, interpersonal relationships with others, and so forth. Mediators might rely more on open-ended questions or directives to encourage more free-flowing discussion when conflict intensity is low. Or, they may use more direct, overt forms of gathering information during heavy conflict intensity to limit disruptive behavior. Nevertheless, gathering information from disputants is a key substantive coherence strategy.

Coherence work contributes extensively to mediator control because adding clarity to a complex dispute gives direction and focus to an impossible, frustrating situation to the disputants. This service creates a dependency on the mediator's skills and draws the couple into a more compliant communication stance. The increased rationality created by this cooperation allows the parties to focus on their problems. It also serves to distract them from the emotional backlog surrounding the issues that have divided them. This use of connecting and linking both clarifies the work of the parties in negotiating their agreement and allows them to begin to change their positions, because the positions have been separated from the emotional baggage by the mediator.

## Procedural Structuring

***Overview.*** Because most couples come to divorce mediation with little understanding of what to expect, and with a long history of turmoil, they need some kind of structure within which to conduct their dispute. Mediators seek to provide a structure capable of reducing person-centered acrimony while focusing on the issue-centered features of the dispute. Structure empowers disputants to interact cooperatively by providing them with a set of principles for organizing the dispute. Such organization decreases ambiguity, allowing the parties to invest some trust in the process so they can give it a chance to work for them. Bearing in mind that the two parties retain control of the outcomes in mediation, the mediator makes structuring choices that direct the flow of the interaction so parties begin complying with the mediator's requests and couples begin interacting productively.

Based on the research reported in chapter 2, three basic structuring strategies appear to dominate mediations: setting agenda, developing and enforcing discussion rules, and directing the modes of information exchange. Each of these strategies is discussed here.

*Agenda Setting.* As indicated in chapter 2, most mediators advocate using a set of phases for leading individuals toward agreement. These phases set an agenda for discussion. They provide the kind of structure needed to increase a sense of direction. This agenda provides this sense of direction by creating interim goals to measure progress. Also, the agenda provides the mediator with a resource in the event of impasse. When they get stuck, mediators can use the structure to summarize their progress and retreat to a prior phase to learn the source of the impasse. Structuring begins when mediators orient parties to mediation by explaining their role and talking explicitly about what they can and cannot do in assisting the parties in coming to an agreement. Agenda setting continues throughout the mediation as the mediator might summarize progress in phases, announce phases, or direct discussions in ways that are consistent with certain phase objectives.

Agenda setting is one avenue that mediators can use to control the substance of the interaction, and in so doing, structure its direction. At a less abstract level, mediators can also manipulate topics within phases as a means of establishing structure to the interaction. In intense conflict, disputants initiate topics suited to their needs as opposed to the needs of the family. Bringing that disputant back to a more functional topic that both maintains the continuity of the discussion and maintains the integrity of the phase reinforces the structure needed for effective problem solving.

***Developing and Enforcing Discussion Rules.*** Structure is maintained in mediation through discussion rules. Mediators seek to establish very basic rules that provide for a fair and equitable decision-making process. A lack of rules encourages exploitation as the more powerful speaker might try to violate politeness rules to dominate the other. For example, in a recent study, Donohue and Weider-Hatfield (1988) found that husbands in more intense conflict situations tended to interrupt their wives and the mediators more than husbands in more cooperative mediations. In these sessions, the mediators were less strict in enforcing such rudimentary rules as "no interruptions," "no slandering one another," "no discussions of past conflict that are irrelevant to the important issues," and "talk time shall be equally distributed." Such rules establish instructions for productive communication. Without such instructions and their continuous reinforcement, individuals are ignorant of how to communicate cooperatively. Rather, individuals revert to rules dominating the interaction prior to mediation. Because the relationship probably experienced some stress due to the divorce, such interactions are not likely to evolve cooperatively.

***Directing Information Exchange.*** Mediators also structure the flow of interaction by directing the manner in which individuals can exchange information. As discussed in chapter 2, many mediators use caucuses to allow couples to vent their emotions and to gather sensitive details that are unlikely to emerge in face-to-face interactions. In addition to caucuses, mediators might promote indirect information exchange between disputants. That is, mediators might insist on speaking after every disputant's statement. This creates a pattern in which disputants rarely exchange information directly with one another. For example, the husband might make a proposal. The mediator would then ask the wife how she likes the proposal and the wife would respond. The mediator is placed in the middle of disputant information exchange. Or, if the mediator feels that the couple is making some progress and can interact cooperatively, the mediator might ask each disputant to direct his or her statements to one another.

Structuring interventions establish a different kind of control for mediators than coherence interventions. Structuring moves seek to gain control by imposing external constraints on the interaction. Enforcing interaction rules, imposing phases, and using caucuses impose external constraints and, in so doing, establish the authority of the mediator. Coherence interventions, on the other hand, establish a more internal form of control by providing parties with insights into their dispute. As parties gain more insight into their problems, they are more likely to attribute competence to the mediator. This increased competence should increase credibility, and therefore, translate into more control.

Regarding time, structuring interventions should dominate initial phases of mediation until a discussion mechanism is established that can carry the disputed issues. Once the structure emerges, the mediator can move to a greater reliance on coherence strategies to move the control from the external hand of the mediator to the internal, rational properties of the disputants. This movement allows a transition from mediator dominance to disputant dominance, and permits parties to take charge of their own dispute.

Throughout the discussions of both the procedural structuring and substantive coherence strategies, it is clear that mediators must be attentive to relational issues in mediation. For the most part, couples come to mediation because their relationship has deteriorated significantly. Facilitating communication between disputants means paying attention to these relational issues. The final set of mediator strategies addresses this problem.

## Interpersonal Distance

***Overview.*** In addition to managing interaction structure and its substantive coherence, mediators might also develop some feel for the level of interpersonal distance needed during mediation interaction. Interpersonal distance is difficult for mediators to manage for two reasons. First, as suggested earlier, distance patterns are very complex and difficult to understand. Consider the comment, "GET THE HELL OUT OF MY LIFE!" Also, assume this comment interrupted the prior comment. This directive is an excellent example of the inconsistent distance messages disputants can send to one another. On the one hand, the comment reduces psychological distance by being very direct and intense. Also, it seeks to establish a very informal level of social distance with the profanity. On the other hand, the intense nature of the directive aims at increasing role distance by trying to dominate the other party.

This comment illustrates a very important principle about the nature of distance in conflict situations. When individuals move toward one another, or increase their intimacy or cooperativeness, they reduce distance and signal a more involved interpersonal relationship. Decreases in intimacy and movement away from one another signals less involvement. In a conflict situation, movement against one another signals inconsistent distance expressions. That is, in conflict, individuals move closer to one another signaling less distance, but they are sending messages that signal a desire to separate themselves from one another.

The second reason distance is difficult to manage relates to the subtle manner in which it influences interaction. Psychological and social distance operate at very microscopic levels of conversation. The former deals with very subtle language features that signal attraction, including verb tense and pronoun selection. The latter focuses on interaction forms that mark a situation as formal or informal (e.g., interruption patterns, use of long sentences, and big words). Processing this kind of information in the face of intense conflict demands a great deal from mediators. Role distance is a bit less difficult to detect because it functions more overtly in conversation. Language that seeks to dominate the other party is relatively apparent.

Even though managing distance is difficult, the need seems critical given that couples enter mediation with deteriorating relationships. The following sections are aimed at exploring how mediators might attend to each of the three forms of distance described earlier.

***Psychological Distance.*** Because this form of distance signals the degree of directness and involvement in the interaction, mediators face the problem of deciding what levels of immediacy are appropriate during intense conflict. As indicated earlier, as parties move against one another in an argument, they use very immediate language. For example, when engaged in very verbally aggressive name calling, parties speak very intensely and directly. Yet, one party may get their feelings hurt during the fight that may, in turn, encourage them to be less open and honest in the future. Thus, if mediators continue to allow high levels of immediacy in a dispute in the form of verbal aggression, they risk a backlash that may push them too far apart to communicate productively in the future.

Strategically, mediators may wish to differentiate levels of immediacy by topic or issue. For example, it might be productive to encourage immediacy regarding the couple's feelings about their children or about their own personal and professional needs. The mediator would increase such verbal immediacy by asking the parents to be explicit and personal in expressions of feelings toward their children. The more personally they tell their stories, the more attraction they express toward their children. At the same time, the mediator may try to encourage the parties to distance themselves from the emotional feelings directed against the other person that could interfere with a productive settlement. To accomplish this task, the mediator might ask each party to label the emotions and not to elaborate on the circumstances that gave rise to the emotions. Detailing the circumstances would make the emotions more explicit and would probably surface a great deal of old conflicts in the process.

*Social Distance.* Managing social distance requires that the mediator select a level of formality that is appropriate for disputants' needs. In highly emotional, intense conflicts, the mediator might wish to create a more neutral tone. Emotional, aggressive interaction tends to look very informal with frequent interruptions and colloquial terms. Yet, disputants can also pursue a more righteous, formal tone in accusing the other of creating problems. Thus, a more neutral tone should function best to focus on problem solving and to avoid interaction patterns that might disrupt collaborative efforts.

Moreover, mediators benefit from establishing a level of social distance from each party that does not jeopardize his or her relationship with the other. Common reference terms for each disputant seem prudent to lend a sense of fairness to the interaction. Name choices (i.e., first name or title and last name) or nonverbal reference through eye contact may be subtle cues of social distance. Or, lapsing into an informal social distance with one party through humor, for example, whereas a more formal tone is maintained with the other party might compromise the mediator's sense of fairness. In less intense conflict situations, individuals generally attribute less significance to inconsistencies in formality because these situations impose fewer constraints on the extent to which the individuals need to focus on the task. Thus, it generally pays for the mediator to remain concerned about appropriate levels of formality during the mediation session.

*Role Distance.* Role distance presents a special challenge for mediators. The challenge is difficult because of the control problem described previously. Disputants in aggressive, intense interaction, pursue powerful and domineering strategies and tactics (see Courtright, Millar, & Rogers-Millar, 1979) intended to punish the other or win the dispute. Changing topics, using imperative directives, or disconfirming tones not only challenges the mediator's role, but also challenges the other's role as an equal participant in the process. As indicated previously, mediators who allow couples to consistently use these role-domineering messages risk role conflict that may result in an inappropriate loss of mediator control.

In general, the mediator's goal strategically is to encourage couples to adopt strategies and tactics that balance power. Walton (1969) indicated that balancing interpersonal power improves individuals' long-term abilities to negotiate because such balancing creates more equity in the relationship, in the sense that rewards become proportionate to costs. In a relationship characterized by unequal power, low power individuals are much more vulnerable to costs and have fewer access to rewards. Balancing power helps such individuals get back some of the energy they invest in the relationship, thereby increasing the likelihood that they will continue the relationship.

Mediators can balance power through one or more of the following options (Hocker & Wilmot, 1985). First, they can limit power attempts of the higher power party by, for example, preventing that party from interrupting the low-power person, or the mediator can make sure that both parties' perspectives on issues are heard. Second, the mediator can empower the lower power party. To accomplish this objective the mediator might caucus with the party before mediation if he or she is unwilling to reveal important information that would bolster a position in a face-to-face encounter with the other party. Third, the mediator could attempt to transcend the win–lose aspect of the conflict that de-emphasizes power. Focusing on the children's needs or on some other aspect of the conflict that bypasses the individual power levels of the disputants might be effective in this regard.

Balanced power improves the chances for productive problem solving because such balance increases both parties' motivation to negotiate. They are more motivated because, through the balanced power, they now have greater access to rewards in the relationship and might be willing to fight harder to achieve those rewards. From another perspective, motivation might be enhanced by the realization that neither party enjoys exclusive control over outcome. They must work together to achieve an agreement.

*Summary.* Through distance work, the mediator tries to develop language patterns that set the context for more productive relationships, both between the parties and between the parties and the mediator. They accomplish this objective in two ways. First, mediators may direct couples to use certain distance levels. For example, mediators might enforce certain structuring rules that reinforce a more formal, decision-making context. This enforcement might also include some comment about the mediator's role in the interaction. On the other hand, the mediator might want to reduce distance to encourage more openness in the negotiation. Mediators often ask couples to speak directly to one another when they appear ready to cooperate. Such direct communication certainly constitutes a basic step in reducing distance. Once they are talking directly to one another, then perhaps the mediator can encourage the couple to make more explicit proposals, or to provide other information that signals trust and a willingness to work together.

Second, mediators may create certain distance levels by example. By using indirect, formal language, mediators send the implicit message that only those distance levels are appropriate in that situation. This more indirect strategy is based on establishing a norm of reciprocity. By example, the mediator creates a context in which it is understood that only certain levels of formality are appropriate. Such indirect approaches are probably only effective when the mediator has sufficient control over the situation, such that disputants will pay attention to what the mediator is doing. When conflict is intense, disputants may be less inclined to take any subtle cues about appropriate ways of interacting.

Although establishing appropriate levels of distance is critical for mediators, they also face the problem of folding these distance decisions into other decisions about interaction structure and coherence. More specifically, any given intervention by a mediator must take into account all three of these performance parameters. For example, when mediators set a decision-making agenda, they must also decide what levels of distance to encourage and how their comments might impact the interactional coherence. Thus, all three performance parameters can function simultaneously in interaction. This model argues that mediators capable of controlling all three stand a much better chance of improving disputant cooperation.

## CONCLUSIONS

Perhaps the overwhelming impression one might gain from this model of mediator-interaction management is its complexity. Is it reasonable to conclude that mediators detect, or are capable of detecting the kinds of interaction patterns identified here? How should mediators respond when disputants launch an attack on the other party to better their position, or when they use certain threatening compliance-gaining strategies and then mix up several issues into those attacks? Should they address the attacks first, or simply pull out the issues and process them? When should the mediator cut off the parties, or ask them to talk directly to one another?

This research program seeks to understand this complexity through description. It seeks to describe disputant communication patterns in each of the following three areas: relational, content, and strategic. Its goal is also to describe which kinds of mediator strategies and tactics respond to these patterns. Is it likely that mediators securing more cooperation from disputants will use more structuring strategies in response to verbally aggressive strategic moves made by disputants? Thus, describing and understanding the key interrelationships between disputant and mediator communication strategies and tactics are the goals of this project.

The next step toward accomplishing this goal is to describe the data on which these series of studies are based. That description is sufficiently detailed to provide an understanding of the issues and special problems mediators faced in those mediations. Chapter 4 presents these descriptions.

# 4

# Background Features of the Transcripts

Chapters 5 and 6 present various analyses of the divorce mediation transcripts described briefly in chapter 1. Because all of the analyses were performed on the 20 mediation sessions described in chapter 1, it might prove useful to describe these sessions in detail to facilitate interpreting the results. This task begins with a description of the court system in which the sessions were conducted. Following this description, several quantitative features of the sessions are reviewed. These features provide the necessary background to present the qualitative features of the 20 mediation cases used in these studies.

## THE LOS ANGELES CONCILIATION COURT

### The Court System

All of the tapes used in the analyses reported in this volume were collected at various branches of the Los Angeles County Family Mediation and Conciliation Court under a grant from 1981 through 1984 administered by Dr. Jessica Pearson, who was then the director of the research unit of the Association of Family and

Conciliation courts in Denver, Colorado. The grant was funded by the Children's Bureau of the U.S. Department of Health and Human Services (90–CW–634). Dr. Pearson's project aimed at evaluating and comparing a variety of established mediation programs around the country. She collected the audiotapes as a means of gaining insights into mediators' actual practices. A summary of the project's results can be found in Pearson and Thoennes (1985).

According to McIsaac (1983), the mediation of child custody and visitation disputes became mandatory in San Francisco, Sacramento, and Los Angeles counties in 1976. For several years before that date, mediation was an option for couples seeking to resolve these issues. In 1978, the Los Angeles Conciliation Court handled 747 of 1,431 disputed child custody cases. In 1981, a state law was passed making mediation mandatory throughout California for contested custody and visitation disputes. The law does not require that parents reach a settlement during mediation. It preserves their option to use the court system to resolve their dispute in the event that mediation is not appropriate for their particular dispute. For example, mediators shy away from cases involving spouse, child, or drug/alcohol abuse, although these issues might arise in the course of discussion. Such cases create tremendous power imbalances among parents and suggest that the abusing party might not be acting in good faith.

McIsaac (1987) indicated that, on a statewide basis, mediators achieve at least 62% partial or full agreements. California handles more than 30,000 mediation cases annually. Most counties find that mediation is a big money saver for the courts and for the parties involved. Court costs per hour can run into the thousands of dollars, whereas mediation costs the court only hundreds of dollars per hour. Because only about 14% of the mediation cases return to the court (McIsaac, 1981), mediation can be a real savings to the state.

Although California's mandatory system ensures that all disputants will experience mediation, it has the disadvantage of forcing couples into confrontations they might normally avoid with their present or former spouses. As a result, the range of conflict intensity is probably greater under mandatory systems than under nonmandatory systems in which couples freely choose mediation, although no data are available to validate this claim. Clearly, when couples freely select mediation, they are probably more motivated to bargain in good faith about the issues, and less motivated to use mediation to punish the other person. The

# BACKGROUND FEATURES OF THE TRANSCRIPTS

transcripts used in this study reflect a wide range of conflict intensity that often arises from a mandatory mediation system.

In addition to being mandatory, the Los Angeles system has other important features that bear upon the results of this study. First, as indicated in chapter 2, mediation in this court is confidential in the sense that mediators cannot testify in court about the mediation's proceedings, and the attorneys cannot be present during the sessions. Attorneys are included in the discussion after an outcome has been reached. Second, because the case load is large in Los Angeles, mediators often feel time pressures to mediate any given case. Couples can come back to mediation in multiple sessions, if they choose. Only one case in this analysis lasted more than one session, and it was completed in two sessions. Most sessions are completed in an average of about 2 hours, although mediators can decide to continue a session for any length of time. Third, the only outcome measure associated with these tapes is whether or not an immediate agreement was reached by the disputants. Data concerning the longevity of the outcome, or any of its perceived effects, were not available.

Finally, perhaps the most important feature of the Los Angeles system that bears upon the results of this study deals with the model of mediation used by the mediators. As indicated in chapter 1, mediators rely on the interventionist model that focuses exclusively on the legal issues and pays little attention to deep-seated relational issues. As a result, couples mired in such issues might experience some difficulty in this court.

## The Mediators and the Disputants

The 20 sessions used in the analyses were conducted by eight mediators, one of whom was a woman. All but one of the mediators had been with the court for 10 years or more. When these tapes were gathered, all mediators had spent most of their time as mediators with the court. One mediator had worked for the court for only 2 years when the tapes were made. However, this person had conducted several sessions prior to the taping. Clearly, this was a very experienced group of family court professionals.

At the time they collected these data, Pearson and Thoennes (1985) noted that the mediation staff consisted of 7 women and 8 men, most of whom hold master's degrees in social work. Six mediators were located at the central branch in downtown Los Angeles, with the remaining 6 mediators working in outlying branches. Pearson and Thoennes reported that this staff enjoys very high professional standards and works very hard to schedule whatever sessions are necessary to help couples. However, mediators experience frustration by the short-term nature of the mediation intervention. Two hours, or even 4 hours is not enough time to help angry parents whose dispute history is long and spiteful.

Each mediator taped at least two sessions. In fact, five mediators taped two sessions, two taped three sessions, and one taped four sessions. All but two of the mediators experienced at least one no-agreement session. This distribution is typical for mediators in that most get their share of agreements and no agreements. Clearly, because most of the cases get settled, mediators experience more "success" than "failure."

The couples in Dr. Pearson's study are typical of the population of Los Angeles County. She reported that about 50% were White, 25% were Black, and 25% were Hispanic. Asian and Native Americans comprised less than 5% of the sample. Educationally, the sample was also quite diverse. About 10% had no high school education, 20% graduated from high school but did not continue, about 40% received some college or trade school education, and 30% of the sample graduated from college.

Pearson and Thoennes (1985) reported that most people who arrived at the Los Angeles Conciliation Court were separated but not divorced, and only 14% were remarried. The predivorce couples (about 40% of those coming to court) had been separated for almost 12 months, whereas the postdivorce couples (the remaining 60%) had been separated for about 3 years, on the average. Most of the marriages lasted about 7 or 8 years. About 50% of the cases involved only one child, with 40% having two children.

Dr. Pearson also discovered in her survey of the mediation clients that about 50% had solved their property and child support issues. The average monthly support payment was about $290. About 60% of the children lived with the mother, whereas 33% of the couples reported that joint physical custody was in effect.

Prior to mediation, clients were asked to estimate their chances of reaching agreement. Most gave themselves only a 40% chance of success. However, after experiencing mediation, about 80% of the clients (even those not reaching agreement) said they would recommend mediation to their friends. About 60% of the clients reported settling in mediation, with 40% indicating that the agreement was "permanent." Most respondents thought that mediation produced a better outcome for them than their preliminary court hearing that specified temporary arrangements prior to dissolution of the divorce case.

## QUANTITATIVE FEATURES

### Tape Selection

As indicated previously, 20 tapes were selected from the group of 95 tapes collected from Jessica Pearson's mediation evaluation project. Because the general goal of the research project reported here involves identifying communication patterns that discriminate between an agreement and no-agreement session, the first goal in tape selection was to select an equal number of tapes in each condition. To accomplish that goal, all the tapes were reviewed and several criteria were used to select the tapes for the various analyses. The selection criteria included:

1. Husband–wife–mediator interaction, only. Several tapes involved attorneys and/or children and/or grandparents in pre- or postmediation sessions.
2. Sound quality. Many tapes were simply inaudible. One party might be audible, but the others were inaudible.
3. Coherence. Several tapes contained inaudible sequences, or the tapes ended without any conclusion, or the session was preceded by another session that was not on tape.
4. Type of session. In many instances, predivorce hearings involving attorneys were taped and included in the group of transcripts. Because these sessions are generally conducted by the attorneys, they were excluded from the sample. Only mediations excluding attorneys were included in the sample.
5. Specific outcome. In a large number of tapes, the outcome was not available.
6. Manageable logistically. The sample of tapes could not be so large that it would be difficult to code the utterances with multiple coding schemes; yet, it needed to be sufficiently large to detect patterns that emerged.
7. Mediator diversity. Because only 13 mediators produced the entire set of tapes, it seemed important to have as many mediators as possible on tape so that no one mediator domi-

nated the transcripts. A limit of four mediations by one mediator seemed appropriate.

Reviewing the tapes with Criteria 1 through 5 yielded 40 tapes that could be used. However, only 10 of those tapes were mediations in which an agreement was not reached. Because the project sought to examine an equal number of agreement tapes, the remaining 30 tapes were examined to determine which 10 to select to complete the sample of 20 tapes. The selection of 20 tapes appeared to satisfy Criterion 6 in that the 20 sessions would yield a large sample of utterances, yet the sample would not be too large to prevent it from being coded over the course of several weeks. By applying Criterion 7, the 10 agreement tapes were selected to come from maximally different mediators than the no-agreement tapes. As a result of this seventh criterion, 8 mediators are represented on 20 tapes, which is a reasonable diversity considering that only 13 mediators produced all 95 tapes.

**Transcribing Procedures**

After selecting the 20 tapes, they were transcribed using the procedures outlined in Schenkein (1978). This transcribing scheme was considered appropriate because it was designed for conversation analysis, which requires very detailed information about how the talk is produced. For example, interruptions, overlapping talk, and pausing were detailed very carefully in this transcribing format. The location where the interruption began and ended was also included. Providing this kind of detailed information was considered essential for the coders who were often asked to make judgments about the speaker's intent. The added information aided significantly in these decisions.

**Utterance Frequencies**

The entire set of transcripts yielded 9,169 utterances. There were 7,511 (62.3%) utterances from the agreement tapes and 3,458 (37.7%) from the no-agreement tapes. The agreement husbands made 1,788 talking turns and the no-agreement husbands made 1,178 turns for a total of 2,966 utterances. The agreement wives made 1,917 turns, whereas the no-agreement wives contributed 1,042 turns for a total of 2,959 utterances. The agreement mediators spoke 2,006 times, whereas the no-agreement mediators made 1,238 utterances, for a total of 3,244.

The most significant features of these totals is that the agreement mediations extended their sessions much more than the no-agreement sessions. Reading the transcripts gives the impression that mediators in the no-agreement sessions made a judgment fairly early on about whether the session was going anywhere. If momentum failed to occur, then the mediators simply bailed out. Again, because California is a mandatory mediation state, and the mediators use only the interventionist model, it is quite possible that mediators are sophisticated at identifying signs of couples who cannot be helped. For example, one sign of difficulty for mediators might be the emergence of difficult relational issues. Barraged with such issues, the mediators might sense that the couple is not ready to focus on the legal issues.

Another interesting feature of these numbers relates to the frequency with which the mediators intervened. In both conditions, the mediators spoke more frequently than either of the two disputants. In fact, mediators intervened after each disputant's utterance about 84% of the time. Mediators rarely let couples talk directly to one another.

## QUALITATIVE FEATURES

Although the numbers tell the technical side of the story, they cannot begin to tell the human side of the story. The 20 families represented on the transcripts have different stories to tell from different perspectives. Rather than provide a description of each mediation session, it might be more useful to summarize the 20 mediations along several dimensions that might provide some insight into the analyses described in subsequent chapters.

These mediation sessions are described along six dimensions:

1. Point in the relationship. Were the couples coming to mediation as a predivorce option, or as a postdivorce option? This distinction is important because couples coming to mediation as a predivorce option have had less time to build animosity toward one another than couples using mediation after their divorce, or well after their divorce.
2. Who wants change? Does the husband want change in the legal status of the child and/or visitation agreement; does the

wife want change, or are both parents seeking change? Accessing this information might account for some communicative differences among the disputants. For example, if the husbands seek change in a custody agreement, the wife might adopt more intense communication patterns to defend the current agreement.
3. Were caucuses used? Chapter 2 indicated that some mediators favor caucuses with the disputants as a means of diffusing tensions that might get in the way of developing an agreement. Differences in caucus use might provide some useful information about how certain outcomes were reached.
4. Disputed legal issue. Were the couples disputing custody, visitation, support (some mediators discuss this issue even though they cannot include such information in the formal agreement), or some combination of issues during the mediation?
5. Other disputed issues. In addition to the legal issues in dispute, what were some of the other subissues and underlying issues that emerged in the course of trying to resolve the legal issues? The relationship among these three strata of issues is discussed in chapter 2. The range of issues that appeared in these mediations were: (a) trust or other relational issues, (b) money, (c) physical or drug abuse, (d) extramarital affairs (beyond relational issues), (e) parenting, and (f) none.
6. Outcome on other disputed issues. Was agreement or resolution reached on any of the other disputed issues, or did they remain contested after the mediation?

Procedurally, these data were collected from two sources. First, data for Categories 1, 2, 3, and 4 were gathered from information that accompanied the tapes. The information needed to code Categories 5 and 6 was gained by performing a content analysis of the tapes. Two coders applied the categories listed in Categories 5 and 6 after extensive training. Procedurally for Category 5, the coders examined each utterance for the presence of any or all of the nonlegal issues. The reliability estimate (Guetzkow, 1950) on the set of categories (.89) in Category 5 indicates that the coders were able to make these issue judgments fairly consistently. For Category 6, two coders made a judgment about whether or not (simply yes, no) these nonlegal issues were resolved by the end of the transcript. The criterion for resolution included some kind of overt agreement from both sides that the issue was resolved to the satisfaction of both parties. The coders agreed on these resolutions in 83% of the cases.

## Point in the Relationship

As it turns out, the agreement sessions differ dramatically from the no-agreement sessions along this dimension. In all but two of the agreement sessions, mediation was a predivorce option for the disputants. The other two families came to mediation to modify existing orders granted after their divorce. On the other hand, three of the no-agreement sessions were predivorce, whereas the remaining seven families came to mediation after the divorce.

Although this finding may make sense from the standpoint that predivorce couples generally have less time to build up animosities with one another, the finding is surprising in another way. Specifically, nearly 40% of the cases coming to the California courts are postdivorce cases. One might expect that the court would develop ways of handling these couples, given that they see them frequently. Perhaps such couples defy standard solutions to their problems so they fall outside of what the court is willing to do to help couples develop a working relationship with one another.

## Who Wants Change

Differences were not readily apparent across this dimension. Of the 10 agreement sessions, 5 were initiated by the husband, 2 by the wife, and 3 by both parties. Of the 10 no-agreement sessions, 5 were initiated by the husband, 3 by the wife, and only 2 by both parties. An interesting feature of these data is that wives seemed a bit less reluctant to initiate actions involving family change. Perhaps the husbands felt that their wives got, or were about to receive a better deal than they deserved.

Comparing the prior category, "Point in the Relationship," with this category of "Who Wants Change," some interesting results emerge. In 6 of the 9 mediations in which the dispute occurred after the divorce, the husband was the party bringing the action that caused the couple to enter into mediation. On the other hand, the 11 predivorce actions were evenly distributed by person with husbands asking for change in 4, the wives in 3 mediations, and both parties seeking change in the remaining 4 mediations. In conversations with many mediators, it was learned that when mediators see postdivorce actions, they generally feel a fight coming on with the husband. The most frequent incident-provoking action is the father seeking custody after divorce because the wife is withholding visitation. In many cases the wives claimed that the husbands were not paying child support promptly, so they did not feel that the husbands deserved visitation with the child. This vicious cycle of the mother holding the child ransom for money and the father not paying until he sees the children appears to be a common problem in mediation.

**Were Caucuses Used?**

In 8 of the 20 mediations, caucuses were used. Three occurred in the no-agreement mediations and 6 were done in the agreement mediations. The 12 mediations in which caucuses were not used were evenly divided between agreement and no-agreement sessions. Although it is impossible to determine whether the caucuses contributed to the increased willingness of the parties to agree with one another, these data suggest that agreement is twice as likely when caucuses are used. Certainly, the 20 mediations represent a small sample of the cases that come before the Los Angeles Conciliation Court. As such, it would be interesting to conduct further research with the caucused sessions to determine (as suggested in chapter 2) whether these private sessions actually reduce tensions between disputants by allowing them to vent their relational frustrations toward one another.

Another interpretation of the observation that caucuses were twice as likely to be used in agreement sessions is that the mediators sensed rather quickly that the agreement couples were worth more effort than the no-agreement couples. A bit of evidence that lends some credibility to this interpretation lies in analyzing which pre- and postdivorce cases received caucuses. Of the 8 caucuses, 6 were among predivorce couples, whereas only 2 were among postdivorce couples. This bit of evidence, although again based on a very small sample size, suggests that some postdivorce couples may have been categorized as "hard to handle," with little chance of success.

Do the mediators' initial expectations about the potential success of a case affect their communication interventions in working with the couples? Although there is no evidence from actual divorce mediation courts, a recent laboratory experiment does shed some light on this issue (Burrell, 1987). In this experiment, students were asked to role-play mediators in actual roommate conflicts between other students. The mediators' expectations about case difficulty were manipulated so that mediators were lead to believe that the cases would be very difficult or very easy to resolve. Burrell (1987) found that these expectations had no effect on outcome, disputants' evaluations of mediator performance, or mediator-intervention strategies.

Although this study was a laboratory experiment involving university students, it does provide some evidence that mediator expectations may not significantly impact mediator communication behavior during the sessions. The study does not address the issue of selecting caucuses or other interventions outside the mediation activities. In talking with mediators it was learned that they generally review files prior to a session and look for case features that may indicate what kind of session they are likely to encounter. In courts with smaller case loads than Los Angeles, court mediators often get to know cases quite well because couples often come back to court on several occasions. Thus, it is probably likely that mediators form expectations about cases. However, the impact of these expectations is unclear at the present time.

## Disputed Legal Issue

Of the 20 cases, 6 were custody disputes, evenly divided between both agreement conditions. Of the cases, 10 were visitation disputes with 4 in the no-agreement condition. One of these visitation disputes discussed the support issue in relation to the visitation problem. The remaining 4 mediations concerned themselves with both custody and visitation disputes.

Of particular interest is the distribution of cases along the pre- and postdivorce category. The custody cases were evenly divided with 3 in each category. However, 7 of the predivorce cases were visitation, whereas only 3 were in the postdivorce group. One predivorce case involved both custody and visitation, whereas 3 postdivorce cases tried to tackle both issues at once. The interesting feature of these numbers is that the predivorce (the agreement cases) focused mostly on the visitation. And, most of the postdivorce (the no-agreement cases) addressed mostly custody issues. Because the custody issue is undoubtedly more difficult to handle, these figures are not surprising.

In fact, the mediators in this study had the best and worst of both worlds. Most of their predivorce cases (7 of 11) already settled the custody issue with only visitation remaining. Some agreement had already been reached, so only the relatively easy visitation issue remained. In contrast, most postdivorce cases (6 of 9) had to fight the custody battle. The hard work was still in front of them, with no foundation of agreement behind the disputants upon which they could build.

## Other Disputed Issues

The remaining nonlegal issues represented in the mediations provide additional insights into the difficulty of the mediator's job. For example, in 8 of the 10 no-agreement mediations, relational issues were prevalent; in only 4 of the agreement mediations did these issues emerge. In half of the no-agreement sessions money was discussed, whereas only 1 of the agreement sessions had to deal with money topics. Similarly, parties in 3 of the no-agreement sessions brought out allegations of physical or drug abuse, whereas parties in the agreement sessions exposed none of these topics. Outside affairs arose in only 1 no-agreement mediation. However, allegations about parental competence were concerns in 6 no-agreement sessions and in only 2 of the agreement sessions.

The reader could easily draw the impression that the range and frequency of these nonlegal issues were greater in the no-agreement sessions than in the agreement sessions. This impression is an accurate reflection of the reality. On average, the no-agreement mediators had to deal with 2.4 nonlegal issues per discussion, whereas the agreement mediators struggled with only .9 nonlegal issues per session. The striking feature of these figures is that the no-agreement mediations were about half as long as the agreement ones. The no-agreement mediators took less time to interact, but were exposed to many more issues.

The most frequent combination of these leftover issues was relationship and money appearing in 5 of the 10 no-agreement sessions. None of the agreement sessions was forced to address this powerful combination. This combination tended to take the form of one person charging the other with lack of trust or good faith, and the other withholding money until some good faith was demonstrated. Given this combination, and the fact that the no-agreement mediators had so much more issue baggage than the other sessions, it seems clear that no-agreement mediators were fighting an uphill battle.

## Outcome on Other Disputed Issues

Given the shorter duration of the no-agreement sessions and the overwhelming number of issues exposed in those session, it is not surprising to learn than none of these nonlegal issues was resolved during the no-agreement mediations. However, in only one of the agreement mediations in which nonlegal issues were discussed did the mediator help the couple resolve those issues, as well. Thus, it appears that mediators focused almost exclusively on the custody/visitation issues to the exclusion of the nonlegal issues. Again, this focus on legal issues stems from the interventionist model of mediation used in the Los Angeles court. The system is not really designed to deal with the full range of couples' problems. When they come in with deep-seated relational concerns, the court chooses not to confront them for a variety of pragmatic reasons (e.g., time and money) and philosophical reasons (e.g., mediation is not relational therapy as endorsed by the facilitation model). It would be interesting to compare the models that deal with relational problems with models that ignore this focus, both from a short-term agreement and a long-term viability perspective.

## CONCLUSIONS

Few would doubt the claim that mediation in the California system is difficult. Case loads are high and the amount of time available to help people is limited. The mandatory prescription further stresses the system. This combination of elements must certainly provide for tremendous variance in the levels of conflict intensity observed in this system. Postdivorce couples who have hated one another for years, and predivorce couples with only a recent history of dislike must all mediate within this time crunch. As the studies in the following chapters attest, these transcripts display this range of conflict intensity. Enmeshed couples who live to fight are represented in the sample. Couples with less conflict-habituated relationships also emerge in the sample.

From the point of view of this book, the critical question stemming from the observation that some cases pose greater challenges than others relates to the relative importance of communication in this mediation process. In general, does communication make any difference, and in particular, does a mediator's ability to manage the interaction exert a significant influence over the outcome?

This critical question is addressed from two perspectives. First, to what extent was communication, and particularly interaction management given a chance to make a difference in these mediation sessions? If it was not given much of a chance to work, then these transcripts probably do not provide a very good test about the extent to which well-managed interaction can make a difference in mediation.

To address this issue, consider the challenges the no-agreement mediators faced and how they tried to face them. They faced a large number of nonlegal disputed issues, none of which was addressed or resolved. These disputants came to mediation well after their divorce, signaling a long history of making problems for one another. This conflict history certainly suggests that these couples might bring a hefty number of nonlegal problems to the table. To deal with these couples, the mediators made three choices. They focused fairly exclusively on the legal issues, they spent less time in the mediation sessions, and they caucused infrequently with these couples.

For the agreement couples, the mediators made some different structural decisions, but their approach was basically the same. They caucused a bit more, and they spent more time with them. But, from a communication perspective, they still focused exclusively on the legal issues. That probably worked for these couples because they came to the table with fewer problems enabling them to focus on the legal issues. Mediators probably sensed that they could make more progress with these couples so they spent more time with them.

Given these challenges, and the decisions the mediators made to meet them, is it fair to say that the ability of interaction management to "cause" an agreement received a good test through these transcripts? The answer is, probably not. None of the mediators thought much about interaction management because none were not trained to use it. They were trained to help couples deal with the legal issues and they did that. So, no one will ever know what might have happened if the mediators had used interaction management techniques more aggressively with the no-agreement couples. Thus, all we really know about these transcripts is that the mediators used the model they were trained to use and it worked for some couples and not for others.

So, we come back to the original issue of what this project can tell us about the role of communication and interaction management in helping couples reach agreement. As suggested here, the first reaction to this issue is that these transcripts may not provide the best resources for addressing this issue. Indeed, perhaps no set of naturally gathered transcripts could serve this purpose very effectively. However, the second perspective for looking at this issue goes back to the purpose of conducting this research in the first place. Specifically, this book simply tries to use interaction management as a template to describe how mediators and disputants interact with one another. Examining the extent to which interaction management "causes" couples to reach agreement remains a fruitful issue for another analysis. This book seeks to learn more about how marital couples communicate when they are very distressed, and how mediators try to manage this distress. These transcripts certainly appear capable of accomplishing this goal. Indeed, by describing these communication differences perhaps mediators can be alerted to the challenges they might face in "difficult" or "easy" cases.

This book now moves to chapter 5 exploring disputant-interaction patterns. Several interesting patterns that stem from the mediator-interaction management model are revealed in this next chapter.

# 5

# Disputant Communication Patterns

Chapter 3 presented the idea that mediators can better serve couples by discriminating between their productive and unproductive communication patterns. This idea comes clearly into focus when talking with mediators about their major communication challenges. Typically, mediators express frustration about their intervention timing. "When do I jump in and when do I let them go?" asked one mediator. What solid criteria can mediators use to make these decisions? As indicated at the beginning of chapter 3, this timing problem is really a discrimination problem. When mediators identify patterns that threaten cooperativeness, some kind of intervention is needed to redirect the interaction. When couples are communicating productively, they should probably be left alone.

Of course, the question is which patterns reflect cooperation and which threaten it? This simple question is the focus of chapter 5. Specifically, it explores the three types of disputants' communication patterns described in chapter 3: content, strategic, and relational. What different choices do couples make along these three dimensions as they move toward building an agreement or confronting a stalemate? To address this key question, chapter 5 begins by examining disputants' content communication patterns. Do the differences found in chapter 4 regarding the kinds of issues couples and mediators discussed emerge under closer scrutiny?

## DISPUTANTS' COMMUNICATION CONTENT PATTERNS

Recall from chapter 2 that the first criterion for a successful divorce settlement negotiation offered by Kressel (1985) focused on the extent to which all relevant issues get resolved. As a result, mediators probably should pay close attention to the issues disputants expose in the course of their interaction. To illustrate the importance of understanding how issues are exposed, interrelated, and developed in mediation, consider this actual husband–wife–mediator exchange:

Wife: [To mediator] There's a boundary line he likes to cross and not respect me as a human being. He shows up at my house unannounced and uninvited. I've tried to tell him as simply as possible, don't come to my house uninvited. He came by at 6 just when we were eating dinner.
Husband: You were not eating dinner. You never eat until 7.
Mediator: [To husband] Is that 6 o'clock time in the current visitation order?

This exchange reflects a main problem that mediators face in managing the substance of disputants' statements: Parties often expose multiple issues in a single statement that mediators must sort out, prioritize, and discuss. For example, the wife began her statement by bringing up a relational issue of respect. She followed this issue with a statement expressing her value for consideration, and concluded with a statement of fact about what time her former husband arrived for his visitation. The husband responded only to the time issue and ignored the others. The mediator also addressed only the time issue in relation to the visitation agreement already in force.

This section extends the very preliminary analysis conducted in chapter 4 about the kinds of issues discussed in the mediation sessions. That analysis did not provide a detailed look at the kinds of issues mediators encouraged disputants to address. Did the mediators concentrate more on the relational issues, or on matters more directly related to outcomes? Did the disputants go along with these directives or set their own discussion agenda?

### Categorizing Issues

What do people fight about? To answer this question, a way of categorizing issues in mediation was needed. Perhaps the most parsimonious scheme for categorizing issues, and one that integrates the discussions presented in this chapter and chapter 1, is found in Wehr's (1979) conflict map. In this map, Wehr identified four types of issues: (a) facts-based, or disagreement about the truth or falsity of some perception/judgment, or the existence or nonexistence of some phenomenon or event; (b) values-based, or disagreement about prescriptions related to policies, relationships, or some other source of conflict; (c) interests-based, or disagreements over wants and the distribution of resources (e.g., power, privilege, rewards, and so forth); and (d) nonrealistic issues, or disagreements originating elsewhere than in these substantive categories including interaction style, quality of communication, or aspects of the immediate physical setting such as discomfort. Although these remain useful categories for exploring the types of issues that arise in conflict, they appear to have generated little research. As a result, their empirical value is unclear, at this point.

Despite their lack of empirical validation, this issue typology appears well suited to categorizing issues arising most often in the divorce mediation context for two reasons. First, the Wehr (1979) categories capture the substantive essence of mediation interaction. Specifically, most custody and visitation disputes center on such problems as desired visitation, custody, and resource-allocation arrangements (interests), the suitability of the other parent (values), the extent to which the parent has complied with past arrangements (facts), and deep-seated emotional issues about prior relational problems, feelings about the other, or past failures that have little or nothing to do with the substantive nature of the dispute (nonrealistic).

Second, these categories can be arranged on a continuum suggested by Coser's (1956) distinction between realistic and nonrealistic conflict. Realistic conflicts arise from frustration of specific demands. They focus on the disputants' interests, and are resolved through negotiation. On the other hand, nonrealistic conflicts arise from a need of tension release. Individuals focus their tension release on the other person with no real objective in mind other than hurting that other person. Thus, realistic conflicts are issue-centered and address disputant goals. Nonrealistic conflicts are person-centered and focus on individual frustrations.

The most realistic, straightforward disputes arise from factual disputes because they are simply based on "what is" in the world. At the next level of abstraction are interests that are based on "what I want" in relation to "what is." The third level (values) goes even further to provide a rationale and a moral foundation for "what I want" to "what's the right thing to do." Finally, we move to the extreme nonrealistic conflicts based on past emotional/relational problems that serve to vent frustrations. Such disputes can border on value imperatives because they deal with problems of trust, control, or intimacy, yet they are not directly relevant to the substance of the dispute. Given this category scheme, the question at this point is how did the mediators manage the issues? This chapter now turns to that question.

## Mediator Issue Management

For mediators, managing disputant issues is critical, as discussed in chapter 2, because in conflict the issues need to be organized. When people are mad about many different issues at once, they become very jumbled. Sorting through the issues is a difficult task. To illustrate this problem, consider the following actual husband–wife interaction sequence:

Husband: You never told the truth about money when we were living together. How do I know you're not lying now?
Wife: Look, all I want is my $50 a week so I can support my son.
Husband: For all I know you're probably spending all your money on that jerk sleeping with you.
Wife: The judge says I should get the money. I've got bills to pay. My son needs things for school.

These disputants are talking about the same *topic*, money, but they are discussing very different money *issues*. The husband treats the money as relational currency and appears lost in relational issues associated with spousal separation. The wife, on the other hand, simply expresses her money needs in a manner unrelated to the marital relationship. Given this confusion about the topic, the disputants lose sufficient focus to make a decision about any of these items. By allowing the disputants to continue interacting, the mediator in effect reinforces this disorganization. Increasing the organization by pulling out one issue at a time and directing the disputants to talk about one issue at a time, the mediator begins the problem-solving process.

Returning to the original goal of this chapter, helping mediators separate productive from unproductive communication patterns, it seems clear that one unproductive communication pattern involves allowing couples to jumble important issues. Not stepping in to stop the interaction and separate the issues denies the couple access to their problems. An additional communication pattern that can also get away from mediators deals with couples' strategic communication patterns. What happens when mediators allow parties to attack one another without intervention? This chapter now turns to this problem.

## NEGOTIATING DISPUTANTS' STRATEGIC POSITIONS

Positioning strategies reveal how individuals try to adjust one another's goals during mediation. What positioning strategies might be expected between the agreement and no-agreement disputants? To answer this question, this section begins by reviewing the kinds of goals and strategies disputants pursue, and the kinds of identities they try to maintain while arguing their points of view.

### Research on Goals

Wilson and Putnam (1990) interrelated two key concepts that help understand negotiation in mediation: *goals* and *strategies*. They defined goals as people's thoughts about their desired end states. These goals can pertain to entire negotiations, or to single sessions or encounters. For example, a husband might want custody of his daughter as his overall goal, but in a particular session he might want to hurt his former wife to make her pay for his grief. Couples pursue their goals using strategies, or specific actions driven by the goals. If a mother repeatedly attacks a father's parenting skills, then the attack becomes an offensive strategy to achieve some overall objective. In summary, goals represent what people want, whereas strategies represent how they try to achieve them.

Most researchers in bargaining and negotiation literature concentrate on two main types of strategies: *distributive* and *integrative* (Donohue, 1981a, 1981b; Putnam & Jones, 1982; Putnam & Poole, 1987; Walton & McKersie, 1965). Distributive strategies seek to achieve individually oriented goals at the other's expense. These strategies assume a fixed set of potential outcomes that must be distributed among the parties. In such negotiations, disputants seek to maximize their own profits that inherently means less for the other parties. Threats, put-downs, demands, blaming statements, and bluffs are common in distributive negotiation as each party tries to compete for the outcomes. Use of distributive strategies assumes that the outcomes are more important than maintaining positive relations with the other party. Friends may threaten or criticize one another on rare occasions when they are angry, but repeated use of these strategies indicates that the outcomes are more important than the friendship.

Integrative strategies, on the other hand, emphasize joint gains. These strategies tap common ground by cooperating to find alternatives that allow both sides to accomplish their goals. Pruitt (1981) listed several integrative strategies that involve helping one another overcome the costs each might incur from some jointly selected outcome, or building a third alternative outcome that bridges both individual goals. Integrative strategies involve open information sharing, joint concession making, and demonstrating flexibility on methods for achieving joint goals. As might be expected, integrative strategies assume that the disputant's relationship is just as important as the outcomes. Individuals using these strategies send the message that they desire a long-term working relationship in which they can continue to help solve one another's problems.

In a custody mediation, the difference between sole and joint custody represents an excellent example of the distributive–integrative distinction. As indicated in chapter 2, sole custody means that only one parent can hold the legal responsibility for the child; joint custody means that both parents maintain that legal responsibility. Before joint custody was implemented by the courts, parents found themselves competing for the "ownership" of their children. This competition encouraged them to use distributive strategies, which in turn further eroded the parental relationship. Joint custody is a legal partnership between parents that allows them to bridge their individual goals in favor of their collective goal. This bridging encourages them to use more integrative strategies while also stressing the need for a long-term, cooperative parental relationship.

It is important to note that disputants in mediation, or in any bargaining context for that matter, do not rely exclusively on either distributive or integrative strategies. Putnam and Poole (1987) emphasized that bargaining contains both kinds of strategies depending on how goals evolve over time. A mother entering mediation without any knowledge of the joint custody option might begin using distributive strategies to win custody of her child. Once informed of the joint custody option, she might change her strategies to become more integrative. Or, individuals might maintain the overall goal of developing a mutually satisfactory visitation arrangement, thereby encouraging them to use integrative strategies.

The question of interest for this research is how do disputants mix integrative and distributive strategies to accomplish their goals? As indicated in chapter 3, bargainers use various position-adjustment strategies for this purpose. Recall that a disputant's "position" is conceptualized as a subjective, moment-to-moment sense of control over the achievement of his or her own goals. The question is, what kinds of strategies do couples use to adjust their own and the other's position to gain a greater sense of control?

## Types of Position Adjustment

As described in chapter 3, couples use a variety of strategies to strengthen their stand or position on various issues. These strategies include: (a) attacking the other's position to make his or her goal attainment less likely, (b) defending one's own position to hold ground in the face of the other's attack, (c) bolstering one's own position to make it stronger and more substantial, and (d) integrating one's own position with the other's to forge a collective position. Each of these strategies and their specific tactics are discussed in detail.

***The Attacking Position Strategy.*** Disputants frequently attack one another's positions in mediation. This strategy is probably the least rational but the most predictable because disputants enter mediation in the context of wounded personal identities. It is predictable because emotions tell them to strike back to win the children or the rights to visit them. It is least rational because until they stop attacking one another's positions, they cannot work on a collective position that can lead toward a solution that is in the best interests of the children. Consistently attacking the other demonstrates a desire to make the interaction highly competitive. Attacking tactics include (see Donohue, Allen, & Burrell, 1985):

1. insulting the other by making a personal affront of some sort;
2. charging fault to make the other appear negligent, incompetent, unfaithful, inconsiderate or improper;

3. making a hostile proposal or an outrageous demand intended to punish the other;
4. asserting rights that appear to have been denied by the other;
5. changing the topic to disconfirm the other's line of thought; and
6. structuring the discussion procedures to assume the role of mediator and to create favorable rules.

These tactics represent various means of attacking the other's identity while taking control of the interaction. The first four tactics seek to belittle or downgrade the other party. Tactics 1 through 3 demonstrate verbal aggression. Tactics 5 and 6 aim at taking charge of the dispute's direction. Controlling the topic and the discussion procedures can be very instrumental in controlling outcome. These controlling tactics also challenge the mediator's role in structuring the interaction.

***The Defending Position Strategy.*** The defending position strategy shifts the discussion away from issues potentially harmful to the individual's position on an issue. This strategy is generally used in response to attacks as the user seeks to sustain the strength of his or her own position and keep it intact. Defending tactics include:

1. rejecting the other's proposal, or in other ways challenging the other's offers;
2. rejecting the other's comment by disagreeing or challenging the prior utterance with counter examples or opinions related to the issue;
3. denying fault or any complicity in wrongdoing;
4. denying the relevance of any issue or information presented by the other;
5. requesting justification of the other's position; and
6. avoiding the issue with sarcasm or humor.

The defending strategy and its attendant set of tactics are somewhat less competitive than the attacking strategy and tactics. Whereas the attacking strategy focuses on breaking down the other's position, the defending strategy brings the focus back to the speaker in an attempt to avoid damage to the speaker's position. The tactics are still competitive in the sense that the speaker directly confronts the other's messages. However, they are not direct attacks on the other's position.

***The Bolstering Position Strategy.*** The bolstering strategy also focuses on the speaker's own position. It represents an attempt to make the position less vulnerable to attack by developing or in other ways broadening the position. However, the development is not confrontational. Rather, individuals strive to appear more credible and more focused on the task at hand and away from the other party. The following tactics illustrate this task focus:

1. proposal making to begin developing alternatives to reach the solution;
2. substantiating one's own position by providing evidence or arguments in support of the position;
3. clarifying one's position in response to a specific request to do so;
4. requesting clarification of the other's statement to learn more about the other's position;
5. extending the prior topic in a manner that does not provide new information or evidence to support a position; and
6. confirming the prior utterance by providing a simple acknowledgment of the utterance or simply agreeing about the truth of the prior statement.

Tactics 1–3 add information to the negotiation, whereas Tactics 4–6 simply keep the interaction moving. These last three might be termed *conversational organizing devices* because they are often used to show involvement in the interaction and to manage the flow of communication.

***The Integrating Position Strategy.*** Unlike the other three strategies, this positioning strategy focuses on the couple as opposed to either individual. It is a cooperative attempt to merge positions and to narrow alternatives. It provides both face-honoring and face-compensating messages in relation to the issues in negotiation. The integrating position tactics that execute this strategy include:

1. supporting the other's proposal by agreeing with, or approving the other's offers;
2. socially supporting the other through approval or acceptance messages that show understanding for the other's situation or position;
3. apologizing for any kind of unacceptable behavior;

4. giving concessions on proposals by showing a willingness to accept less than the previous proposal; and
5. proposing flexibility by indicating a willingness to look at alternative positions.

These tactics support the other party substantively and personally. They demonstrate respect, acceptance, and acknowledgment of the other's general position. By the time these tactics are used, the disputants have probably already developed a solution and are working toward selecting it openly. As a result, these tactics are most often visible during the final stages of bargaining in mediation. In addition, by selecting these tactics, couples acknowledge the need to work on improving their relational ties. They begin to reduce personal barriers and to concentrate on building a cooperative outlook. Clearly, then, relational messages are an important part of position adjustment strategies. This chapter now moves to a more explicit examination of how relational messages are exchanged in the mediation context.

## DISPUTANTS' RELATIONAL COMMUNICATION PATTERNS

As suggested in chapter 3, mediators face very difficult challenges in understanding and managing the way in which disputants relate to one another. One party might try to move closer, whereas the other party tries to signal a desire to move further away. For example, mediators often face parties who have very inconsistent commitments to maintaining a marital relation. In the segment at the beginning of chapter 1, the husband seemed interested in remaining married, whereas the wife simply wanted out. In the terms used in chapter 3, the husband wanted to become more psychologically attached to the wife, whereas the woman wanted to reduce this attachment.

What language features can be used to indicate how close or distant parties wish to define their relationship in mediation? The two language features that appear most capable of identifying how parties feel about one another include *verbal immediacy* and *language intensity*. Both of these language features and their functions in mediation are discussed in detail.

## Dimensions of Verbal Immediacy

The body of research related to verbal immediacy is dominated by the work of Mehrabian and Wiener (Mehrabian, 1966a, 1966b, 1967, 1971; Mehrabian & Wiener, 1966; Wiener & Mehrabian, 1968). These authors described the principle of immediacy by proposing that people are drawn toward persons and things they like, evaluate highly, and prefer, and they avoid things they dislike. Such preferences are reflected in, or marked by, verbal choices. In general, the immediacy cues of interest here focus on linguistic signals that propose drawing the person closer to the things preferred, and further away from the things not preferred. The signals are not explicitly stated proposals, but tacit, or understood proposals as described in chapter 3. If the other person reciprocates the level of distance, then the proposal is accepted and the context becomes altered to accept that new definition of the relationship.

***Types of Verbal Immediacy Markers.*** Although the scholars exploring the verbal immediacy construct use several different kinds of markers to examine relationship patterns, only two are discussed here: *spatial* and *implicit immediacy*. Spatial immediacy focuses on demonstratives that specify spatial relations in the communication context. Grammatically, a demonstrative is a part of speech that singles out or references the object of the sentence. The words, "the," "this," and "those" are demonstratives. Demonstratives are useful in revealing spatial relations because they provide information about how individuals view their relationship to the object in the sentence. Consider the following two sentences: (a) "I am speaking about *THIS* agreement we signed," versus (b) "I am speaking about *THAT* agreement we signed?" In sentence b, the speaker's use of the demonstrative "that" instead of "this" suggests an attempt to conceptualize the agreement as something that exists at some distance away from the speaker. Use of the demonstrative "this" brings the agreement psychologically closer to the speaker.

Demonstratives that bring objects psychologically closer to the individual include: the, this, these, and here, and are coded as spatially immediate and given a value of 3. Demonstratives that conceptualize objects as separate from the individual include: that, those, and where, and are coded as nonimmediate. If an utterance contains no reference to spatiality, or if both an immediate and nonimmediate spatial reference is contained in the same unit of analysis, then the unit is viewed as neutral, or neither immediate nor nonimmediate.

Implicit immediacy explores the extent to which the speaker specifies the subject of the sentence. If the speaker is very clear about the subject, the speaker gives the listener access to his or her actual views of the object of the statement. In essence, this more open approach gives listeners greater access to the speaker's thoughts. As a result, by being direct, the speaker is tacitly reducing distance between speaker and listener by sending the message, "I want to be more open and direct with you; I don't want to hide my thoughts." For example, if a husband claims in a mediation that "I believe you should grant me custody," he is clearly tying himself to the specified belief and giving the listener direct access to his thoughts.

However, the husband proposes a different level of relational distance in the following statement by making the subject and the object more implicit: "Some people believe you should change the custody arrangement." This increased ambiguity tacitly divorces the husband from the stated view that he, the husband (instead of some people), believes that the wife should grant him custody (as opposed to change the custody arrangement). This increased ambiguity proposes distance between the husband and the wife because the husband is giving his wife much less access to his thoughts. Less access means greater distance.

When the speaker specifically states the subject of the action, then the statement is conceptualized as highly immediate. If both the subject and object of the action are implicitly stated (the subject is understood as in the statement, "It is generally understood that"), then the statement is viewed as nonimmediate, or distance producing. If the object of the action is explicit, but the subject remains implicit, then the statement is conceptualized as neutral because the speaker strikes a balance between an implicit and an explicit statement.

***The Functions of Verbal Immediacy.*** As individuals interact, it appears that verbal immediacy choices are influenced by general relational goals and situational constraints. Research addressing the situational issue (Donohue, Weider-Hatfield, Hamilton, & Diez, 1985) found that when decision rules are imposed on conflicting dyads, the participants reduce their verbal immediacy. This impact makes sense because rules impose structure and structure creates formality. Under such formal constraints, people use more distant language to depersonalize their contributions.

More personal statements are left for after the meetings when people can interact freely.

With respect to relational goals, Donohue, Diez, Stahle, and Burgoon (1983) found that decision makers reciprocated immediacy. When a person perceived that the other wanted to become closer interpersonally, the person increased verbal immediacy. The opposite also happened. Specifically, when the subject received a cold reception, verbal immediacy decreased. This study demonstrates that people adjust their verbal immediacy as a generalized relational response to the perceived relational goals of the other. This finding makes sense because most people are cautious and formal when they are treated that way by the other. The research on reciprocal communication patterns among marital couples referenced in chapter 2 reinforces this point. People control one another's responses. We generally accept the other's relational definition of the situation and adjust accordingly.

These studies lead to an interesting conclusion. Verbal immediacy is probably not under the discriminatory control of interactants; it is more likely to follow from alterations in the interaction context, or in response to changes in global relational desires. Does this pattern hold during intense conflict? Will disputants use verbal immediacy the same way in conflict as in more cooperative interpersonal contexts? In addition to the impact of conflict on the generalized use of immediacy, what about the behavior of each individual dimension of immediacy? Will each of the four dimensions become consistently immediate or nonimmediate, or will some become very immediate while others are very nonimmediate? To answer these questions, consider the following husband–wife sequence in an actual divorce mediation:

Wife: You won't pay any utility bills cause you moved out. Not one!
Husband: That's my business. I wasn't the one who ran those up. I had those cancelled, and she had 'em turned back on.
Wife: Then what are you worried about?

It is probably easy to notice that the levels of immediacy are quite mixed within each utterance. For example, notice the explicit nature of the attacks. Also, notice that neither party qualifies his or her remarks. These explicit, unqualified comments reflect an attacking–defending interaction cycle. Typically, when people are mad they are not careful about what they say. This highly explicit, unqualified speech indicates high verbal immediacy on the implicit dimension. Yet spatially, the husband is distancing himself from this wife by referring to "those" utility bills his wife "ran up," indicating that he is marking his language with low spatial immediacy.

This example suggests that intense conflict often yields very inconsistent immediacy proposals. Spatially, the disputants are distancing themselves from one another. Yet, the implicit immediacy dimension reflects a desire to reduce distance. Their language reflects a history of caring and intimacy, but it also shows an aggressiveness to defend against the hurt, anger, and other emotional reactions couples face in divorce.

## Dimensions of Language Intensity

A second feature of language that marks relational distance is language intensity. Bowers (1963) defined *intensity* as "the quality of language which indicates the degree to which the speaker's attitude toward a concept deviates from neutrality" (p. 345). Intensity signals magnitude of feeling unlike immediacy, which signals direction of affect (positive vs. negative).

***Types of Language Intensity Markers.*** Bowers (1964) specified four features of intense language: (a) obscurity, or uncommon word choices made for rhetorical or stylistic effect (e.g., rare words or exceedingly long words may fall into this category); (b) metaphors, or words that seek to transfer the meaning of one concept to another concept in a different situation (e.g., "The couple was a study in the sand trap of jealousy"); (c) qualifiers, or words that modify other words lending to them a more extreme meaning than if the modified word stood alone (e.g., instead of accusing the other of making a "bad argument," the person would be accused of making a "ridiculous, insane argument"); and (d) profanity, or words that approach or cross the bounds of good taste and include obscenity, vulgar language, religious profanity, and metaphorical references to excrement, urine, intimate body areas, genitalia, or sexual acts are classified as profanity (e.g., "Hey, asshole, you scared the shit out of me").

Bowers (1964) divided the metaphors into three categories because his research revealed that some metaphors were more powerful than others at signaling intense language. He identified both sex and death metaphors in addition to those that did not contain such references. Sex metaphors denote the practice of sexual acts or events that refer to a broader context (e.g., "All you salesmen are whores for the company"). Death metaphors denote associations with death, decomposition, or the afterlife (e.g., "You killed our marriage"). Bowers did not identify different forms of qualifier, profanity, or obscurity markers because those appear to function unidimensionally.

***The Functions of Language Intensity.*** Bradac, Bowers, and Courtright (1979) indicated that most research using intensity has tried to assess the extent to which intensity enhances persuasion. These authors indicated that intense language enhances effectiveness when: (a) the sources try to sell messages that are consistent with the audience's views, (b) the sources have relatively high initial source credibility, and (c) receivers are high in need for social approval. Language intensity decreases persuasion when: (a) sources try to sell messages that are inconsistent with the audience's views, and (b) sources judged as less competent use obscenity in their messages. Thus, it appears that when people who do not like each other start fighting and using intense, obscene language, they simply increase their dislike for one another. Conversely, when people perceive that they have similar interests and they use intense language, they increase their attraction toward one another.

For divorce mediators, the implications of controlling language intensity seem quite clear. When couples enter mediation, they probably do not like each other very much. Allowing highly intense language while individuals vent their frustrations appears quite capable of inciting more animosity. In contrast, some disputants may need to increase their level of conflict intensity to confront very difficult individual perspective issues. At that point, mediators might consider intense language to create this conflict.

This chapter proposes the idea that understanding a couple's communication patterns in mediation requires an examination of three communication dimensions: content, strategy, and relationship. After reading about these three dimensions, it seems reasonable to form the conclusion that these dimensions are not independent. Various kinds of topics typically stimulate certain strategy choices that in turn influence the kind of relational language disputants might use to frame their contributions. For example, consider the husband's discussion of his wife's extramarital affairs and how she lied to him about these affairs. The husband will probably try to pursue this topic by attacking his wife to weaken her claim for custody. Using highly integrative language in pursuing this topic seems a bit unusual here. Relationally, the language is likely to be explicit (with the husband trying to pull the wife into the dispute) and yet spatially distant (with the husband trying to push the wife away to deal with the hurt and pain of separation). Given these kinds of integrations, perhaps it is appropriate to explore them in more detail as a means of integrating these three communication dimensions.

## INTERRELATIONSHIPS AND EXPECTATIONS

This chapter focuses on three sets of communication patterns that are likely to influence a mediator's ability to pull disputants into the problem-solving process. Unfortunately for mediators, these dimensions function simultaneously, making the timing problem that much more complex. However, if interrelationships can be specified and identified in the research, perhaps mediators can look for fairly obvious communication markers indicating that cooperation is either building or deteriorating.

Perhaps the best way to identify these interrelationships is to address them from the perspective of disputants' content patterns. The reason for selecting this perspective is that the issues that couples discuss are probably the most easily identifiable interaction feature for mediators to recognize.

### Issue Development and Position Adjustment

When couples begin discussing the various types of issues (relational, value, interest, or fact), what kind of position adjustment strategies might they use to frame these issues? To address this question, consider the nature of the divorce context and the stakes involved in negotiating for custody and visitation rights. For example, when couples discuss such relational issues as trust, respect, and consideration, or value issues including the best way to raise children, they probably refer to some problem that precipitated the need to surface such issues. In addition, these issues probably arose in the first place to discredit the other's behavior as opposed to criticizing the party's own behavior.

As a result, it seems reasonable to assume that couples will discuss their relational and value issues through the development of attack—defend cycles. For example, a husband claims he can no longer trust his wife because she is sleeping with her boyfriend in the same house in which the child is living. This attack about a relational issue stimulates a defensive response so the wife can protect her position in the mediation. She might respond that the boyfriend and the child relate well to one another and the child is accustomed to the new living arrangement. The husband might then counter with a value issue about the most appropriate way to raise the child and again, the wife hears the issue as an attack on her maternal skills and tries to defend herself.

However, when discussing interest or factual issues, parties generally pursue different strategic agenda. For example, when exchanging proposals or disclosing factual information, parties probably have less need to attack the other's position. Proposal and factual information sharing signal more forward-looking, problem-solving kinds of actions. However, as several examples listed earlier illustrate, couples can fight a great deal about specific factual issues and attack one another on these issues. Even various interest statements can stimulate attack–defend cycles. Nevertheless, the nature of divorce mediation is likely to encourage more attack–defend cycles surrounding relational and value issues because these issues are so central to divorce and to the task of creating custody and visitation agreements. Thus, although some attack–defend cycles might surround issue and interest statements, it seems more likely that parties would select bolstering and integrating strategies to frame their interest and factual contributions.

## Issue Development and Relational Distance

Turning to the links between issue development and relational distance, similar observations seem appropriate. For example, it might be expected that relational and value issues would stimulate the "push–pull" verbal immediacy process described earlier, in which couples seek to both physically separate themselves from one another while accessing the intimacy of their relationship. They want to push away from while pulling toward one another. This dilemma presents couples with a potentially difficult paradox to resolve. Pulling closer creates more fear and the need to push further away. This paradox can yield tremendous frustration as individuals vacillate between moving against one another and moving away from one another.

It might be expected that discussions about relational and perhaps value issues would stimulate this paradoxical situation simply because these discussions show increased spatial and temporal immediacy, and increased directness at the same time. Conversely, discussions of facts and interests may show less spatial and temporal distance while also emerging with more implicit immediacy. In addition, it would be reasonable to assume that as the discussion becomes more relationally oriented, the disputants would use more intense language. Part of the pushing away process should involve more intense language. Thus, when relational issues dominate, language intensity should increase.

## Examining Communication Patterns

This chapter discusses the relational, content, and strategic dimensions of interpretation with respect to "patterns" of communication that are likely to emerge. Detecting patterns is done by exploring trends over time. For example, decreases in language intensity are expected over the course of the agreement mediations. As issues get resolved and couples move away from distributive strategies and relational issues, the language intensity should drop. Given the need to detect patterns, the analyses conducted in this chapter separate each mediation transcript into equal thirds, on the basis of total utterances divided by 3 for each transcript. This chapter now examines the results of coding the 20 transcripts using the relational, issue, and position-adjustment category schemes.

## ANALYSES AND FINDINGS

The transcripts were coded using the various schemes reported previously. The specific coding procedures and several data analysis issues and results associated with those procedures are contained in Appendix A. This appendix also contains reliability information for each of the coding schemes and some other analyses related to the immediacy dimension.

This section begins by identifying how all three dimensions of disputant communication functioned independently of one another. This analysis provides an important overview of each area. Following these individual analyses, this section concentrates on how they fit together from the perspective of the issue development data. The first set of links explores the ways in which the issue data overlap with the position adjustment results. Next, the links between the issue and relational distance data are examined. This chapter now turns to this analysis.

### Issues, Positions, and Relationships

#### *Types of Issues Discussed*

To begin, what did disputants talk about in the mediation sessions? By simply counting which issues arose across the three time periods (facts, interests, values, relationships), the data reveal that couples who forged an agreement concentrated on facts and interests (see Table 1 in Appendix A for this analysis). Their communication centered on the task at hand and tended to avoid relational and value issues. In contrast, couples in the no-agreement sessions lost sight of their negotiation task. Instead, they chose to discuss relational issues with factual issues second, interest issues third, and value issues again last.

As confirmed by the analysis in chapter 4, it appears that the no-agreement disputants arrived at the sessions with more relational baggage to unpack. The analysis from chapter 4 found that the no-agreement disputants exposed many more nonlegal issues than the agreement couples. These couples generally entered mediation several years after divorce in response to some specific problem. Mediation for them became a forum to look back to the event precipitating the need for mediation. The agreement couples entered the process looking ahead toward wrapping up the circumstances of the divorce.

Second, the analysis of issues provided some interesting insights about what mediators directed couples to talk about. In the agreement sessions, the mediators directed couples to discuss interests. They spent much less time asking couples about factual, value, or relational concerns. On the other hand, the no-agreement mediators allocated much more time to discussing factual issues. Reading any of the no-agreement transcripts reveals that couples often framed their relational problems in the form of factual disputes. For example, couples often fought about trivial logistical issues such as what time the husband returned the child after visitation. These kinds of arguments can be termed *toothpaste cap* disputes (i.e., many couples fight about who forgot to put the cap back on the toothpaste tube). The real issue in these disputes is typically not the toothpaste cap. Rather, the issue relates to some deeper underlying relational concern about trust, respect for private space, and so forth.

Unfortunately, the no-agreement mediators often chose to get involved in these toothpaste cap disputes. They tried to solicit facts about the factual dimension of the dispute. For example, one couple fought for several minutes about whether the husband dropped off the daughter after visitation at 6:15 or 6:30. Instead of probing the deeper issues (e.g., trust and reliability) the mediator tried to determine which of the two times was correct. Did the mediator miss an opportunity to pull the couple out of the past and to help them understand more important issues affecting future agreements?

Clearly, the no-agreement mediators appeared less able to pull their couples into substantive problem solving. This observation was reinforced with an additional analysis of issue development across the beginning, middle, and end time periods in the mediation sessions (Table 2 in Appendix A contains this analysis). The agreement couples and their mediators stayed with interest issues throughout the entire mediation. However, the no-agreement couples acted very differently. They quickly moved away from facts and interests toward value and relational issues immediately after the first time period and stayed with these issues to the end. But, their mediators moved further away from processing or developing these relational issues. During the last time period, these no-agreement mediators concentrated exclusively on facts, while the couples waded even deeper into their relational abyss. The divergence of couples and mediators in this analysis was quite remarkable.

## Types of Position Adjustment Strategies Used

Across the agreement sessions, were couples more likely to attack the other's positions or to integrate positions? Specifically, disputants in both agreement sessions began their interactions using the same level of cooperativeness (see Table 3 in Appendix A). They concentrated their contributions mostly on defending and bolstering strategies. This concentration is reasonable, given that most mediators used this initial period to orient couples to the process and to gather some preliminary information about expectations.

Then, at Time 2, the picture changed dramatically. The no-agreement disputants significantly escalated their strategic moves toward an attack–defend cycle. Recall that this is the point at which the relational issues really started to dominate for the no-agreement group. In contrast, the agreement couples became significantly more cooperative in Time 2. They pursued integrating and bolstering strategies as they exchanged information and proposals. These couples continued their cooperative interaction at Time 3, whereas those in the no-agreement sessions retained their competitive, attack–defend cycle at Time 3.

The attack–defend cycle that burdened the no-agreement couples may have its roots in the "accounting" process. In a recent paper, Zappa, Manusov, Cody, and Donohue (1990) analyzed these same 20 mediation sessions by focusing on how couples handle attacks. Following an attack, these authors discovered that most individuals provided the attacker with an "account" or justification for bad behavior alleged in the attack. After the account had been offered, the other provided an evaluation of the acceptability of that account (i.e., did it explain the bad behavior?). These "evaluations" often took the form of other attacks, thereby perpetuating the cycle.

For example, consider the following sequence:

Husband: You're an unfit mother the way you used drugs around my son!
Wife: I never used any drugs and you can ask Todd (the son) if you want.
Husband: I don't have to ask him. I've seen it myself.

In this sequence, the husband attacks, the wife defends herself with an account that includes reference to the son as proof. The husband follows the account with a statement negatively evaluating the account's credibility and further attacking the wife. In the Zappa et al. (1990) article, the authors discovered that after the initial attack the agreement mediators often moved in to prevent the cycle from escalating. They would redirect the topic, or more carefully process the issue. The no-agreement mediators simply allowed the cycle to play itself out. They often did nothing to stop it. Often, mediators would let couples exchange 15 or 20 utterances before intervening. Whatever the reason for the difference in mediator-intervention strategies, it seems clear that when the cycle is left to play itself out, the context for cooperation appears to dwindle considerably.

### Types of Relational Messages

**Verbal Immediacy.** The data confirmed expectations about verbal immediacy. Specifically, the spatial analyses revealed very high scores for the mediators, indicating that they were trying to be very immediate spatially, perhaps in an attempt to bring the parties closer together. However, the husbands and wives seemed to reject these proposals because they demonstrated significantly lower scores spatially. They wanted to stay apart from one another. In contrast, the opposite pattern was observed for implicit immediacy. The husbands and wives showed high immediacy by framing their ideas very directly without much ambiguity about their intentions. They were mad and showed it by not taking the time to carefully craft their comments. But, the mediators were implicit; they tried to phrase their interventions very carefully, and the couples simply ignored these relational proposals.

Together, these results reflect the push–pull process of relational development in intense conflict. When conflict becomes more relationally centered, people become more direct and more spatially distant. They try to push one another away while moving closer to the other in an attempt to defeat the opponent.

**Language Intensity.** The data reveal a much more complex story about language intensity than verbal immediacy across the various mediation sessions. Recall that language intensity provides insight about how individuals use language to persuade one another because this variable signals a desire to take charge of the situation–to move in and command the task. For example, when people swear at one another, they send the message, "Hey, I mean what I say and you better believe it too!"

As might be expected, the overall analysis of language intensity in the sessions revealed that the agreement couples significantly reduced their language intensity over time (see Table 4 in Appendix A for the means on this analysis). They sought less to force options on one another, particularly as they moved more toward agreement. Perhaps the couples were less afraid that their needs would be ignored. Unfortunately, the no-agreement couples reacted quite differently. Their language became much more intense from the start of interaction, and peaked at Time 2. They came into the mediation all charged up and ready to fight, and let it all out, particularly during the second time period. This no-agreement group retreated to their original intensity levels at Time 3, perhaps in response to mediator demands to discuss case facts.

Reading the no-agreement transcripts revealed a sad story in many cases. The intense language in these sessions often accompanied comments about how the other was threatening the child's well-being. It was easy for the reader to create a vision of the father pulling on one arm and the mother pulling on the other, as they fought about parental abuse and neglect. Couples expressed fear and often hopelessness about how their children were being raised.

Based on these analyses, should mediators pay attention to either verbal immediacy or language intensity independently of either the issue or the strategic dimensions of communication? These analyses found some interesting differences, but the real test of the importance of these variables probably rests in being able to complete an overall picture of how couples communicate in mediation. Certainly, these variables are difficult to focus on independently because they generally gain only passing attention from mediators. However, as the next section indicates, when combined with the other two dimensions of communication, these relational variables provide important insights about the evolution of more cooperative and competitive interaction styles among couples.

**Interrelationships Among the Three Dimensions**

*Issues and Positions*

As it turns out, the type of issues discussed had a great deal to do with the types of position-adjustment strategies individuals used to talk about the issues. Consistent with expectations, when couples began escalating their concerns to value and relational matters, they became more competitive strategically. They escalated conflict by moving quickly into their accounting cycle, while recalling their relational problems. In contrast, as couples cooperated, their discussions became more interest-centered. These findings make sense because it was clear from reading the transcripts that couples could not discuss relational issues without attacking one another. It was difficult for them to isolate the issues and to solve problems about this subject matter. Certainly, interests tend to dwell on less emotional matters that encouraged couples to use more cooperative strategies.

At this point, then, the content and strategy dimensions of communication merge. That is, by focusing on the content or topics of communication, mediators can also gain significant insight into the strategies couples use. Specifically, the more relationally based issues appear to trigger more verbally aggressive strategies. As people get hurt, they strike back and then defend themselves against further attack.

### Issues and Relational Distance

***Verbal Immediacy.*** The data largely sustain the expectation that the immediacy variable would interact significantly with issue use (see Table 5 in Appendix A for specific statistical data). Specifically, as participants moved toward more relational issues, they used more direct, less implicit language to do so. They pressed one another very directly about specific relational concerns. The transcripts show very little thoughtful qualification or abstractness about their comments. They had a message and they were not going to sugar-coat it.

However, the spatial and temporal variables moved in the opposite direction. While framing issues very directly, couples sent messages revealing a desire to increase spatial and temporal distance, particularly at the beginning and ending segments of the mediation. Their language expressed pushing away in space and time. Yet, their directness accessed the intimacy in the relationship. Thus, it appears that the push–pull, paradox problem described earlier reared its troubling head during these mediations. Specifically, as the topic approached relationally sensitive issues, disputants increased their spatial and temporal distance while becoming more direct with one another. In other words, they accessed both their personal fears and the intimacy left in the relationship. Two opposing forces were pulling at them. They might be feeling: "I fear and mistrust you, but my feelings for you are still strong." Coping with these discrepant signals only enhances the ambiguity in conflict.

***Language Intensity.*** Consistent with this vision of intense conflict, the data also indicated that the couple's language became much more intense as they moved toward discussing relational and value issues. Couples in this initial time period laced their comments with various qualifiers and metaphors to frame their demands. Both agreement and no-agreement groups used this intense language, probably to communicate their commitment to their respective positions.

However, this observation held only at Time 1. At the second and third time segments, language intensity did not vary with issue type. At these later time periods, couples and mediators spread their intensity across the various issues. That the relationship held only for Time 1 is somewhat surprising, particularly because, for the no-agreement couples, their focus on relational issues ballooned at Time 2. Perhaps when Time 2 rolled around, the couples became intense regardless of the issue. They were angry and fearful and they showed it repeatedly.

## CONCLUSIONS

This chapter focused on discerning disputant communication patterns. The basic underlying assumption of this chapter is that managing interaction in mediation is founded on understanding these patterns. What communicative behaviors dominate interaction when couples are out of control and headed for deadlock? Which behaviors typify constructive problem solving among couples headed for agreement?

### Reviewing the Major Findings

The analyses revealed fairly clear responses to these questions. When considering content, the immediate escalation to relational issues dominated the no-agreement sessions. Consistent with their agreement counterparts, the no-agreement couples began mediation by exchanging factual information and describing interests. However, at the first opportunity the flood gates opened for the no-agreement couples. They escalated quickly into exposing their relational problems. Their mediators tried to pull them back by asking them to focus again on facts and issues, but the couples ignored these requests and continued fighting despite the mediators' efforts.

The immediacy analyses provide some insight into how these

relational problems spiraled out of control. As couples fought about these relational issues, they spoke very directly, yet remained very spatially distant. The more this "push–pull" process entered into framing the content, the more emotional confusion entered the discussion context. By pulling the other closer with directness and pushing the other away by increasing spatial distance, the speaker's actions were caught in a trap of intimacy and fear. This intimacy and fear confusion may have stimulated further relational struggling, perhaps because the need to confront the confusion became overpowering as it expanded.

Contributing to the emotional energy inherent in these relational issues are the strategies couples use to frame these relational issues. Recall that the no-agreement couples exposed their relational issues strategically through attack–defend cycles. The data do not reveal that disputants and mediators dispassionately discussed relational problems in some kind of detached manner. Couples were mad when these problems came up. As a result, the relational issues framed in attack–defend cycles took on the appearance of the verbal aggression cycle described in chapter 2. One party makes an accusation, the other defends and then attacks back until either a third party intervenes or violence breaks out. Because the motivation behind verbal aggression is ego protection, perhaps the relational issues being discussed through aggressive strategies stimulated this identity challenge. Couples saw the relational issues coming, they became afraid, and they attacked to protect themselves. Allowed to continue, the discussion quickly escalated out of control until the mediator had very little, if any, influence on the discussion.

## A Content Focus

Does this pattern suggest that mediators should concentrate their interpretive attention on all three dimensions on disputant communication—the content, relational, and strategic dimensions? This complex effort is very impractical. Few people can be trained to look for many signs at once. Furthermore, the data seem to say that looking in three places is probably not necessary.

Indeed, the data reveal that mediators should probably concentrate on the issues and how the parties express them. Specifically, mediators should probably watch for both relational and interest issues and the fallout that accompanies each. For example, when relational issues arise that are not requested from the mediator, they can signal the beginning of a destructive conflict cycle. One relational issue turns into another until multiple problems confuse and perplex the interactants. These issues often arise in the context of some story about a past problem. The story may involve disloyalty, trust, infidelity, and so on. This past relational problem probably contains some kind of provocative attack that will stimulate a defensive response and another attack. If the relational problem is not addressed in time to prevent the defensive reaction, the destructive cycle is likely to take off.

On the other hand, the repeated emergence of interest issues seems to characterize more cooperative interaction. When these issues arise, they signal a cooperative problem-solving context. They reveal a couple's desire to put the past behind and focus on the future. These issues are generally framed by bolstering and integrative strategies and increased levels of spatial and temporal immediacy. Couples generally pull together with this future focus.

What kind of interventions stimulate a movement toward an interest focus? Chapter 6 focuses on the intervention strategies mediators used in both agreement sessions.

# 6

# Mediator-Intervention Strategies

Chapter 5 stressed the need for mediators to closely monitor couples' issue development. If couples began moving toward difficult relational issues without mediator assistance or intervention, they risk lapsing into verbal aggression and emotionally laden language. The data suggest that more active mediation can redirect couples away from these problems. As a result, chapter 5 was probably most useful in offering mediators information about when to intervene. The mediator-interaction management model stresses this timing concern. If mediators cannot effectively "chunk" interaction into productive and counterproductive parts, their intervention effectiveness drops considerably.

So, this chapter concentrates on the intervention part of the interaction management model. It looks at the types of mediator interventions that typify both kinds of agreement sessions. However, as indicated in chapter 3, the approach does not focus on interventions in isolation. Rather, it explores mediator interventions in response to disputant negotiation strategies. When disputants act, how do mediators react? This dyadic or interactionist approach is needed to translate the results of this research into practice.

To address this need, this chapter begins with the development of a coding scheme for exploring mediator intervention strategies. The scheme focuses on how mediators structure their sessions and develop the content or substance of the interaction. In addition, this chapter addresses the phase question. Recall from chapters 2 and 3 that many researchers and practitioners encourage phase development. Do these phases work? This chapter now turns to these interests.

## INTERVENTION TYPES

### A General Coding Scheme

Recall from chapters 2 and 3 that two important intervention priorities for mediators involve adding both coherence or issue clarity and structure to the mediation session. The clarity problem really requires meeting three important communication needs: framing, and reframing the parties' comments, and managing information effectively. *Framing* involves encouraging parties to see an issue from a different perspective. Usually, mediators like to frame parents' problems with one another from the children's perspective, or from the other parent's perspective. This new view can dramatically change a parent's position on these problems. Reframing refers to the task of exposing hidden issues. For example, it might involve pulling out an important relational issue in what appears on the surface as a factual problem. Mediators experienced difficulty with this task as evidenced in chapter 5. *Managing information* involves exposing the facts and parties' perceptions of the facts, and keeping them organized gives parties better access to the information they will use to build their agreements.

Structuring work relates to agenda setting, enforcing interaction rules, and directing the modes of information exchange. Agenda setting directs disputants to discuss topics in some progressive order that helps build momentum toward agreement. Enforcing rules keeps disputants within acceptable and productive bounds of problem-solving behavior. Directing the modes of information exchange, or how parties should talk to one another, helps them find communication channels most comfortable for them. Without interaction structure, building coherence grows increasingly difficult because the mediator loses control over the substance of the interaction.

The coding scheme that explores these coherence and structuring intervention needs will be organized around three primary content strategies: structuring the process of mediation, reframing the disputants' positions, and expanding the information resource. The tactics listed under each primary strategy are not intended to be comprehensive; rather, they represent those tactics that are most frequently cited by the researchers and practitioners in divorce mediation listed earlier and other researchers in the area of conflict and negotiation (e.g., Hocker & Wilmot, 1985) that appear capable of accomplishing the general objectives previously cited.

### Structuring the Mediation Process

The objective of this first general strategy is to empower the mediator to gain control of the session. If the mediator permits the couple to control the session before they are prepared to focus on substantive problem solving, the interaction can degenerate into name calling (Saposnek, 1983). The consequences of relinquishing control were evident in chapter 5. The no-agreement mediators asked couples about factual issues, whereas the couple wanted to dwell on relational concerns. The couple went in one direction and the mediator in another. Clearly, the no-agreement sessions did not give the appearance of structured problem solving. Based on several of the compliance-gaining strategies outlined in Saposnek's (1983) recommendations for effective mediation, the tactics that provide such structure include:

1. Identify or enforce the interaction rules (e.g., "Please do not interrupt." or "Let me establish some discussion rules here.").
2. Terminate or initiate discussion (e.g., "Let's stop the discussion there because we are not getting very far." or "Why don't you tell him what you think instead of talking with me?").
3. Identify or enforce the agenda or topic ("Let's move to the issue of support." or "Let's talk about the child's welfare.").
4. Delineate role definitions and the process of mediation (e.g., "My role in this discussion is to. . ." or "I can't give you that information because I won't be evaluating your case.").
5. Provide a listening or involvement marker to signal attentiveness, or encourage the person to continue with that train of thought (e.g., "Um, hm." or "I see.").

## Framing and Reframing Interventions

A key mediator responsibility involves both framing the couples' perspectives on issues and organizing their issues. Restructuring ideas and proposals provides valuable insight to couples who may not understand the underlying concerns reflected in their comments. The wife who voices a concern about her husband's girlfriend may still feel emotionally attached to him. She may not understand that her reaction is both normal and reasonable and must be confronted. By lending insight and structure to complex, sensitive issues, and looking at issues differently, individuals can expand their problem-solving opportunities. Recent research reveals that when couples receive insight about these complex issues, their desire to cooperate with one another increases (Thoennes & Pearson, 1985). The following tactics seek to tap these framing and reframing interventions:

1. Create alternative proposals (e.g., "Wouldn't it be better if you began the visitation?").
2. Negatively evaluate the disputant's proposal or position (e.g., "That isn't very realistic." or "I think you are being a little unreasonable here.").
3. Reframe proposals or reframe prior utterances as a proposal (e.g., "What I hear you saying is that you want to see the children more often.").
4. Identify and reinforce points of agreement and support for the utterance (e.g., "You both seem to agree that . . . ." or "I think that proposal is very workable.").
5. Provide orientation information about the situation, mediation, or counseling (e.g., "Sometimes children do strange things. For example . . .").

## Expanding the Information Resource

Although mediators use framing and reframing tactics to take the information already given and restructure it in a more usable form, the expanding directives work to increase information available for decision making. Research in mediation and negotiation cited in chapter 3 makes a compelling case that a large pool of task-relevant information is necessary to explore alternatives so disputants can create more integrative agreements (e.g., Pruitt, 1981). A lack of information can lead quickly to impasse as potential solutions do not become apparent. The expanding tactics explored in this chapter include:

1. Request opinion or evaluation of the other's proposal or opinion (e.g., "What do you think of his proposal?" or "Can you go along with that idea?").
2. Request proposals (e.g., "What do you have in mind for the children?").
3. Request clarification of a proposal or topical situation (e.g., "What further information do you have on that proposal?").
4. Request relational or feeling information (e.g., "What are your feelings about mediation?" or "What have you gotten out of this relationship?").
5. Request clarification of a prior utterance (e.g., "What do you mean by that statement?").

## *Intervention Timing*

Recall that the mediator-interaction management model focuses on mediator interventions in relation to disputant negotiation strategies. Considering these interventions apart from the context of the couple's behavior violates this key timing principle. To address this key principle, mediator-intervention strategies are assessed in relation to the couples' position-adjustment strategies and to the types of issues they discuss. Implementing this timing principle involves examining the couples' strategies and issues immediately prior to, and immediately subsequent to, the mediator's intervention. This procedure places the intervention in its context in the on-going stream of interaction. According to Kressel and Pruitt (1985) "...it is important to measure not only what the mediator does at critical moments, but what *the parties* are doing when the mediator intervenes and what they are doing after an intervention" (p. 196).

For example, the study on accounts described in chapter 5 (Zappa et al., 1990) found that some kind of intervention is needed immediately following an attack. If the mediator waits for the attack–defend process to develop, conflict escalates out of control. In response to attacks that violate the rules, mediator-structuring interventions should result in more collaborative follow-up responses by disputants. Reminding couples of the rules should switch them back on track to perhaps a bolstering move that provides some information.

Although keeping people on track from comment to comment is important, mediators also seek to structure decision making more globally by directing couples to move through phases of interaction. Chapter 2 identified a variety of phase prescriptions based on practical experience in the mediation context. This chapter now moves to exploring this more global means of structuring disputants' decision-making activities by developing a procedure for understanding phases in mediation.

## Phases in Divorce Mediation

### An Overview

Should mediators try to move disputants through specific interaction phases? What are the advantages and disadvantages of phase development? Chapter 2 revealed that nearly every professional mediation text supports moving disputants through some kind of phase development because the structure breaks them away from their old, destructive decision-making habits. It provides them with a new framework for communicating productively with one another. A phase model provides disputants and mediators with general guidelines for communicating. If disputants get stuck in a particular phase, the mediator can retreat to a prior phase and attempt to develop it further so the dispute can move forward. Of course, if the mediator tries to force disputants to use phases that are not suited to their dispute, this structure might prove less valuable, as indicated in chapter 2.

Unfortunately, few studies provide any information regarding the effectiveness of phases. The only study that has really examined this problem rigorously appears in Jones' (1988) analysis of phase structures in agreement and no-agreement mediations. Using an expanded version of the same data set reported here, she found that the agreement mediations worked through a systematic set of phases. They began with agenda building, moved to information exchange, and then finally progressed to substantive decision making in which agreements were negotiated. In contrast, the no-agreement disputants failed to move past blaming each other for various problems and paid little attention to process issues. They turned away from the substantive problems and never really developed the structure necessary for decision making.

Although these results tend to support the need for phases in divorce mediation, many important questions remain. First, do these data show similar results to the Jones' study? Do the mediations progress fairly systematically? Second, how do mediators move disputants through phases? Do they rely mostly on asking questions to move couples along, or do they mix tactics and use a broad repertory to induce cooperation? This chapter tries to address these questions with a coding scheme that traces both the mediator's phase directives and the disputants compliance with those directives. To understand the logic of the coding scheme it might be useful to review the variety of phase recommendations mediators forward about phases.

## Phase Descriptions

Thoennes and Pearson (1985) indicated that most professionals advocate moving systematically through *phases*, defined as specific, intermediate goals intended to structure the interaction process. Although the number of phases varies widely from author to author, all appear to agree that phases are necessary to build structure and clarity into the dispute. Lack of structure and clarity jeopardizes the disputant's commitment to mediation because any sense of progress would be unlikely to arise out of such disarray.

***Phase 1: Orientation.*** Table 6.1 summarizes several published recommended phases or stages mediators should actively pursue to reach satisfactory agreements. The contributions of these authors can be organized into four phases, or intermediate mediation goals. Most authors agree that this first phase should provide disputants with an orientation session. They should be given information about rules for interacting, the extent to which the session protects confidentiality, and alternatives to mediation. Most couples are unfamiliar with the mediation process and what to expect, so this orientation is very necessary. Mediators should also talk about their role in dispute (i.e., what model of mediation they prefer, and perhaps what goals they wish to achieve). Hopefully, this orientation can calm nervous parents and motivate them to work together.

***Phase 2: Gathering Background Information.*** Once the couple understands the objectives and structure of mediation it is possible to begin developing the informational foundation of the

## Table 6.1.
### Review of Phase Recommendations from Professional Mediators

| Mediator | Phase/Stage | | | |
|---|---|---|---|---|
| | Orientation | Background Information | Issue Processing | Proposal Development |
| 1. Kessler (1978) | Setting the stage | Defining the issues | Processing the issues | Resolving the issues |
| 2. Black & Joffee (1978) | Engagement | Assessment & direction | | negotiation; education |
| 3. Haynes (1981) | Set the tone: Orientation | Collect basic data; identify goals; expose hidden agenda; develop family profiles | Negotiating basic issues; reviewing progress | Gaining accommodations |
| 4. Bienenfeld (1983) | Intake: Meeting the family | Preliminary conference | Parental interviews to identify concerns; children's interviews; | Negotiating an agreement; wrap-up conference |
| 5. Saposnek (1983) | | Gather information | Family conference | Describe options; shape proposals |
| 6. Folberg & Taylor (1984) | Creating structure and trust | Fact finding | Isolation of issues | Creating options and alternatives; negotiating |
| 7. Moore (1986) | Setting the agenda orientation | Background info is collected prior to mediation | Defining issues; generating and assessing options | Final bargaining; achieving formal settlement |

```
TIME        : Sun Mar 10 2002 04:21PM
TERMINAL    : 310
TITLE       : Communication, marital di
CALL NUMBER : HQ834 .D65 1991  tocir
BARCODE     : 30516020181714
STATUS      : IN TRANSIT
Received. Belongs at UST-OSF Stacks
```

dispute. As Pruitt (1981) contended, information is the primary resource on which agreements are built. The more information couples have available, the more options parties create for constructing agreements. Also, sharing information signals that trust has expanded between the parties.

Although the authors represented in Table 6.1 recognized the need to build an information resource in the second phase, some differences are apparent concerning when to collect it. Kessler (1978) emphasized gathering information about critical issues soon after the orientation concludes. Her logic in taking this position is that the key issues dividing couples should be exposed as soon as possible so couples can understand the foundations of their dispute. In contrast, most of the other authors recommended collecting basic background information about couples' situations before asking them to discuss key issue differences. They argued that after orientation, couples are not ready to launch quickly into controversy. Discussing relatively uncontroversial background information (e.g., the number of children, where they attend school, family role responsibilities, etc.) helps build a more cooperative interaction context. It also helps the mediator begin to assert control over the structure of the interaction in two ways. First, the couple is following the mediator's agenda. Second, the couple can begin to develop some faith in the mediator's ability to move the dispute forward.

Another important difference lies in the extent to which settlement objectives should be addressed in the early phases of mediation. Haynes (1981) and Folberg and Taylor (1984) advocated using either the first or second phase of mediation to state settlement objectives. The logic of discussing such objectives sooner rather than later lies in the need to expose hidden agenda that can undermine cooperative interaction later in the mediation. For example, consider the couple who came to mediation, not to solve their visitation problem, but to punish and embarrass the other person as a way of dealing with their hurt. When asked about their objectives for the session the couple was unable to articulate any. After repeated probing, the mediator learned that neither party had any problems with a suggested visitation arrangement offered by the mediator. They simply wanted to continue fighting to vent their hurt. Learning this up front, the mediator was able to suggest an alternative intervention aimed at helping the couple deal with this hurt.

Other conflict specialists (Fisher & Ury, 1981) suggested that negotiators avoid getting locked into specific positions during the early phases of interaction. Becoming locked into positions makes it more difficult to listen to the other's options. Once a position is expressed, it becomes a filter for interpreting the other's point of view. It creates a mindset that stimulates defensive thinking about what the other person is proposing. Also, as individuals lock themselves into positions, they risk losing face when it becomes necessary to retreat from those positions to reach an agreement. Couples who propose sole legal and physical custody of the children lose face when other custody plans are proposed.

***Phase 3: Issue Processing.*** The basic data gathered in this phase lays the foundation for disclosing and processing issues underlying the dispute. Most of the authors represented in Table 6.1 express the need to pull out and resolve, as much as possible, those issues that can serve as road blocks to cooperative interaction. This is an extremely difficult task because, as observed in chapter 5, couples mix complex issues into single, relatively simple statements.

Black and Joffee (1978) and Saposnek (1983) remain unclear about the role of issue processing in mediation. They move from gathering information to negotiating alternative proposals. However, the four remaining authors appear firmly committed to this phase. Bienenfeld (1983) even extended her discussion of issue processing to identify those groups that should be involved in this process. She argued that possibly children and other family members can provide important insights into underlying issues dividing family members.

***Phase 4: Proposal Development.*** Finally, the resolution of key issues provides the context for proposal development according to most of the authors in Table 6.1. Once the key issues have been addressed, the couple is in a position to prepare and decide upon specific options for overcoming these issues.

The authors cluster their recommendations around two distinct approaches to the proposal development process that are represented by these authors. Saposnek (1983) and Folberg and Taylor (1984) emphasized the need to develop more integrative options in proposal development. Integrative options are those that seek to accommodate all parties' needs. The more options that are created, the better the odds that one can be created that can serve as the foundation for the agreement. More options also prepare the couples for negotiation by simply giving them more to negotiate. On the other hand, Haynes (1981) emphasized gaining accommodations from disputants by asking what they are willing to give up. The emphasis is on backing away from original goals to show both good faith in bargaining, and to encourage the other to act cooperatively.

Finally, Black and Joffee (1978) and Bienenfeld (1983) included some sort of educational debriefing at the conclusion of mediation. These authors recognized that informing disputants about the implications of their agreements may have a positive impact on their willingness to live with them in the long term.

Collectively, these four phases of mediation can be viewed along a time continuum that reflects both the mediator's and the disputants' orientation toward the conflict. That is, the categories move progressively toward a more future, problem-solving orientation regarding the conflict. For example, the process issues and historical development of the dispute are rooted largely in the past as disputants discuss why they came to mediation and review the circumstances surrounding their dispute. The issues underlying their current dispute are rooted in the present as disputants seek to learn what currently divides them. Proposals center on what can be done in the future to manage the dispute and how the various individuals affected by the dispute are likely to respond to the proposals.

### *Communication Tactics*

In addition to arguing that effective mediation moves progressively toward agreements focusing on managing the future, the authors represented in Table 6.1 also list a variety of communication tactics that can be used to facilitate such movement. Coding will also include an examination of these tactics to determine how mediators accomplish phase objectives. The tactics include listening cues, requesting directives, evaluation tactics, and framing tactics.

**Listening Cues.** This group of tactics emphasizes four primary communication needs. First, tactics such as active listening to encourage more information and absorbing angry talk can be accomplished through the use of backchannels. *Backchannels* are comments made "in the background of the conversation" that signal attention and involvement. The most common backchannels in a negotiation situation might include such comments as "Well," "OK, I see," "Uh huh," and so on. These comments try to reduce interpersonal distance by indicating that the hearer is involved in the conversation, endorses the topic, and wants to hear more. This signal establishes a context that encourages information sharing.

***Requesting Directives.*** The second group of tactics center around the act of requesting information. A *directive* is a statement that asks or tells someone, more or less explicitly, what needs to be done. For example, the comment, "Tell me your children's ages," is a very explicit directive to determine children's ages. On the other hand, the comment, "I need to know the ages of your children," is a less directive way of gathering information. Clearly, requesting directives play a prominent role in building information (Donohue & Diez, 1985). Because the phase authors reviewed earlier indicate that requesting serves several very important functions in mediation, it would be useful to track their frequency in relation to the substantive phases listed here. Are there any differences with respect to when directives are used?

***Evaluation Tactics.*** A third communication tactic that emerges from the list can be termed *evaluation*. Complementing the couple, enforcing interaction rules, and commenting on disputants' commitments to the mediation process all serve to maintain control and to provide structure to the interaction. Evaluation is needed to positively reinforce productive, and to negatively reinforce unproductive, communication habits. This behavior is also consistent with the interventionist assumption about the role of the mediator described in chapter 3.

***Framing Tactics.*** The final tactic, also consistent with the interventionist assumption, can be termed *framing*. As the most frequently cited contributor to mediation success, framing includes such behaviors as giving information, restatement, offering suggestions, deflecting angry comments, providing reflection, and reframing utterances as proposals. These framing tactics are more broadly defined than the reframing tactics listed at the beginning of this chapter. Those reframing tactics focus on restructuring individual comments. These framing tactics include a broader set of behaviors aimed at creating the couple's insight about their problems. When the mediator judges that the interaction has moved in a less than productive direction, the framing tactics slow down the conflict and provide disputants with the insights necessary to see their own positions, concerns, and so on, in relation to the other. According to the authors reviewed here, such insight improves flexibility and, therefore, cooperativeness.

## RESEARCH QUESTIONS

Two basic research questions guide the mediation analyses provided in this chapter. The first question relates to the links between disputant communication patterns and mediator strategies and tactics that respond to these patterns. Specifically, what kinds of disputant position adjustment and issue development strategies trigger which kinds of mediator-intervention strategies? Recall that this question really lies at the heart of the interaction management model presented in chapter 3. It is concerned with understanding what couples and mediators do in relation to one another. For example, mediators need to know whether reframing in response to disputant attacks helps convert the attack's competitive energy into a more cooperative follow-up behavior.

The second question relates to the phases of mediation. What kind of phase development do the agreement mediators pursue in comparison to the no-agreement group? Although some professional mediators disagree about timing issues, most seem to hold the view that mediators should proceed in some kind of systematic fashion as they mediate. Perhaps many of the troubles the no-agreement mediators faced in keeping couples focused on interest issues stemmed from enforcing phases in mediation.

## ANALYSES AND FINDINGS

The transcripts were coded using the intervention strategies and the phase-analysis coding schemes. The coding procedures, reliability, and statistical information used for these two coding schemes are presented in Appendix B. In addition, Appendix B presents several tables that are referenced in this analysis section.

### The Intervention Strategies Coding Scheme

The first research question, focusing on the interventions mediators select in relation to couples' actions, is particularly interesting to mediators. They want to know what actions to take in moving couples toward more cooperative interaction. Providing this information is probably best achieved by examining the three types of intervention strategies separately, as opposed to looking at them collectively. The actual analysis procedure involves comparing the disputant's comments just before and immediately after each intervention. This analysis is conducted across the three time periods. If the mediator's interventions are effective, the competitiveness should drop when comparing the strategy preceding the intervention with the one that followed it.

For example, consider a sequence in which the husband attacks his wife's parenting skills during a custody mediation. The mediator reframes the attack away from the parenting problem and asks the husband to focus instead on his wife's commitment to the children. In response, the husband acknowledges that he harbors no doubts about his wife's commitment to the children; after all, she cared for them in many difficult situations. This sequence would be coded as: (a) a husband attack, (b) a mediator reframing strategy, and (c) a husband integration move. In this sequence the mediator moved the husband off the attack and on to a more integrative orientation toward his wife. This chapter now proceeds to explore the way in which disputants respond to mediator structuring strategies.

## *Structuring Interventions*

Recall that the structuring moves keep people on track by enforcing the rules and topics, initiating discussion, and establishing role definitions. You might think of these strategies as getting organized and keeping people in line (Tables 2 and 3 in Appendix B contain the means and other statistical information for mediator strategies and tactics across all three time periods).

Interestingly, the mediator's ability to get organized and keep people in line appeared to vary with time. During the first period, couples in both types of sessions became much more cooperative in response to mediator-structuring moves. When the couples started to charge ahead with competitive comments, the mediators responded mostly by reminding couples about the rules. These reminders seemed to work fairly effectively at keeping couples on track with more cooperative comments. Most of the follow-up comments couples made in response to structuring interventions were bolstering comments aimed at more information sharing. Also, the issues couples discussed were primarily factual, again focused on information sharing. This kind of quick impact resulting from structuring moves is not particularly surprising. After all, couples meet with mediators in a court setting, the mediators represent the court, and at least for the first few minutes of interaction, they are going to step in line with the mediator's wishes. Couples show some deference to the mediator, it appears, at least for the first few minutes of interaction.

However, at Time 2, the picture changed dramatically, at least for the no-agreement mediators. Their couples became significantly more competitive strategically during this second time period. Any initial apprehension about attacking one another and defending sacred positions disappeared in this second phase. Couples simply paid little attention to mediator-structuring moves. In contrast, the agreement mediators faired much more successfully. Their structuring moves proved effective in developing increased cooperativeness. As in the first phase, when these mediators jumped in after defensive comments or attacks with a structuring move, couples become more cooperative by sharing information about the situation.

Did the mediator's selection of structuring tactics influence this big turnaround for the no-agreement mediators? The data reveal that both groups of mediators clearly deemphasized rule enforcement during this second phase of interaction. Instead, both sets of mediators relied mostly on the less directive tactic of providing listening markers, or backchannels to indicate that they were listening to the disputants (see Table 4 in Appendix B). Recall that these comments, "I see," "Uh huh," and so on signal that the mediator is paying attention. Mediators used these frequently in the first time period, but they used them more in this second time period, particularly at the expense of enforcing the rules.

Backing away from the more powerful tactic of enforcing the rules essentially transfered control of the interaction's direction over to the couples. For the agreement couples with few relational issues to air out, transferring control at this important second time period seemed productive. They were ready to work more toward constructive solutions on their own. However, the no-agreement couples were not ready. Because they carried heavy relational baggage into the mediation, they were unprepared to take control of the interaction at this second time period. They still needed more guidance to keep on track, whether the track involved discussing their relational problems, or working through their legal issues.

At Time 3, the picture continued to brighten for the agreement mediators as couples again emphasized proposal and information sharing in forging their agreements. Even the no-agreement couples became slightly more responsive to mediator-structuring interventions, although their cooperativeness improved only marginally as they still battled one another with destructive attack–defend cycles. Perhaps the reason for this slight improvement was the switch in rule enforcement from Time 2 (see Table 5 in Appendix B). During this third period, all mediators concentrated more heavily on rule enforcement and less on providing listening markers. The mediators once again tried to retake control of the interaction's direction by enforcing the rules. The agreement couples needed the rule reminders to keep on track in negotiating the details of their agreements. Certainly, the no-agreement couples needed this structure, as well, and perhaps these rules contributed to the slight improvement in cooperation. However, these couples were lost by the second time period and probably not capable of regaining the cooperativeness they expressed in the first time period.

## *Reframing Interventions*

In contrast with the mediator's structuring interventions, their reframing interventions did not yield increased cooperation for either the agreement or no-agreement mediators. The level of cooperativeness and the kinds of issues couples discussed following reframing interventions were about the same as before the interventions were given. Given these results, what role did reframing play in the mediations? Were they useless, or did the study simply not pick up their value? Mediators certainly feel that reframing is necessary to provide couples with insight about their dispute. However, giving such insight did not seem to pay off in directly affecting cooperativeness among couples.

The data seem to suggest that reframing may not have directly encouraged couples to use more cooperative strategies. Indeed, reframing an utterance in some particular way might even stimulate more uncooperative strategy use by couples. For example, consider the no-agreement mediators. They relied mostly on two reframing tactics: negatively evaluating proposals and creating alternative proposals for couples (see Table 6 in Appendix B). Telling one party that his or her proposal is unreasonable, or giving him or her a proposal to evaluate might not stimulate many cooperative responses from couples. In fact, it might even emphasize differences among disputants. As a result, it is not surprising that these reframing tactics did not immediately stimulate improved cooperation among parties.

Perhaps a more interesting way of looking at these reframing tactics is to compare them with the structuring tactics. Recall that mediators emphasized structure in the second time period. For couples with few relational problems, this deemphasis probably worked because they were capable of focusing on the legal issues of custody and visitation. As a result, the mediators for this group could work with the proposals generated by these couples. At least these couples had some ideas about solving their problems because they were not burdened with endless relational squabbles. Not blessed with much disputant cooperation, the no-agreement mediators were forced to generate ideas for the couples. The discussion surged out of control, and perhaps the mediators felt that they could refocus couples on the task by generating proposals for them and asking for their responses. Unfortunately, the data reveal that this strategy paid few dividends.

## *Requesting Interventions*

Finally, the requesting intervention patterns proved interesting in these transcripts. For example, at Time 1, the data once again revealed the challenge of working with couples that harbor deep relational problems. Specifically, the no-agreement couples became more cooperative strategically following requesting interventions. They moved away from defending strategies to use more bolstering or information-sharing comments (see Table 7 in Appendix B for all requesting intervention data). However, the issues these couples discussed centered more on relational topics following mediators' requests. In contrast, the agreement couples changed neither their level of cooperativeness nor the kinds of issues they discussed. They answered questions and focused on interests. The kinds of requests both groups of mediators made generally fell into two categories: requesting proposals and clarifying proposals (see Table 8 in Appendix B for all requesting tactical information).

This interesting finding highlights what can happen when mediators ask relationally troubled couples for proposals and proposal clarifications early in the interaction: They signal cooperation by giving and clarifying their proposals. Then, they stimulate conflict by surfacing relational issues. As a result, mediators gain some initial cooperation, but at the expense of pulling out sensitive topics. If mediators wish to explore these issues early, then this strategy is useful. However, if they wish to suppress these issues until later, requesting proposals may not be a good idea early in the interaction.

At Time 2, agreement couples became more defensive, whereas the no-agreement couples turned more toward attacks. Similarly, couples' comments centered more on relational issues following requests. What specific tactics stimulated this movement toward more competition? Instead of concentrating on proposals, mediators directed their search toward gathering situational and feeling information about problems that brought them to mediation. This change gave couples an even more specific forum for making accusations about relational problems. So, instead of revealing what they wanted as they did in Time 1, they supported their demands in Time 2 by their telling stories about the problems that brought them to mediation. Problems that bring people to mediation can generate very intense battles.

At Time 3, the situation turned around for the agreement couples. They began to use more integration strategies and focus on interests, following the requesting interventions. Unfortunately, the no-agreement couples stayed bogged down in their competitive, relational problems at Time 3. They could not negotiate these problems, and deadlock resulted. Tactically, mediators continued to request situational and feeling information in Time 3. The agreement couples appeared ready to reveal the more varied kinds of information requested by the mediator at Time 3. Opinions about the other's proposal as well as relational information, might assist the agreement couples in developing more options. However, these same requests may have given the no-agreement disputants an opportunity to continue their attack–defend trend established in the second time period.

### *General Observations*

What do these data reveal about how mediators coped with the different kinds of couples they saw every day? Perhaps the most interesting observation is that mediators reacted about the same way to most all couples. They used a fairly standard set of strategies and tactics. They do not seem to adjust a great deal to couples with severe relational concerns. This lack of adjustment is understandable because the Los Angeles mediators, as revealed in chapter 1, are interventionists and not involved in counseling, or any type of mediation that smacks of counseling. They were trained to remain task centered, and their strategy and tactic use reflect this priority.

For example, the mediators established a set of rules early on and reinforced them periodically during this initial period. They then solicited information about goals, and couples provided this information. However, after this fairly structured approach was out of the way the couples began telling their stories to support their goals. So, mediators decreased requests for proposals and started asking for more details about the stories. As revealed in chapter 5, if the stories took a relational turn, the mediators started requesting more factual information and avoiding the relational issues. If the stories did not take this turn, the mediators continued to probe couples' interests. All during this second time period, the mediators deemphasized structural interventions by letting the rules slip a bit, and allowed couples to exercise more control over the situation.

For the mediators forced to confront couples with big relational concerns, this more permissive, factual focus following the opening period resulted in big problems. These couples became more competitive in response to inquiries and the mediators simply could not bring them back to the legal issues. The other couples were fine because they were willing to stay on the legal issues and hammer out specific proposals. Should the mediators have adopted a different focus in dealing with couples with severe relational concerns? This question is addressed in chapter 7.

## The Phase-Analysis Coding Scheme

### Introduction

The purpose of this section is to focus on mediators' phase directives. The prior analysis revealed that mediators seem to have some kind of game plan, but the couples with severe relational problems reject that plan. They have their own plan (i.e., to blast away at one another), and the mediator just seems to get in the way. Is this tendency also reflected in mediator-phase directives? Does the deemphasis of structure in that second time period plague the mediator's ability to move couples through phases? This section seeks to address these questions.

### Comparing Future Orientations

Recall that mediator phase analysis really focuses on a "future orientation" continuum. As mediators press on toward proposals, they express that future orientation. By asking couples to talk about concerns that brought them to mediation, they develop a "past-problem orientation." This first analysis tracked the future orientations for mediators in both agreement groups in relation to their disputants' position-adjustment strategies. The question of interest here is whether the mediator's phase directives are associated with the kinds of strategies couples used in their sessions.

This first analysis revealed statistically significant differences across the two mediation sessions. Mediators in each agreement group developed very different phase orientations over the course of their mediations. Figures 6.1 and 6.2 track the means over the eight time periods for both of these groups.

The "M" line represents the mediator's average "future orientation," whereas the other two lines represent the husbands' (H) and wives' (W) levels of competitiveness as reflected in their

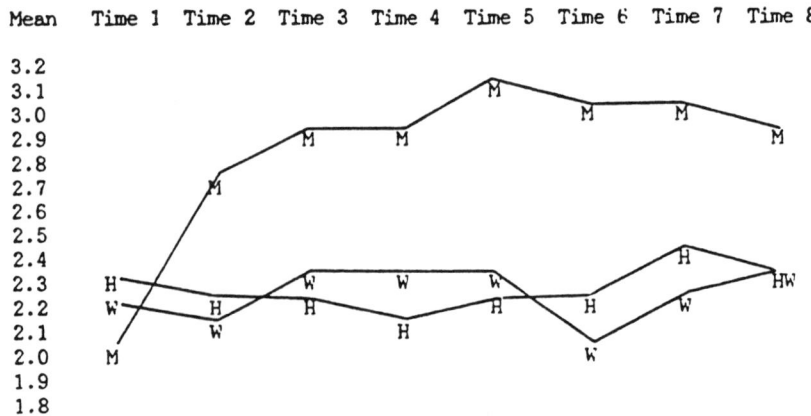

*Figure 6.1.* Mediator phase means and disputant position-adjustment means for agreement sessions.

position-adjustment strategies. As the mediator values climb, the mediator moves toward a higher future orientation. Higher values for the couples reflect increased cooperativeness. Because both of these variables were coded on a 1 to 4 scale, they can readily be compared on the same chart.

Figure 6.1 reveals that the agreement mediators escalated their future orientation very quickly during the second time period and then leveled off. Half way through the mediation, they escalated their future focus and reached another plateau before coming down slightly at the end when the decision had been made. This line shows a very consistent future orientation for the agreement mediators.

The couples' behavior mirrored this pattern. Up to the fifth time period, the agreement disputants maintained a relatively stable level of cooperativeness. At Time 6, the wives developed a more attacking orientation, but they returned to a more cooperative level at the end of the mediation. Clearly, these disputants did not vary significantly from their original positions across the eight time periods.

In contrast, the no-agreement mediators and disputants demonstrated very inconsistent orientations across the eight time periods as revealed in Fig. 6.2. These mediators also escalated their future orientation quickly, but not to the same level as the agreement mediators. Then, from the third to the fourth time period, these mediators significantly decreased their future orien-

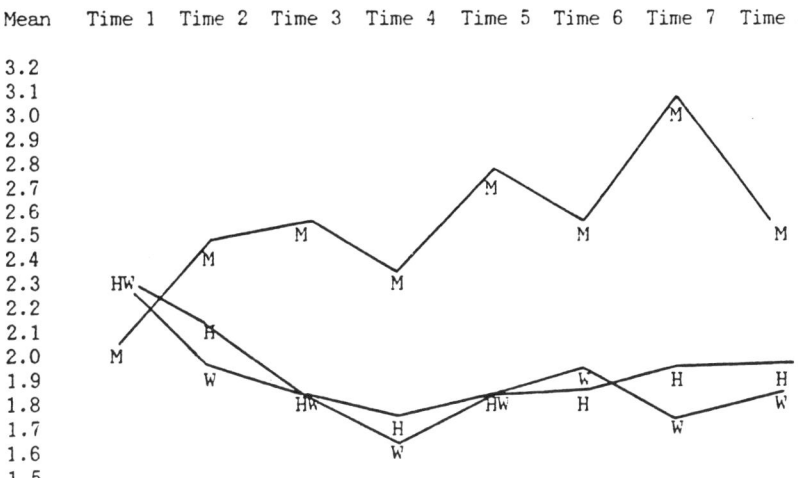

*Figure 6.2.* Mediator phase means and disputant position-adjustment means for no-agreement sessions.

tation. They escalated again up to the fifth period, only to decrease again in the sixth period. In the seventh period they escalated even further, but fell dramatically at the end, probably reflecting the lack of agreement on the part of the disputants.

The disputants' position-adjustment means across these same eight time periods are also very different than the agreement disputants' patterns. The no-agreement couples fell dramatically through the fourth time period to develop a highly attack-oriented strategy, as discussed in chapter 5. They rose only slightly toward the end, but finished well below their initial starting position.

Some interesting features emerge from these two graphs that are consistent with prior analyses. For example, the issue data in chapter 5 revealed that the no-agreement couples trapped mediators into discussing factual issues when the relational problems were the issues of most concern to the couples. The no-agreement chart reflects the control couples exerted over their mediators. Specifically, the agreement couples showed steady levels of cooperation until about half way through the session. Their mediators kept the focus on the problem and the disputants increased their cooperation.

However, the no-agreement mediators got pushed around in their sessions. As the no-agreement couples dropped their cooperative interaction in favor of more attacks at Time 3, their mediators also dropped their future orientation and went down after them by asking questions about their problems. This retreat by the no-agreement mediators lies in sharp contrast to the agreement group. In fact, the up and down phase-intervention focus by the no-agreement mediators reflects a very different style than their agreement counterparts. This difference is reflected in the issue data from chapter 5 and the structuring and requesting data from this chapter. The no-agreement mediator style consisted of probing factual issues inherent in the couples' problems, getting into trouble with more relational outbursts, and suggesting proposals for resolving the factual issues. Unburdened by these intense relational problems, the agreement group pressed on with the interest issues and sustained their future orientation, for the most part. Unfortunately, the no-agreement mediator style failed to succeed in building cooperation among couples.

### Comparing Mediator Phase Decisions

Because mediators developed different intervention styles, it might be useful to track the individual phase categories to clarify further the mediator differences. Figures 6.3 and 6.4 contain the comparison of agreement and no-agreement mediator phase decisions. The numbers on the left of the figures reflect the percentage of each category's usage during that particular time period.

**The Agreement Mediators.** Figure 6.3 presents the agreement mediators' phase allocation decisions. Clearly, the two most prominent features of this graph include the dominance of proposal making and the decreased emphasis on gathering background information. The rise in proposal talk took off from the very first time period and reached an early peak in the fifth time period. It slowed briefly by the increase in process talk from the fourth to the sixth time period. Nevertheless, it stayed strong throughout the entire negotiation. Requests for background information also dropped off dramatically from the first to the third time period. Then, these requests dropped again to almost nothing from the fifth period on.

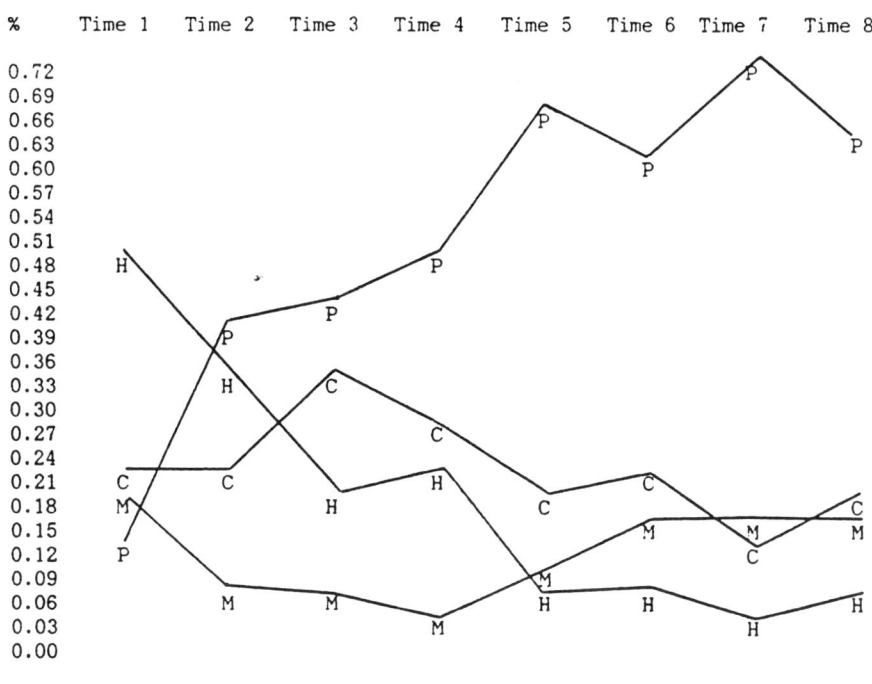

"P" line indicates proposal making
"H" line indicates history of dispute interaction
"C" line indicates problems in the current dispute
"M" line indicates focus on process of mediation

Figure 6.3. Percentage of agreement mediator-phase interventions.

This development is somewhat consistent with expectations in two respects. First, several of the mediation professionals represented in Table 6.1 advocate the need to identify goals early in the dispute and continue the proposal negotiation toward the latter stages of the dispute. The data indicate that the agreement mediators adhered to this priority. They kept a proposal focus from the first minute to the last. Second, the mediation professionals also advocate gathering background information early to serve as a foundation for the disputes. The mediators also pursued extensive background information early, then terminated this interest when the information picture was complete.

However, the issue development observations were somewhat inconsistent with expectations. Clearly, the individuals represented in Table 6.1 recommend discussing the issues underlying the proposals. This happened from the second to the fourth time period, but then dropped off considerably. For these mediators, the issue talk never dominated the proposal talk, probably because the underlying issues were minimal. The couples came in ready to focus on the task and the mediators obliged them. However, the no-agreement mediators allocated their phase directives very differently, as reflected in Fig. 6.4.

**The No-Agreement Mediators.** Although the agreement mediators may not have adhered to all of the phase recommendations in Table 6.1, it seems clear that they were at least following some kind of game plan. They kept their focus on the future and processed those issues that seemed relevant at the time. Unchallenged with difficult relational problems, these mediators sustained control of the process and moved it systematically along to agreement. A look at Fig. 6.4 tells a different story. At first glance, this graph warrants the comment, "Gee, what a mess." No consistent game plan, or movement, developed for the no-agreement mediators. The only trend that was even somewhat consistent with the agreement mediators dealt with gathering background information about the dispute. The no-agreement mediators pursued this information actively from the first to the second time period, and then dropped it from the fifth time period on.

Dominating the no-agreement interventions at the fourth time period were the issues underlying the dispute. These issue discussions never allowed the future-oriented proposal talk to take over. The agreement mediators dropped the issue discussions as time progressed and developed a future orientation fairly quickly. The

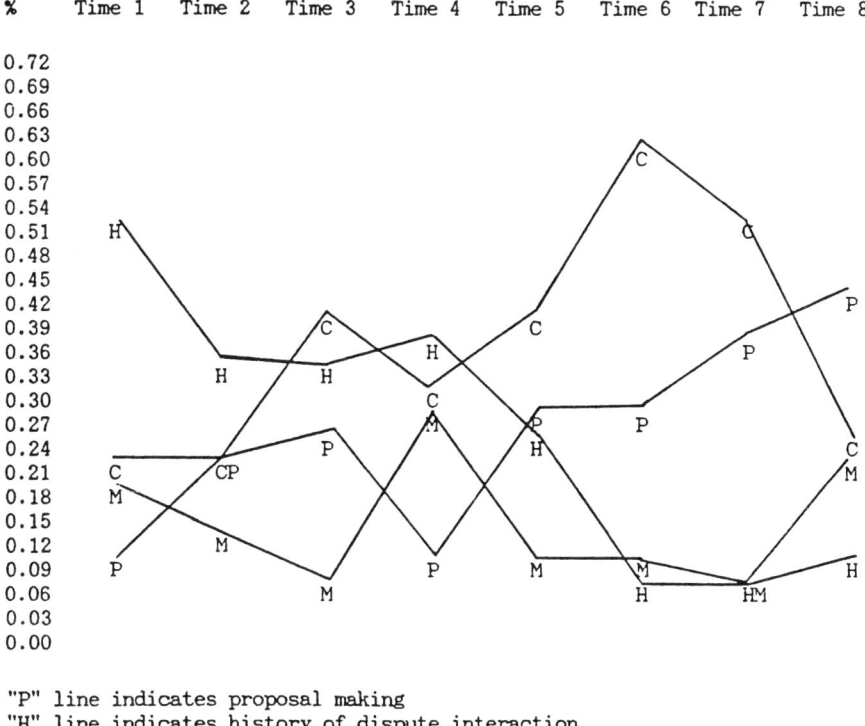

"P" line indicates proposal making
"H" line indicates history of dispute interaction
"C" line indicates problems in the current dispute
"M" line indicates focus on process of mediation

*Figure 6.4.* Percentage of no-agreement mediator-phase interventions.

no-agreement group became burdened by issues from about the mid-point of the mediation on and was unable to shake them. From Time 7 to 8 the no-agreement mediators made a mad rush to develop proposals. However, by then, it was too late.

### *Comparing Mediator Tactical Decisions*

Comparing the mediators' communication tactics across the eight time periods also reveals some interesting differences. Specifically, the agreement mediators pursued questioning—framing tactics during the first two time periods. These tactics were clearly used to identify background information, clarify goals, and provide orientation information. As the mediation continued, the agreement mediators relied more on their framing skills and less on their questioning skills. In contrast, analyses reveals that the no-agreement mediators peaked in their use of framing tactics at the mid-point of the negotiation. They relied much more extensively on their questioning skills, particularly toward the end of the mediation.

This analysis suggests that when mediators were burdened with relational problems, they concentrated on contributing useful information capable of helping couples understand and evaluate their legal positions. When burdened with these problems, the mediators concentrated on them by asking questions, mostly about factual issues surrounding these problems. No consistent plan seems apparent for this group. Perhaps, as indicated in prior chapters, these mediators got caught up in the dispute and allowed the disputants to control the flow of interaction.

## CONCLUSIONS

These intervention analyses reveal an interesting story about what happens when couples control a mediation with their relational problems and mediators ignore these problems. Before the relational problems surfaced in the initial phase of mediation, the mediations looked about the same. The mediators structured the situation with rules, orientation information, and requests for proposals. Soon after this initial period, the mediations diverged considerably. The couples with relational problems quickly began discussing them, and the mediators responded by asking questions about the factual dimensions of these relational problems. The underlying relational issues such as trust, fairness, equity, and so on were not processed. Instead of processing these relational issues to regain control, the mediators tried to suggest a variety of proposals that might resolve the factual issues. Unprepared to look toward the future, the couples ignored the proposals and continued their attacks.

The couples without the relational problems breezed through mediation because they were prepared, for the most part, to put the past behind them and to focus on the future. Mediators talked about interests because the couples were ready to hear one another's interests. The mediators translated these interests into specific proposals, and they were readily accepted by the couples. The mediators kept the couples focused on the future, which is where they wanted to be.

# 7

# Lessons from the Data

The research presented in chapters 4, 5, and 6 tells us much about divorce mediation, interaction management, and conflict. For example, the data reveal some interesting insights about how divorce mediation is handled in Los Angeles County, and about how couples enter mediation with very different goals and concerns. The data also inform us about the interaction management process that might help mediators and parents enhance their communication skills in very intense conflict situations. And, the results provide communication students and scholars with some perspectives on highly emotional conflicts that have largely been ignored in the conflict literature. The purpose of this chapter is to identify these lessons and hopefully to pull together the research findings in a way that makes this study of communication in divorce mediation more meaningful.

## LESSONS ABOUT DIVORCE MEDIATION

### Lesson 1: Different Folks Need Different Strokes

The case analyses from chapter 4 provide a compelling profile of the kinds of people and the kinds of problems they bring to mediation in Los Angeles County. Recall that most of the agreement couples entered the process just prior to their divorce, whereas most no-agreement couples came to mediation after several years of divorce. The agreement couples also appeared to enter mediation with minimal relational and other nonlegal issues to cloud the focus on the legal issues. In contrast, most no-agreement couples entered mediation several years after their divorce. In addition, they brought with them a variety of fairly severe relational difficulties that played havoc with the mediation process.

As indicated previously, the connection between these two variables is fairly clear. Couples entering mediation after years of divorce have just that much more time to build animosities toward one another. They have lived for years with custody and visitation orders that were probably unsatisfactory in the first place and have simply grown worse over time. Communication between such couples has also had years to deteriorate, making constructive problem solving that much more difficult.

The point of these differences is that perhaps these different folks need different strokes. That is, those coming to mediation after years of divorce may need to be screened to assess the extent to which they can work together in mediation. Are there significant relational issues left unresolved in the mediations? To what extent are they interested in dealing with the legal issues of custody and visitation? Mediators seem to function very effectively when couples come to mediation ready to bargain. They keep couples focused on their interests, they stimulate information exchange, and they work very hard to hammer out specific details on agreements. However, when mediators sense that the couple really wants to use the mediation session to blast each other about severe relational problems, the mediators terminate these sessions rather quickly and let the judge decide. Perhaps some kind of screening for these couples would help make better use of a mediator's time.

## Lesson 2: The Deck Chairs on the Titanic Really Don't Need Arranging

A second lesson about divorce mediation relates to the strengths and limitations of the interventionist model of mediation. This model, as practiced in the Los Angeles Court, focuses fairly exclusively on resolving the legal issues. As suggested previously, some very important pragmatic considerations (e.g., time, staff, money) prevent incorporating parts of the facilitation model into this interventionist model. As a result, the staff is not really prepared to enter into prolonged discussions about couples' relational problems.

Despite the fact that this strict interventionist model is not set up for relationally difficult mediations, the mediators use it anyway. After all, what choice do they have? For the most part, they do not find out about the problems until they get into the process, and by that time most of the damage has been done. Although the Los Angeles mediators have the option of scheduling more sessions, this option is unlikely because mediators would not use the extra time for "counseling" aimed only at addressing relational issues. As a result, they take the interventionist model as far as it goes and then drop the case. The fact that the no-agreement sessions are half as long as the agreement sessions suggests that the mediators make a judgment fairly early about the viability of the mediation process.

So, faced with these relational problems and their interventionist model, what approach do the mediators use? When relational issues arise, they focus on the facts, aimed generally at details of agreements. The transcripts are filled with examples of couples waging war with one another while the mediators ask for specific details about potential custody or visitation arrangements. Instead of probing about the deeper issue of trust, the mediators are often stuck with the more superficial details about a variety of concerns. Thus, probing such facts that hide deep relational divisions is akin to arranging the deck chairs on the Titanic. The ship is going down, but the deck looks neat.

Certainly, the interventionist, or more appropriately nonrelational development model of mediation used in the Los Angeles Court handles about 75% of the cases rather well. In most cases, couples can focus on the problem and work out an agreement that lasts at least a year. So, on balance, the interventionist model is probably the most useful option for the Los Angeles Court. It breaks down fairly quickly only when couples come to mediation with real problems. If, as suggested in the first lesson, such couples could be screened and prepared for mediation, then the interventionist model is probably most useful.

## LESSONS ABOUT INTERACTION MANAGEMENT

### Lesson 3: Don't Treat Mediation as a Spectator Sport

The analyses also revealed many important lessons about the model of interaction management presented in chapter 3. The first, and perhaps most important, lesson gained from the data is about control. In the no-agreement sessions, the mediators often lost control of the interaction in several ways. In many cases, they simply watched as the couples ripped away at one another. This strategy turned the mediator into a spectator at a tennis match, by watching one side and then the next side slam away at one another. This constant head turning to watch the fight allowed the couples to control the mediation's pace and substance. Second, the no-agreement disputants talked about relational problems while their mediators pursued factual issues. Their interest in talking about similar topics in mediation diverged considerably as time progressed. Third, these no-agreement mediators chose not to interfere with attack–defend cycles. After one side attacked, the mediators let the couples play through the cycle and then intervened after the cycle had been played out.

Were these couples controllable? The answer to this question is difficult. Certainly, there are no data to follow up on these couples to determine if anyone successfully aided in dealing with the couple's dispute. Perhaps the better question is, were these couples controllable with the model of mediation used in the Los Angeles Court? The answer to this question is probably not. As indicated earlier, the interventionist model does not deal with everyone's needs because no model of mediation meets everyone's needs. Some of the no-agreement couples may have been controllable in the sense of being able to focus on the legal issues if they had been exposed to some kind of counseling prior to mediation. It appears that draining off the relational energy from the mediations would have been necessary for mediators to have an impact with these couples.

**Lesson 4: Don't Give Me Just the Facts, Ma'am**

Does managing relational problems with factual inquiries work very well? The data reveal that the no-agreement mediators failed to focus couples on substantive problem solving by asking them about the factual details of their disputes in response to their relational concerns. When they just asked for the facts, the couples ignored them and simply went on fighting. This trap is easy to fall into because couples often disguise relational disputes in factual questions. Mediators may feel that if they somehow get agreement on the factual problem, the relational problem will simply disappear. The mediations studied here tend to reject this view. Continuously pursuing factual questions does not seem to hide the deeper relational concerns because the no-agreement disputes dealt with deeply troubling personal problems and not logistical details. Couples had fundamental objections about whether one another could be trusted. With such fundamental difficulties, a factual focus is not likely to rescue the mediation.

### Lesson 5: The Beef Is in the Issues

The saying, "Where's the Beef?" is an appropriate question for mediators. What should mediators focus on when trying to understand couples' interaction patterns? Should they concentrate on the relational messages, strategic ploys, or substantive issues? The data from this project suggest that tracking the substantive issues is most appropriate. In most cases, the nature of the substantive issues appeared to influence both the relational messages couples sent to one another and the kinds of strategies they used to send those messages. For example, when couples discussed relational issues, they became locked into the highly competitive attack–defend strategy exchange. They framed these relational issues with very direct yet spatially distant levels of verbal immediacy that send a very competitive message. Conversely, when couples focused on interests, they used more information-exchange strategies and more cooperative forms of verbal immediacy. As a result, mediators can probably get a sense of what couples are doing by focusing on the most obvious feature of the interaction, the issues they are discussing.

### Lesson 6: Take Couples to the Outer Limits

The outer limits for couples is simply the future. The data tell us that couples capable of, or directed to focus on, the future also express their interests instead of their relational concerns, and they engage in more information sharing. In the agreement sessions, the data from chapter 6 are remarkable in their clarity about directing couples through phases. These mediators kept a sharp focus on the future while also deemphasizing discussions of past problems that plagued the couple. As suggested previously, perhaps these couples were simply more amenable to this kind of future focus. Nevertheless, when couples sustained a future focus, many additional benefits resulted. For example, because informa tion sharing was more associated with discussing future interests, the future focus appears to stimulate problem-solving skills. This connection makes sense because couples need more information to decide what to do in the future.

This lesson is a deceptively simple one, because it is difficult to achieve, particularly for couples frought with relational problems. Mediators were able to gain control of couples coming to mediation while in the process of divorce and secure their focus on the future. Unfortunately, this control and the ability to steer couples into the future were much more difficult for the relationally centered couples. As suggested in the first lesson, these kinds of couples might be able to focus on the future if they were better prepared to focus on it instead of bashing away at one another.

## LESSONS ABOUT CONFLICT INTERACTION

### Lesson 7: Double Binds Mean Double Troubles

One of the more interesting lessons about conflict emerging from this study deals with the kind of relational language that couples use to discuss various kinds of issues. When the no-agreement couples brought out sensitive relational topics, they framed them with very direct, yet very spatially distant, language. This language use reflected a desire to pull the other into the conflict while simultaneously pushing him or her away physically. In contrast, when couples were focusing on interest issues and engaging in substantive problem solving they were much less direct and they used more spatially immediate language. The push–pull process was not evident when couples focused on substantive problems.

### Lesson 8: Breaking Up Really Is Hard to Do

Breaking up is hard to do because once relational issues develop, they acquire a life of their own. They escalate quickly out of control and feed on one another. Many other conflict researchers have noted this escalation cycle as indicated in chapter 2. The escalation was particularly apparent in the no-agreement sessions. Typically in these sessions, the cycle looked something like this: (a) a substantive relational issue emerged, (b) that was framed strategically as an attack, (c) the attack stimulated a need to defend face, (d) the face and relational problem stimulated the relational double-bind problem, and (e) the other returned the attack with more verbal aggression while the mediator failed to intervene in the process and redirect the couples toward more substantive problem solving.

This pattern indicates that breaking up is hard to do because, first, the focus is on the relationship and these kinds of problems spiral out of control very quickly. Second, the mediators watched them spiral out of control. They allowed the attack–defend spirals to develop to the point that couples were distracted from substantive problem solving. Even if the problems involved the relationship, the mediators chose not to address these problems to get on with problem solving.

The interesting feature about these nine lessons is that they seem to center around the no-agreement interactions. Perhaps we learn more about the system's capabilities when the system breaks down. This chapter now moves toward a better understanding of these no-agreement sessions. The concept of crisis bargaining is used to examine how the no-agreement sessions spiraled out of control so quickly.

## CRISIS BARGAINING IN DIVORCE MEDIATION

Recall that the no-agreement couples came to mediation many months or years after their divorce was final. What brought them to mediation? In each case, couples came to mediation because of some specific event that deeply disturbed one of them. For example, a daughter might have told her mother that her father and his friends were smoking marijuana during her weekend with him. Upon learning this from the daughter, the mother decided to seek sole custody or in some way limit the father's visitation with the daughter. In none of the no-agreement cases did a parent enter mediation because the couple agreed that they had simply "outgrown" their agreement and it needed some fine tuning. Some really big problem brought them back to court.

The fact that some specific event precipitated their mediation suggests that the no-agreement couples were in crisis upon entering mediation. It seems appropriate, then, to think about how couples bargain while in crisis. How does bargaining in a crisis differ from bargaining performed in more "normal" circumstances? Most of the work dealing with bargaining in crises comes from a political science perspective. For example, in their book dealing with international crises, Snyder and Diesing (1977) lay out a model of crisis bargaining designed specifically to understand such international crisis bargaining events as the Cuban Missile Crisis of 1962 when President Kennedy bargained with the Soviets to remove their nuclear missiles from Cuba.

Although their model generally concentrates on international crises, it also appears applicable to an interpersonal bargaining context such as divorce mediation. The rationale for using it to understand divorce mediation is that Snyder and Diesing conceptualized bargaining in a crisis as a traditional two-party interaction in which parties use various strategies to gain advantages and to "win." The key differences between the international situation and the divorce situation seem to center around two issues. First, the international situation can become much more complex as parties have many difficult choices to make and many people and issues to consider in defining their positions. Second, the stakes can become considerably more important because large numbers of people are affected by the bargaining outcomes. Nevertheless, the essential principles of crisis bargaining as developed by Snyder and Diesing appear applicable to couples experiencing particularly bitter custody and visitation disputes. At this point it might be useful to identify these principles and to apply them to the divorce mediation context to better understand the results presented in these chapters.

**Principles of Crisis Bargaining**

Snyder and Diesing (1977) defined a crisis as: (a) a sequence of interactions between individuals who, (b) are confronted with a specific challenge that threatens their high priority goals, (c) the situation catches them by surprise, (d) they feel intense resistance from the other party regarding those high priority goals, and (e) normal, more cooperative structures for resolving the problem have broken down and are not available for managing the crisis. This definition intends to exclude a variety of other situations from inclusion in this chapter. Specifically, the definition excludes those personal "crises" in which intense conflict is not a part of the situation. For example, in a suicide crisis, the person considering suicide generally is not in conflict with the mental health professional seeking to talk that person out of suicide. The person may be at war with him or herself, but not with the caseworker. The definition provided here intends to capture those situations in which the adversarial process escalates to a point beyond which normal decision-making structures are useful, but short of the point in which disputants resort to physical violence to resolve the dispute.

Within this crisis "twilight zone," disputants generally interact to resolve their conflict. When the disputants chose this course of action, Snyder and Diesing (1977) termed this behavior *crisis bargaining*. Although other scholars have examined the general problem of bargaining in a crisis situation (e.g., Janis, 1989), the principles offered by Snyder and Diesing seem particularly useful in understanding the bargaining process when mediation fails to make progress toward agreement. The following is a list of crisis bargaining features taken largely from Snyder and Diesing, but tailored to this particular divorce mediation, in general, and this data set, in particular.

***The Prominence of Coercion.*** Snyder and Diesing (1977) contended that one of the major features of crisis bargaining that separates it from normative bargaining is the prominence of coercion as opposed to accommodation. The Putnam and Poole (1987) distinction between distributive and integrative communication is similar to the coercion–accommodation dichotomy. In essence, Snyder and Diesing believe that in more normatively based bargaining, the disputants begin with the assumption that both sides will ultimately work together in an accommodating or integrating mode. In contrast, crisis bargainers believe that accommodation is not ultimately feasible; coercion is needed to force the other side into a suitable course of action.

Snyder and Diesing (1977) indicated that the first act of severe coercion is called the *challenge*. Challenges are actions that propose a state of extreme conflict between parties. A divorced father may challenge the mother by bringing a custody suit against her to force her into relinquishing the children. Challenges are stimulated by precipitants or circumstances that motivate an individual to take extreme actions. The precipitant might include the father's belief that the mother is not properly raising the child. Sometimes a specific precipitant, often called "the last straw," can motivate a challenge, such as the father coming for weekend visitation and finding mom smoking dope in the house with a boyfriend.

When the challenge and the resistance collide, it produces what Snyder and Diesing (1977) termed a *confrontation*, which remains at the core of the crisis. The confrontation severely escalates conflict and brings it from a possibly latent, hidden state to a very overt, manifest state. This confrontation may continue for some time and is often characterized by rising and falling tensions and predominately coercive tactics on both sides. Each side stands firm with his or her initial positions by engaging in a variety of threatening actions and warnings to communicate firmness of position.

For divorce mediation, three outcomes of confrontation are possible. First, the individuals can pursue the divorce equivalent of war by kidnapping the children, or resorting to violence to get their way. Once war has been declared, the crisis-bargaining phase is over and individuals move into a different phase of interaction that moves beyond the scope of divorce mediation. Second, one side can capitulate to the other's demands. The following "resolution" phase of the interaction involves a variety of accommodative tactics including bids, concessions, and settlement proposals. The third option, a negotiated or tacit compromise in Snyder and Diesing's (1977) terms, involves individuals' moving away from the confrontation into hard bargaining with some mild coercive moves as displays of determination. Pruitt (1981) indicated that these bargaining behaviors might hopefully adopt a more integrative form in which individuals are able to work through both the crisis and the underlying conflicts of interest. If the bargaining or the resolution only ends the crisis and leaves the conflict of interest unresolved, then the confrontation may rise another day.

Snyder and Diesing (1977) indicated that the aftermath of crises can assume four different forms. First, the power between the parties may change. Parties may lose resource control or even a loss in face or credibility. Second, the resolution selected may reduce or increase the relational strength of the parties. Some individuals grow from crises because the air is cleared and emotions are displayed, whereas others intensify their anger toward one another. Third, the outcome can affect alignments. The children or other members of the family may decide to align with one party or the other, depending on how they viewed the crisis and its outcome. Finally, several emotional effects emerge in the aftermath of crises. If one side used unnecessarily severe or humiliating threats and the injured side is not permitted some face saving in the course of managing these threats to retain some dignity, then emotional disdain is likely to linger after the crisis is over. Hopefully, the course of divorce mediation increases disputants' relational ties and offers them an opportunity to address key issues underlying the dispute so the crisis will not escalate to war.

***Bargaining for High Stakes.*** The second feature of crisis bargaining that often separates it from more normative bargaining involves the size or importance of the issues at stake. When the issues are very important, such as the custody of children, then individuals become very motivated to do whatever is necessary to win. These stakes are often very personally involving, such that if the stakes are lost a very important part of that individual's psychological and physical stability is also lost. Parents would certainly argue that their children constitute one of the most personal parts of their lives. Normative bargaining may at some points dwell on very important issues. However, most of the interaction in this mode revolves around issues that are not centrally tied to each bargainer's most important human identity.

The key to understanding the role of high stakes in developing a crisis bargaining orientation focuses on each disputant's flexibility. This point is very clear in the marital interaction literature (see chapter 2). If disputants remain fairly flexible in their demands, then the stakes are not particularly high. If disputants remain unrelenting and extremely attached to the stakes, then flexibility is low and a crisis may emerge.

***Focusing on the Prominent Alternative*** The psychological attachment disputants make toward their high stakes encourages them to focus only on what they want (i.e., their prominent alternative). They have defended their position repeatedly, making their desired end states very focused in their mind. This prominent alternative discourages them from engaging in what Herek, Janis, and Huth (1987) termed *vigilant problem solving*. This kind of problem solving includes considering a wide range of alternative outcomes and weighing their advantages and disadvantages. When individuals get focused on one alternative, their information processing about other alternatives gets distorted, or terminates altogether. In less coercively based bargaining in which individuals are not forced to repeatedly defend a position, and the stakes are not as high, disputants are generally more willing to look at other alternative proposals. However, as the crisis escalates, this desire is quickly lost.

Another problem of focusing on the mutually prominent alternative is that the alternative may discourage individuals from identifying long-term goals. The coercive strategies used to attain the prominent alternative can actually subvert the long-term goals. For example, consider the father suing for custody (the prominent alternative) to provide what he perceives as a better living arrangement for the children. The conflict generated through the crisis bargaining process can create more damage to the children's well-being than anything the mother might do to the children. Because the father fights vigorously for the prominent alternative, he becomes blinded to his original objective. In more normative bargaining, the father would be able to step back from the process and see that the original goal of providing a better home for the children has given way to punishing the mother through the crisis-bargaining process. Thus, in crisis bargaining the short-term goal associated with the prominent alternative dominates the individual's thinking; long-term goals become elusive and irrelevant at this point.

**High Degree of Emotional Content.** Because both the stakes and resistance from the other are high, coercion dominates strategic thinking, and the prominent alternative is so imposing psychologically on the disputants, bargaining in a crisis situation generally remains very emotional. When individuals lay down challenges associated with personally involving high stakes, Snyder and Diesing (1977) contended that two principal emotions appear: anger (hostility) and fear. The anger stems from the opponent's coercive actions aimed to defeat the highly prized and protected outcomes. Fear enters the situation because individuals have little sense of predictability toward the outcome. In addition, because the crisis revolves around the couple's divorce, they are likely to experience the whole variety of emotions identified in chapter 1.

Once individuals become highly emotionally aroused for a prolonged period of time, their ability to think and act is modified considerably (Roth, 1982). According to Roth, psychophysiologists (those studying the physiology of the brain) use the concept of psychological activation or arousal to describe the complex of physiological, emotional changes that affect performance. When psychological activation or emotions are low, the individual is relaxed and drowsy. When activation is high, the body prepares itself to meet some stressful, challenging situation. If the activation is too low, performance is low because the individual is too relaxed. On the other hand, if activation is too high, the individual is too stressed out to think logically; the mind and body prepare to fight off danger through primitive impulses rather than through creative problem solving. For example, in a hostage negotiation crisis bargaining, the initial moments of the crisis are particularly difficult because the hostage taker is typically activated beyond the point at which he or she is ready to negotiate. The police negotiators typically try to calm the person before asking the person to think logically and clearly.

**The Preponderance of Face Issues.** As indicated earlier, the use of coercive strategies and tactics creates identity problems for the bargainers. The verbal aggression literature summarized in chapter 2 and Folger and Poole (1984) make the point that once face issues enter the decision-making process, the interaction quickly escalates into unproductive conflict. Quite simply, face issues are focused on self-protection. Individuals feel disinclined to discuss substantive issues when their identity is being threatened. Only when identity is secure can individuals problem solve over substantive issues.

Crises not only create face issues between disputants in conflict, but they also create problems for disputants and their constituents. Disputants might continue a torrent pace of coercive actions as a means of convincing constituents that the disputant is remaining tough. For example, the father might continue coercive acts against his former wife to show support for his girlfriend's position that his former wife is despicable. These kinds of face issues make dealing with disputants that have multiple family ties very difficult as McIsaac (1986) indicated.

**The Feeling of Urgency.** Snyder and Diesing (1977) argued that individuals generally find crises as unfortunate, noxious interruptions in their "normal" lives, and the longer the crisis continues the less control individuals will be able to exert over the crisis. The crisis gains a life of its own, much like a runaway freight train, and the rush of events remains marginally subject to control. A false move could lead to disaster. Such perceptions create a powerful incentive to resolve the conflict as soon as possible. More normative bargaining carries with it some sense of urgency as strike deadlines approach in labor—management bargaining, for example. However, such actions are seen as traditional and logically flowing from the normal course of events. In such predictable circumstances, individuals still maintain a sense that they can control the situation. Certainly, some strikes escalate into crises as coercive strategies start to dominate accommodating ones. However, the feeling of control is key in sustaining the perception that something must be done about the crisis.

In addition, disputants or other circumstances may impose deadlines on one another. Logically, any threat carries with it either an explicit or explicit sense of time urgency. Compliance is demanded soon or consequences are likely to follow, sooner than later. The feeling of urgency is also exacerbated by the disputants' emotional states generated by the crisis. Their excitement about the crisis does not encourage a thoughtful, slowed pace of events. The emotional intensity creates a sense that something must be done soon.

***Lack of Complete Information.*** When bargaining in crisis individuals tend not to systematically gather information needed to better manage the crisis. The forces of battle (i.e., emotion, face, the prominent alternative) combine to bias the individual in selecting information about the crisis. For example, the father might not want to hear about how children suffer when their parents fight too much. The father may not be able to see the risks associated with trying to achieve his prominent alternative. This kind of biased information seeking is typical of crisis problem solving, according to Herek et al. (1987). In vigilant problem solving, individuals obtain the necessary information to critically evaluate the pros and cons of the preferred course of action and the alternatives. They conduct a systematic information search to gain expert opinion, critical evaluations of their positions, and a full range of ideas regarding their goals. In crisis bargaining, individuals generally fail to complete this very important task.

***Failure to Work Out Detailed Implementation and Monitoring Plans.*** The final aspect of crisis bargaining is that individuals generally fail to follow through on specifically how any agreements will be implemented and monitored. This inability to implement vigilant problem solving also discourages individuals from specifying contingency plans in the event of the agreement breaking down (Herek et al., 1987). The other forces associated with crisis bargaining combine to sabotage such efforts. When the crisis is resolved such that individuals get most of what they want, they are so emotionally drained from the experience that they check out of vigilant problem solving at that point. In a normative bargaining mode, individuals are more likely to focus on the objective features of the agreement and follow through with monitoring adherence to the agreement and of developing contingency plans in the event that the agreement breaks down.

## Summary

To summarize, couples create a crisis bargaining context when they:

1. pursue coercion more than accommodation;
2. bargain for high stakes;
3. focus on their prominent alternative;
4. exhibit a high degree of emotional content;
5. exchange many face-oriented messages;
6. feel urgent about resolving the situation;
7. lack complete information; and
8. fail to work out detailed implementation and monitoring plans.

In all likelihood, other conditions for crisis bargaining are readily apparent to those familiar with disputants involved in this context. Nevertheless, these features provide a good starting point for understanding what mediators face when dealing with couples who have a particularly difficult time working together.

Can mediators manage interaction to move a couple's bargaining from a crisis to a more normative bargaining mode? Normative bargaining, like that observed in the agreement sessions, assumes that couples negotiate to problem solve and not hurt one another. It assumes that, although the stakes are still high, they are not rushed for time, and they do not need to rely on emotion to make their point. To understand how mediators might help couples make the transition from a crisis to a normative bargaining mode, it is necessary to first qualify the no-agreement divorce mediations as a crisis bargaining situation?

## Mediator Interaction Management and Crisis Bargaining

### *Divorce Mediation as Crisis Bargaining*

***The Prominence of Coercion.*** Instead of labeling any given mediation as either a crisis or a normative bargaining event, it might be more useful to view mediations along a bargaining continuum with "normative" at the more cooperative end, and "crisis" on the more competitive end. Those mediations in which couples merely need some guidance in working through custody arrangements might not exhibit many coercive strategies. These couples begin with the assumption that they are going to work through an arrangement with one another. This course discourages coercive tactics, keeps emotions under control, and encourages systematic information gathering to inform couples about important custody/visitation alternatives.

For the most part, the agreement couples seemed to bargain more toward the normative end of the continuum. They came to mediation in the course of their divorce so they were creating new proposals for custody and visitation as opposed to changing any intact agreements. This point is critical because the driving force behind crisis bargaining is some specific challenging event that triggers the crisis. For the agreement couples, their divorce was certainly a crisis, but it was a long-term process that hardly took anyone by surprise. They had time to prepare psychologically for the mediation process. With no specific challenging event, resistance to the challenge is not stimulated. When challenge and resistance fail to collide, no confrontation ensues. As a result, the agreement couples were much less coercive. There was no need to coerce, only a need to solve the problems associated with the divorce.

In contrast, the no-agreement couples entered mediation in response to a specific crisis event with a desire to change intact agreements. In many cases, the fathers sued the mothers to change specific aspects of their agreements because of some specific problem the fathers were experiencing with the agreement. Often, the fathers sued because the mothers withheld custody, and very often these suits happen very quickly and take the mothers by surprise. When this happens, the mothers react very quickly and decisively, often filing counter charges that the fathers are not paying child support. This challenge and resistance cycle sets the stage for confrontation in mediation. Unfortunately, mediation is often the first opportunity couples have to meet face-to-face following the suit. They have no option but mediation because it is mandatory in California. So, when such couples begin their face-to-face discussions in mediation, they are in a fighting mood. They are not interested in cooperating with the other party because they have been challenged, or they believe the child's welfare is at stake.

***Bargaining for High Stakes.*** Second, all couples in mediation bargain for high stakes. After all, can there be any higher stakes than bargaining for children? For the agreement couples such bargaining was included in the whole divorce process. Couples getting divorced must also bargain for a variety of other issues including child support payments and division of property. So, for the agreement couples, although the stakes were certainly high, bargaining for the children was one more problem to be solved. The fact that mediators had little difficulty getting these couples to focus on the future, deal with their interests and exchange information suggests that they were more or less ready to problem solve.

However, the no-agreement couples came to mediation specifically to deal with the surprise lawsuit over custody and visitation. They had already come to terms with the other aspects of the divorce many years before. They had nothing to distract them from really going after one another surrounding the legal challenge. This focus probably served to elevate the importance of the high stakes for the no-agreement disputants.

***Focusing on the Prominent Alternative.*** Which couples were most likely focused on a single way of resolving the dispute? Clearly, the no-agreement group came to mediation to change intact agreements. So, it was their responsibility to indicate what they wanted to change from the prior agreement. The agreement couples had not forged an agreement yet making them more open to alternative proposals. Reading the transcripts reveals that the no-agreement group came to mediation wanted severe and drastic changes in the agreements. For example, in some cases where the agreements specified joint custody, the no-agreement couples wanted to change the order to sole custody with no visitation rights for the other party. In one no-agreement session, the mediator kept probing for openness among the parties regarding their desires, and neither waivered a bit from their original positions. In response, the mediator simply terminated the session.

***High Emotional Content.*** Given the confrontational nature of the no-agreement sessions, it is not surprising to see that emotional/relational issues dominated these sessions. These couples came to mediation steaming mad and ready for action. Parties violated one another's trust, broken life-long confidences, and constantly attacked one another. It was clear in most of the no-agreement sessions that parties looked for opportunities to punish the other. Each wanted the mediator to see what a loser the other side had become. And, once the slashing and cutting began, it developed a life of its own that the mediators were unprepared to handle. The emotions carried the sessions away after the mediators made their opening comments. Clearly, these couples were hurting a great deal. In contrast, the agreement couples entered mediation with fewer relational concerns, resulting in fewer attack–defend cycles. They did not allow relational issues to cloud the legal problems and settled their disputes with relative ease. Avoiding the attacks also avoided destructive emotions from overtaking the sessions. Emotional issues will dominate in the form of face attacking, saving, and defending. Disputants will become more committed to their prominent alternative causing them to remain unconcerned about additional information that might challenge the prominent alternative. This path actually describes virtually the same pattern of events associated with verbal aggression and marital conflict between clinic couples discussed in chapter 2.

**Face Issues.** Were face issues a problem in these mediations? Certainly, because of the emotions, the confrontations, and the high stakes, the no-agreement couples were constantly challenging one another's face. The dominance of the attack–defend cycles in these sessions provides some evidence to support this conclusion. In fact, a case could be made that these attack–defend cycles constituted verbal aggression. We know from the Felson (1984) research cited in chapter 2 that verbal aggression stems from challenges to one's identity or face. Particularly, in front of the mediator, no-agreement couples had to prove that the other party was unworthy of sustaining the current agreement. By not living up to the original agreement, the other party was violating the law. Parties could not look foolish in this context, thereby making "face" a particular problem in mediations conducted under the cloud of changing intact agreements.

**A Feeling of Urgency.** Did the couples feel an urgent need to resolve their dispute? Certainly, the no-agreement couples probably felt a greater need to resolve things more quickly than their agreement counterparts. After all, they came to mediation in the rush of a specific lawsuit to change the custody/visitation arrangements. They wanted satisfaction now! The agreement couples came to mediation in the course of their marital breakup with a much longer term approach to the problem. Thus, the no-agreement couples probably felt a more urgent need to deal with the problem, which for them was also a crisis. We know from classic negotiation literature (see Pruitt, 1981) that bargaining under time constraints increases the likelihood of coercive strategies. Parties begin feeling desperate and are willing to try anything to get their way.

***Lack of Complete Information.*** Focusing on a prominent alternative and relational issues framed in highly coercive and emotional strategies also served to paint the no-agreement couples into another corner (i.e., a lack of substantive information). Unburdened by these concerns, the agreement couples were able to exchange information much more readily than the no-agreement couples. Mediations for the no-agreement couples were much shorter because they were unwilling to share basic information with one another about their problems. They used the time to punish one another, as opposed to dealing with the legal issues.

***Detailed Implementation Plans.*** Finally, it is self-evident that the no-agreement couples were unable to develop detailed implementation plans. They demonstrated an inability to form any kind of agreement or cooperation with one another. Asking these couples to work on any kind of details was very difficult as evidenced by the mediator's insistence on discussing factual issues. These couples cared less about factual issues and simply went about their business of attacking one another. The agreement couples worked through their specific details, which was another reason why these sessions were so much longer than the no-agreement sessions. Much of the time in the last third of the sessions were devoted to working out the details of the agreement.

### Interaction Management Goals

Was it possible for mediators to transform the interaction in the no-agreement sessions from a crisis to a more normative bargaining mode? As indicated in the lessons that began this chapter, making this transition for these couples probably required changes that the mediators were unprepared to make given the nature of their court system. However, given that the system is more difficult to change than mediator's interaction management strategies, perhaps it is most appropriate to propose a variety of interaction management goals mediators might consider when dealing with the type of couples found in the no-agreement sessions. In other words, what goals might mediators pursue to make the transition from crisis to normative bargaining mode?

First, mediators might try to reduce the couple's feeling of urgency regarding their case. The goal might be accomplished by encouraging couples to take a much more long-term approach on their problem. For example, mediators might pursue questions that take couples away from the specific short-term problem and move them toward longer term issues. A longer term issue might involve the child's future needs, or even the future needs of the parties themselves. After all, the lives of all parties involved in the dispute are changing right along with their needs. Perhaps starting with such long-term concerns might help keep the current crisis in perspective.

Second, mediators might try to process at least some of the key relational issues. Certainly, the system and the model of mediation used in this court is not set up to deal with relational issues. However, couples who come to mediation with these needs seem incapable of simply setting them aside to focus on substantive issues. But, what exactly does it mean to "process relational issues"? As suggested in chapter 3, this task involves first separating the relational from the nonrelational issues and then labeling the issue. For example, if one party seems upset about the other dropping off the child 15 minutes late from visitation, the mediator might probe whether this lateness communicates a lack of consideration from the other party. If that message is sent, then perhaps something needs to be done about it. This probe also gives the issue a label and makes it easier to confront later on.

A third goal mediators might consider in moving couples away from a crisis-bargaining mode involves reducing their focus on a prominent problem-solving alternative. If parties commit to an option early on and then repeat that option, a prominent alternative has emerged and will probably block substantive problem solving. Moving the parties away from the prominent alternative by banning such discussions until all the issues have been heard might help solve this problem. The goal here is to open up couples' thinking as much as possible. Some mediators in the transcript tried to move couples away from repeating single options by simply telling them that the judge will not entertain such an option. Does this strategy serve to open people's minds? Perhaps it might for some, but for others it might present another force of resistance that needs to be overcome.

Fourth, mediators might strive to reduce the need for face-saving in mediation. How can mediators accomplish this goal? Perhaps the primary means of dealing with this problem is cutting off face issues before they escalate too quickly. Face issues emerged in the transcripts as relationally centered attack–defend sequences. When mediators allowed these sequences to play themselves out, they quickly gained control of the interaction. Another way of avoiding such attacks is to focus the first several minutes of mediation on uncontroversial issues, gathering information about where the parties live, their jobs, the child's school, and so on. Couples need practice at simply communicating substantive information in one another's presence without blowing up. Perhaps when they practice these skills extensively, they are better prepared to problem solve and to avoid face threats.

Fifth, mediators facing difficult couples might try to greatly expand substantive information exchange. Not only will such information exchange decrease face-saving needs, but it also provides a better foundation for building agreements later on. Agreements are built on a foundation of information. When couples fail to generate such information and spend their time making accusations and reviewing past problems, they have nothing of value to work with. Mediators in the study were not particularly firm with couples in making them exchange information. Most mediators simply asked questions, but they became easily sidetracked when one of the disputants changed the subject. Sticking to such requests can only help couples down the road.

Finally, mediators might try to establish a more coherent mediation structure at the beginning of the sessions. The agreement mediators used a phase model, but they never really marked phase conclusions or beginnings. They seemed to ease out of one general discussion into another. This loose approach may have worked well for couples able to problem solve, but the strategy seemed less effective with more relationally torn couples. For this group, the mediators advocated one direction and the disputants took another. These interaction management recommendations are meant to serve as points of consideration for mediators. Clearly, all mediations are different, and each requires special treatment. However, making the transition from crisis to normative bargaining appears to be the mediator's most critical need. Mediators appear to perform impressively when they can move quickly to a normative bargaining mode. When couples prevent mediators from moving to this mode they experience difficulty getting on track. The following section is intended to illustrate how mediators might use interaction management to move from the crisis to a more normative bargaining mode.

## AN INTERVENTION ILLUSTRATION

Consider the following slightly edited transcript sample from one of the mediations used in the analysis:

Mediator: OK. Mrs. Jones, let's hear from you. What kind of plan do you think we could reach here?
Mother: Well, I'd like for them to live a normal. . .
Father: What's normal? Is being a cocaine addict and a mental patient and doing tricks [prostitution] normal?
Mother: Where did you hear that? Those are all wild lies.
Father: Your neighbor, Sally Smith told me. Those are your neighbors, not mine.
Mediator: OK, I think you have to be quiet and let her talk about the plan that she's thinking of.
Father: OK.
Mother: Well, I have to sell the house, because since my husband moved out he hasn't paid any of the payments. . .
Father: I have too.
Mediator: Wait, wait. Let's not talk about the house, and let's not talk about money right now. Let's talk about the children being with you and what do you propose in terms of the children's time.
Mother: Well, I'd like the kids to basically live with me and give him visitation rights on weekends.
Mediator: So, you would like them to live primarily with you and to go to school in your area and then set up a plan for them to be with him on weekends and holidays, is that right?
Mother: Yes.
Father: She can't afford any of that stuff.

This interaction begins with a request for a proposal. This request touches off an attack–defend cycle between the father and mother. This pattern is similar to the one found in the data in which basic requests for information give disputants a forum to argue. But, of greater interest is the substance of the father's attacks regarding drugs, mental illness, and prostitution. What's behind the father's comments? Is he simply trying to provoke a response from the mother, is he making serious allegations about drug abuse, and so forth, or is he expressing an important relational issue that needs to be addressed? Perhaps he is trying to accomplish all three objectives. Nevertheless, the coercive nature of the allegations suggests, at minimum, that the couple is leaning toward a crisis-bargaining orientation, and that the mediator's control is about to be challenged. Perhaps the mediator could have at least acknowledged the father's comment and suggest that if he did have serious allegations, he would be able to present them when the time was appropriate (i.e., when the mediator would have a chance to better gauge their validity).

Instead of acknowledging the comment, the mediator uses a structuring tactic that enforces the "no interruption" rule to get the couple back on track. This structuring move, like the data indicate, is very effective in reducing the immediate level of conflict in the interaction as the woman begins explaining about the need to sell the house. However, within this speaking turn, the mother takes another shot at the father about not paying the bills, moving away from the topic about what to do with the children. The father takes the bait and they continue their attack–defend cycle. Again, the mediator must sense that this couple has some serious relational difficulties. Neither can trust one another to properly raise the children or follow through on monetary commitments.

Again, the mediator moves to provide some structure to the discussion by asking couples not to speak about the monetary issues, but instead to focus on the children and the mother's plan in that regard. The mother complies with the request and follows the intervention with a cooperative response in the form of a proposal. The mediator appropriately moves to reframe the proposal to expand its limits and to frame the mother's language into more "agreement-oriented" language. However, the father's follow-up comment once again attacks the mother's position and rejects her comments out of hand with a snide comment.

This bit of interaction was taken from the first few pages of a no-agreement transcript. The mediator continued the request for proposals early on, and it severely incited the couple to make the kinds of comments seen in the transcript. Even though the mediator was using appropriate structuring and reframing moves, the couple still appeared to languish in a crisis-bargaining mode. Soliciting these kinds of proposals early on probably works satisfactorily with couples who are not relationally impaired. But, it seems less effective with relationally difficult couples. Following the goals set earlier, the mediator might have been more effective avoiding these proposals early on. Instead, the mediator might have asked the couple to share some uncontroversial information about one another just to get the discussion off the ground. Then the mediator could have moved to substantive issues that would give each party a chance to air his or her concerns about the other parent. The couple represented in the transcript was in no position to begin laying out proposals at that point in the mediation.

## CONCLUSIONS

The studies reported in this book suggest that the single most important threat to building cooperative interaction in divorce mediation involves the mediator struggling with disputants for *control* over both the process and substance of the dispute. The process struggle involves who secures the right to define the interaction structure (e.g., who controls topics and floor time). The substance struggle involves who controls the ideas for building an agreement (e.g., who creates proposals).

The series of studies reported in this book suggests that interaction management comes down to controlling the process, but not the substance of the interaction. When mediators recognize that disputants are beginning to sabotage the process, and they take steps to more systematically structure the interaction, they may have a better chance of moving away from a crisis-bargaining mode. Structuring is needed to move couples away from sensitive topics early in the dispute. It is needed to direct couples to talk about relational issues when the time is appropriate to do so. Structure gives couples goals to understand if they are making any progress in working toward both becoming more cooperative and building an agreement. In short, structure empowers couples to cooperate.

Although mediator control of the interaction process appears instrumental in moving away from crisis bargaining, mediator control of the settlement options does little to move away from crisis bargaining. In fact, it may even promote such behavior. Often, the no-agreement mediators tried to control disputants' emotional display of relational issues by forcing them to discuss settlement terms. In most cases, the disputants were not ready to discuss such terms. They were too busy venting concerns about past problems, the mediators were very uninterested in processing. In the agreement sessions, the mediators more often worked with disputants' ideas by pulling proposals out of disputants' utterances through the various reframing tactics. This activity established a context in which the disputants controlled the substantive part of the mediation. Reframing disputant contributions into proposals gives them control of alternative courses of action, which in turn, increases disputants' responsibility for their own destiny.

These differences suggest that an effective mediator "leads" the disputants and avoids "pushing" them toward agreement. When pushed, couples in crisis ignore the mediators' directives to focus on agreements because they want to discuss key relational issues. The net effect of this pushing is that it intensifies the struggle for control of the process. One group wants one topic, whereas the other wants another topic. However, when the mediator leads the couple, the struggle for control of the process is uncontested. Because the mediator does not try to impose terms of agreement, there is no need to resist, thus giving the mediator the opportunity to work through phases.

Chapter 8 tests the reader's interactive management skills by providing a simulation of a divorce mediation. After completing the simulation, the reader should have a better idea about how the principles of mediator interactive management can be implemented. The simulation asks the reader to interpret key communication patterns, and then provide interventions based on those interpretations. Hopefully, this exercise will encourage the reader to pursue mediation further.

# 8

# The Mediation of Ted and Betty Johnson

The purpose of this simulation is to provide an introduction to intervening in a divorce mediation. For new mediators (those who have never mediated), it provides a perspective on mediation that is based largely on the interventionist model presented in chapter 2. The simulation should help new mediators see the complexity involved in making critical intervention decisions. For experienced mediators, the simulation provides an opportunity to evaluate intervention values. Experienced mediators may disagree with intervention decisions offered here, which is certainly appropriate for this exercise. The exercise hopes to stimulate a dialogue about mediation, intervention techniques, and intervention values.

Listed here are a series of 30 father–mother interaction segments. Each segment includes a series of utterances that a father and mother might say during a divorce mediation. The reader assumes the position of mediator, and as a result, must decide if and when to mediate the interchange. The reader can choose to intervene after any utterance during the segment. The intervention points are indicated by the letter "M" with a number after it, specifying the intervention point. Choosing to intervene before the end of the segment assumes that the utterances following that intervention point are never presented. This affords the participant the luxury of indicating what the disputants should and should not say. Of course, this is a luxury actual mediators do not enjoy. For example, if the participant decides to intervene after the second utterance of a four-utterance exchange, then it can be assumed that Utterances 3 and 4 were not spoken by the couple.

After that intervention point is selected, then the mediator needs to identify which strategy or set of strategies would work best to move the mediation along most productively. After each segment, a suggested intervention point, a suggested intervention, and a rationale for both of those decisions are provided. These decisions and the rationales are based largely on the research results summarized in chapter 7 and on the interventionist approach to mediation described in chapter 2. Again, it is appropriate to disagree with the intervention decisions offered here because the purpose of the simulation is to stimulate discussion about intervention choices.

## THE SITUATION

Ted and Betty Johnson have been separated for nearly 1 year. Their only child is 12-year-old James, who is currently living with Betty. The temporary visitation arrangement includes Ted seeing James every Friday night and Saturday until 6 p.m., and every other Sunday. Ted recently filed for divorce and for full custody of James, a move that Betty wishes to contest in court. The case has been sent to mediation by the judge who feels some progress in this dispute can be made through mediation.

## INTERACTION SEGMENTS

### Segment 1

Father: Now that I'm in here, I don't really know much about mediation or why I should cooperate in this activity.
M1:
Mother: Yea, I feel the same way. What is this mediation thing all about anyway.
M2:
Father: [To mediator] Aren't you going to help me get my son back? He really needs some decent guidance.
M3:

Mother: I came here because he keeps trying to get my son away from me. My lawyer said I didn't have to do this.
Recommended Intervention: M2
Content: Introduce self, provide orientation about the goals of mediation and the role of the mediator. Explain the process and the phases that will be attempted. Explain the limits of confidentiality to the couple.
Rationale: The mediator needs to begin taking control of the interaction by explaining the goals and functions of mediation, and the rules for interacting responsibly. Allowing the father to attack the mother in his second utterance serves no purpose here, and, if allowed to continue, could threaten the mediator's control. The mediator also needs to begin providing structure to the interaction by specifying the phases and providing goals for interacting. The limits of confidentiality also need to be identified to reassure the disputants of their privacy.

## Segment 2

Mother: I understand about mediation and I guess I see how you are going to try to help us.
M1:
Father: I suppose it is better than going after one another in court and letting my son take all the abuse.
M2:
Mother: [To mediator] But, what happens if we don't settle? Are you going to testify in court or what?
M3:
Father: I'm not going to talk about anything if you are going to testify in court about our case.
M4:
Mother: [To mediator] My lawyer said you could really hurt me.
M5:
Suggested Intervention: M3
Content: Provide additional information about confidentiality and then ask if this information is understood by the disputants.
Rationale: The disputants, or at least the mother, is still unclear about the limits of confidentiality and needs further explanation. The last two utterances expose some feelings of fear, but at this point, it is probably best to put aside the confidentiality fear before processing other fears.

## Segment 3

Father: OK, so what we do here is strictly confidential. I guess I will go along with this if she will.

# MEDIATION OF TED AND BETTY JOHNSON

M1:
Mother: Well, I am tired of the adversarial process. We had really aggressive attorneys that made us further apart in our views.

M2:
Father: I guess we really have had our problems in working out this custody thing. I just want the best for my son.

M3:
Mother: We had some friends go through this and it worked for them pretty well. They stopped fighting as much after the divorce.

M4:
Father: We fight more than we probably should.

M5:
Mother: That's because our son's life is being all screwed up by this divorce thing. This never should have happened in the first place.

Suggested Intervention: M4:
Content: Reinforce agreement by commenting positively on their desire to work together; ask each for some background information about the son.
Rationale: The couple's cooperativeness needs to be reinforced to further commit them to the mediation process. This reinforcement of progress may also encourage the couple to be more dependent on the mediator in addition to the mediation process, thereby increasing the mediator's control. At this point, the couple probably understands the mediation process fairly well and is ready to move to the next mediation phase: developing the information foundation of the dispute by soliciting some background information from them.

## Segment 4

Mother: We have one son. His name is James, and he is 12 years old. He and I get along very well. See, I don't really know why he wants custody now. I want custody because I can provide a better environment for James.

M1:
Father: [To mother] Wait just a minute. What do you mean you can provide a better environment than I can. James and I are great together. I am the one who should have custody because he needs those special things I have to offer.

M2:
Mother: [To father] Look, Ted, you are the one who deserted us. You don't deserve to be involved in James' life anymore. That really hurt him.

M3:
Father: You were the one who really didn't care.

M4:
Suggested Intervention: M1
Content: Remind the couple that options for parenting James will be discussed later, but right now it is necessary to continue gathering background information. Ask the mother to continue her description.
Rationale: With the mother pushing ahead to discuss proposals, the interaction is in danger of degenerating into a no-win mother–father dispute in which the mediator would likely lose control of the mediation. The mediator needs to reinforce the phase orientation of the interaction and press on. Notice also how the push–pull, double-bind process associated with the last three utterances is beginning to assert itself. The disputants are saying exactly what's on their mind by telling one another very directly how they feel. They are also expressing considerable spatial distance by using such demonstratives as "that" and "those" instead of "this" and "these," indicating fear of getting close to the other person. As a result, it is probably best that the disputants not make these comments, if possible, because the context is probably not appropriate yet to expose and process these relational issues.

## Segment 5

Mother: OK, I'm sorry for getting off the track. Well, James and I are pretty close. He does well in school. He really likes his computer courses and wants to be a programmer when he grows up. He is a good athlete and gets along well with his school buddies. I would really hate to disrupt his life right now.
M1:
Father: James' life would not be disrupted if he lived with me. I have a place near his school. He could continue to go there and be with the other kids. Come on. He and I are close too. In fact, he's told me he would rather live with me than with you.
M2:
Mother: [To husband] James never said that to you. He told me he didn't like your girlfriend around all the time. You two should be more careful what you do around James.
M3:
Father: [To mother] Why do you make up stories like that? I can't believe you.
Suggested Intervention: M1
Content: Thank the mother and ask the father about his relationship with the child.
Rationale: Now that the mother has provided her perspective on James, it

is necessary to learn the father's perspective on his relationship with James. Some valuable issues emerge in the other three utterances. However, the father's proposals about custody and his comments about James' preferences might be inappropriate here because the mediator does not have sufficient background information about the couple's situation. The couple's talking to one another is probably a good idea, but this interaction could degenerate into unproductive conflict very quickly.

## Segment 6

Father: Well, I also think I have an excellent relationship with my son. He spends every other weekend with me, and that just isn't enough time. We have always communicated well with one another. He tells me all about his school and how he would like to have more time with his friends. He has his own room in my apartment and he really seems to like it there. Plus, in the long run I think I will be able to support him better...

M1:
Mother: Wait a minute! I have a pretty good job right now, and it looks like I am going to get a promotion soon. I am able to handle most of the bills without much child support. My situation is stable and works best for James.

M2:
Father: I don't think her situation is very stable at all. Every time we fought about this thing she did it in front of James. He gets really upset about all this.

M3:
Mother: He doesn't get any more upset at that than he does when you walked out on us. You had your chance and you blew it.

M4:
Father: I never walked out on him, just on you, and you know why I did.

Suggested Intervention: M2
Content: Remind the couple about interruption rules and the need to continue laying the foundation for agreement. Summarize the information to this point.
Rationale: To maintain control and to focus the couple on the appropriate topic, the mediator needs to enforce the interaction rules. The conflict also needs to be slowed down a bit here so the interaction does not degenerate into a display of dirty laundry. Summarizing the interaction not only slows down the interaction but it provides needed agreement and a sense of progress.

## Segment 7

Mother: OK, I'm sorry for interrupting. But, I think I should be able to tell my side of the story too. Especially when what he's saying isn't true.

M1:
Father: Betty, the way I understand it, we'll both get a chance to do that. Let's face it, we both have different stories to tell. But, if we can do it here, it's a lot better than fighting about it in court, isn't it?

M2:
Mother: Yeah, I guess so.

M3:
Father: I'm willing to try to be reasonable, but I don't think I should be accused of not telling the truth here today.

M4:
Mother: Well, I don't think you are being totally candid about how you have treated me and James all these years. Why don't you talk about that?

M5:
Suggested Intervention: M3
Content: Reinforce points of agreement, and reinforce the desire to mediate. Ask the husband to continue.
Rationale: The couple has shown significant progress in their commitment to mediation, and that commitment needs to be reinforced here. The final two utterances probably do not need to be said because they do not contribute much to the substance of the relationship or the issues.

## Segment 8

Father: OK, as I was saying, I think I'm a good father. I know I haven't always been a good husband [to mother] but that's not what we're here for. I feel James is at an age now where he needs his father. We do things together that a father and son should do. He loves the water and so do I. We sail together in the summer. [To mediator] You know, it would be different if we had a daughter, but she has always been over-protective of him and you can't do that to a boy. James belongs with me.

M1:
Mother: Oh, that's good! I'm the one who took care of him all this time when you were climbing your corporate ladder. Now you want to take him away from me.

M2:
Father: Oh, Betty, don't give me that trash. You're just trying to get the

|          | mediator on your side. All I'm saying is that I think James would be happier living with me right now. I'm not trying to take him away from you. In fact, you could see him as much as you want to. |
|---|---|

M3:
Mother: It's not like I live miles away. In fact, James can even ride his bike when the weather is good.
M4:
Suggested Intervention: M1
Content: Summarize the father's information, and ask the mother to tell more about her relationship with James.
Rationale: Summarizing the father's information adds greater clarity to the dispute and reinforces the mediator's contribution to the progress that is being made in the interaction. Also, because the mother has more information to contribute she should be encouraged to do so here.

## Segment 9

Mother: Well, James and I are real close, too. I'm the one who always helps him with his homework, and besides, I have always provided him with stability. I mean, the family has had a structure because of me. Our lawyers have already worked out our property settlement. I get the house in town and Ted gets the summer house up north.
M1:
Father: Betty, I don't think the property settlement should enter into this at all. What we're trying to do is come up with an agreement about James. What house he lives in doesn't matter.
M2:
Mother: Well, what I was trying to say is that you can have James on the weekends, and I'll have custody during the week. On school nights, James needs that stability. And, besides, you aren't even home much.
M3:
Father: Oh, Betty, you just want a weekend babysitter. You know it might be good for you if you sat down with him and tried to develop some interests together.
M4:
Father: I mean, I really don't think you have anything in common with him. In fact, you're so concerned about discipline and structure that you don't know your son.
M5:
Suggested Intervention: M1

Content: Compliment couple on demonstrating an ability to work out agreements. Ask mother to comment on whether the father appears to have a positive relationship with the son.

Rationale: Pointing out the substantial agreement in positions installs further confidence in the mediation process and adds clarity to the information resource being developed. Also, by asking the mother to evaluate the father–son relationship, and predicting that the evaluation will be positive, the mediator can begin to sew the seeds of cooperation. Allowing the couple to continue with accusations linked with proposals might compromise some of the good will that has accumulated to this point.

## Segment 10

Mother: Well, I guess I do have to agree that James and his father have a lot in common. And, yes, they do both like the water. James does have fun with his father, but there's more to life than fun.

M1:

Father: Sure, there's more to life than fun. James and I share a special bond, and I would really like to take advantage of that.

M2:

Mother: I would like you to take advantage of that, but do you need to have James living with you to be his father?

M3:

Mother: I think you two would get along perfectly well with your current arrangement. I really don't know why you are doing this.

M4:

Father: I'm doing this because he really needs to grow, and not be over-protected. I can't really continue to have this kind of parenting role.

M5:

Suggested Intervention: M3

Content: Summarize the parents' perceptions of their relationships with their son and ask father to evaluate Betty's role as a mother.

Rationale: Summarizing common perceptions about the relationships each parent maintains with the son provides the couple with insight about their parenting philosophies. They both appear to want the other parent in the child's life. To reinforce this point and build more cooperativeness between the parents, it is probably appropriate to ask the father about the mother's parental competencies. Because the mother commented positively on the father's parental capabilities, there is some hope that the father would reciprocate.

## Segment 11

Father: Well, yes, I would have to admit that Betty has been a good mother [turns to Betty], is a good mother. She is better at disciplining him than I am. And, her work schedule allows her to be with him more than I can since she's a teacher and I work for a corporation.

M1:

Mother: That's right. And that's why I'm the best one to have custody.

M2:

Father: Betty, you're missing the point. I was about to say that where we work shouldn't matter. I still have free time in the evenings. And, I would like to share it with James.

M3:

Mother: I was just stating how I felt. That's what we're supposed to do here, isn't it?

M4:

Suggested Intervention: M2

Content: Summarize positive parenting attributes each party has identified at this point. Remind both not to use the words "custody" and "visitation" and speak instead about parenting. Request information from the mother regarding current parenting arrangements.

Rationale: Because each parent has identified positive attributes of the other parent's skills with James it is important that those attributes are clearly defined, and that there are no issues in dispute about parenting competence that could undermine the dispute later. Given this agreement, it is likely that sufficient information about the parent's relationship with James has been revealed so that the mediator can move on to learning more about the temporary visitation arrangements and to learn more about the positive and negative perceptions of these arrangements.

## Segment 12

Mother: Well, as I see it, our situation is OK most of the time. I have custody, oh, excuse me, I parent James during the week and Ted gets him every Friday night and Saturday and every other Sunday. We alternate holidays. James just goes to his father's house right after school on Friday.

M1:

Father: Yeah, I get 3 out of every 14 days. And, I hardly ever get any phone calls during the week. It's tough on me. How can I just be a father on the weekends?

M2:
Mother: Well, you know, if you'd spend more time with your son and less with Lucy, maybe it would feel like more time. I think you really ought to get your priorities straight. And, I think it's terrible that she spends the night when James is over.

M3:
Father: I don't know where you get your information. I do not spend all my time with Lucy when James is there. But, Lucy is part of my life now and I want James to know her.

M4:
Mother: Oh, so you admit that she does spend the night when James is there.

M5:
Suggested Intervention: M2
Content: Summarize situation; ask the father if weekend parenting is a major issue or concern to him.
Rationale: It seems like an appropriate time to pull out the issue of the flexibility of the current agreement because it appears to be at the foundation of the father's position at this point. Also, this point probably marks the transition from gathering information to pulling out and processing issues. Summarizing the situation adds clarity to the situation while increasing the value of the mediator to the disputants. The issue of the mother's feelings about Lucy needs to be exposed, particularly because the mother is thinking so heavily about this issue. However, is the time right to expose this issue and process it? Perhaps later after the father's position has been clarified because he is close to suggesting flexibility in the suit he brought against Betty.

## Segment 13

Father: Yeah, that's the situation. And, I don't think it's right. I want James to know me and be part of, well you know, day-to-day life. I don't want to be a weekend father. That's why I'm suing for custody, or whatever you call it.

M1:
Mother: [To father] Your schedule is pretty lenient. Most fathers only get every other weekend. You get an additional day every 2 weeks.

M2:
Father: But Betty, that makes me a weekend father. Is that the kind of father you want for James? You said a minute ago that we have a special relationship. Don't you want that to continue?

M3:

# MEDIATION OF TED AND BETTY JOHNSON 197

Mother:     Sure, I do. I just think you two are doing just fine the way you are going right now. Your schedule is really pretty liberal.

M4:

Father:     Yeah, but he is getting older now, and he comes to me with things that really require more time. I just can't grow with him when I see him for such short periods. Can't you see that he's grown beyond you?

M5:

Mother:     My son has not grown beyond me. His needs haven't changed that much. And, if you were honest about the time you spend with him, that would be one thing. But, you are still with Lucy when you are with James. What about those times?

M6:

Suggested Intervention: M5

Content:     Reframe father's position to indicate that he would like more time, and summarize mother's perceptions on the issue. Ask father to point out main advantages and disadvantages of current arrangement.

Rationale:     Because the couple appears to be communicating productively here it seems useful to allow them to continue. Reframing the father's position provides a sense of clarity to his concern and puts it in a framework that is understandable to the mother. By asking for strengths and weaknesses of the current arrangement the mediator learns what can be built upon and what needs to be changed. Excluding the mother's final comment is probably appropriate here since it is rather defensive and not really phrased as an issue to be addressed. But, it will surface soon and the mediator will have to deal with it.

## Segment 14

Father:     The main disadvantage of weekend parenting is that James is getting older and his life is getting more complicated. My guidance is really needed now, and it is needed at times that are really spontaneous for us. You just can't expect James to say what he feels just on weekends. The main advantage of the arrangement is that I have my time during the week to pursue my career. But, I am at a point now in my career that I can devote more time to James.

M1:

Mother:     I am just not sure about that. James is open and will speak his mind most all the time. He talks to his father now.

M2:

Father:     But, he comes to me with things that are important right when we have to come back to your house, and you won't extend the time for us to talk further.

M3:
Suggested Intervention: M1
Content: Ask mother about her perceptions of the advantages and disadvantages of current arrangements.
Rationale: Because the father has given a balanced, detailed account of his perceptions of the current arrangements, it is appropriate, for equity purposes, to solicit the mother's perceptions. In addition, the final two utterances are rather defensively stated and could disrupt progress to that point.

## Segment 15

Mother: I think that the main advantage of the current arrangement is that James' life is not disrupted now. He has his home and his friends. It's hard for a boy to just pull up his roots after 12 years of life. The main disadvantage of the arrangement is that I can't go away on a weekend with my son. We really want to go to visit my relatives at times, and this arrangement makes it impossible.
M1:
Father: Why haven't you mentioned this before? I would have gladly let James go with you to visit his grandparents.
M2:
Mother: I don't know. You've just been so unreasonable lately. This suing for custody business has made me so angry I haven't wanted to talk to you at all.
M3:
Father: Well, I just didn't know what else to do to get some time with James.
M4:
Mother: Well, if you would have just talked to me maybe we could have worked something out without going through all this suing business.
M5:
Suggested Intervention: M5
Content: Summarize each person's perceptions of the advantages and disadvantages of the weekend parenting issue: advantage from father's perspective includes extra time to pursue his career, whereas a key disadvantage is the lack of a normal father–son relationship. The advantage of the current arrangement from the mother's perspective is stability, whereas the main disadvantage is her inability to visit relatives on weekends. Indicate that the situation has not been very ideal for either parent. Ask the mother if this is also her perception?
Rationale: Because the couple has made several insights about their

arrangements without the mediator's help, it is probably appropriate to allow them to continue interacting. The timing is right for the mediator to step in and provide the insight that the current arrangement has not been very useful for either person. Confirming this insight with the parties will help gain consensus about this issue.

## Segment 16

Mother: Yes, I guess this isn't the most ideal situation for either of us, but I can't see giving him more time with James when all he does is spend it with his girlfriend.
M1:
Father: I really wish you'd leave Lucy out of this.
M2:
Mother: I wish you would leave her out of it too. But, since you don't, I can't.
M3:
Father: We didn't come here to talk about Lucy. We came here to talk about James!
M4:
Suggested Intervention: M2
Content: Pull out the girlfriend issue and promise to discuss it as soon as the flexibility issue is understood. Ask the father if the flexibility issue is his primary concern.
Rationale: With the flexibility issue mostly resolved, it is probably valuable to get closure on this issue. However, because the girlfriend issue is so critical to the mother, it is time to pull it out and establish it as a priority. However, that issue cannot be discussed until the flexibility issue has been completed, which involves asking the father if the mediator's insight about the current arrangement is correct.

## Segment 17

Father: Yes, that's why I went back to my lawyer to begin with. I don't want to wait nearly a week to see my son. I am missing so much of his life.
M1:
Mother: Well, your situation isn't any different than it was before. When we lived together you really didn't spend much time with James. Your sudden interest probably has something to do with your new girlfriend, I suppose.
M2:

Father: I asked you not to bring her up. I don't want to discuss her with you. James likes her and that's all that's important.
M3:
Mother: That's not what James tells me. He says you spend all your time with her and you don't pay any attention to him.
M4:
Father: I don't know where you get your information, but James tells me he really likes spending time with Lucy.
M5:
Recommended Intervention: M1
Content: Indicate that there is agreement about the flexibility issue and that the situation is not ideal from either person's perspective. Ask for details about the girlfriend issue.
Rationale: Now is the time to pursue the girlfriend issue in greater detail because the flexibility issue has been resolved. It is probably best to bring it up before the mother starts attacking with it again. It shows that the mediator is listening to the mother and cares about this critical issue.

## Segment 18

Father: I really don't see why we have to discuss this. We are here to discuss James and not Lucy.
M1:
Mother: Well, if Lucy is going to spend time with James, then I feel it's appropriate to discuss this.
M2:
Father: I just don't think that Lucy is an issue, and I don't want to talk about her here.
M3:
Mother: Sure. You only want to talk about the things you want to talk about. But, as soon as something important with me arises, you clam up. Half the reason we're here is because of her.
M4:
Father: You know that's not true. Our marriage was in trouble before I even met Lucy.
M5:
Suggested Intervention: M2
Content: Suggest that all issues of concern to each party need to be discussed as a means of reducing conflict so James can be raised in a more cooperative environment. Ask mother about specific concerns regarding Lucy.
Rationale: The issue of the other woman is an integral part of the dispute. Although the father is reluctant to discuss it, the mediator can override the father's objections because the mediator has

already worked with the father to discuss the dimensions of the flexibility issue over the objections of the mother. The rationale for avoiding the discussion about Lucy is that it brings up dirty laundry about the marriage that needs to be avoided here.

## Segment 19

Mother: I'm concerned about Lucy spending so much time with James. She's over every weekend, as far as I can tell. When James comes home, he never mentions anything that he and his father do together. He only talks about the things that he and his father and Lucy do together.
M1:
Mother: I think it's a little ridiculous that he's suing for custody and claiming that he doesn't get enough time with his son. He'd get more time with his son if he'd not spend so much time with his girlfriend.
M2:
Father: [To mother] I wouldn't spend so much time with Lucy except that James likes her so much. She takes him shopping, sends him birthday cards, buys him gifts when she goes away on business. She even helps James with his homework sometimes.
M3:
Mother: That's supposed to be the time you spend with James, not the time Lucy spends with James.
M4:
Father: I don't think it's really any of your business what James does when he's with me. We don't live together anymore, and soon we'll be divorced.
M5:
Suggested Intervention: M3
Content: Identify and legitimize the mother's concerns about Lucy and ask the mother whether she feels Lucy is a poor influence on James.
Rationale: The mother's concerns need to be clarified for her so she can better understand them. Some evaluation of Lucy's influence will help identify the mother's true objections to Lucy's presence.

## Segment 20

Mother: That's not what I meant at all. I don't feel that she is a bad

202                                                                         CHAPTER 8

M1:
Mother: influence on James, necessarily. I just object to how much time she is spending with him.

M2:
Mother: I mean, I think that his visitation is time Ted should be spending with James.

Father: I do spend time with James, you know that. I don't see anything wrong with Lucy being there, too.

M3:
Mother: You don't see anything wrong with anything you do, do you?

M4:
Suggested Intervention: M2
Content: Restate mother's position, and ask the mother if James and Ted should spend all their time together without anyone else present.
Rationale: Given that Lucy as a person is not the problem, the issue becomes one of parental influence on the child's life, and the mediator needs to pull that out of the mother so she can better understand the parameters of her fears on this issue. Intervening at this point is probably useful because the father simply gets defensive after the mother's second utterance.

## Segment 21

Mother: No, of course that's not what I mean. I just don't think she should spend that much time with James.

M1:
Father: I told you, she doesn't spend all her time with me. Last week, Lucy had to go away on business and we didn't see her all weekend.

M2:
Mother: Yes, and James really enjoyed that time with you. He said he enjoyed spending time alone with his father for a change.

M3:
Father: The time we spend alone really isn't that much different than the time we spend with Lucy.

M4:
Mother: All I know is what James told me. I think he really resents Lucy and doesn't want to tell you.

Suggested Intervention: M1
Content: Reframe the mother's comment to pull out the issue related to Lucy replacing Betty as James' mother. Ask Betty if she perceives that to be true.
Rationale: The mediator needs to quickly reframe Betty's comment to get to the heart of the issue, which is her perception that Ted

wants to replace her as a mother. This issue appears to have been a major stumbling block to Betty's willingness to be flexible. Allowing the interaction to continue might distract from processing that issue carefully. After the first utterance the couple circles around on an attack–defend cycle that ends with the mother intensifying her anger about Lucy. Unfortunately, the mother doesn't quite yet understand the parameters of that anger, while the parameters are probably clear to the mediator.

## Segment 22

Mother: [Starts crying] She took my husband away from me, and now she wants my son too. How much should I be asked to give up?
M1:
Mother: [After a lengthy pause for drying eyes] I want to raise my son as I see fit. I have been a good mother [to father], can't you see that?
M2:
Father: Betty, the last thing I want to do is take James away from you. I am not trying to replace you as a mother. You have been a fine mother for James. I just want to see him more often, and have him become a part of my new life.
M3:
Mother: When I hear all the things Lucy does for him, it hurts me. I can see that if I let this go on, James will pull further away from me [sobbing].
M4:
Suggested Intervention: M4
Content: Restate the father's intention not to have Lucy serve as a substitute mother for Betty, and ask father if that is correct as a means of reassuring mother. Ask the father to tell that directly to the mother, once again.
Rationale: Significant progress has been made here. The father is helping and comforting the mother, and the mother needs to have that point reinforced by the father speaking directly to the mother.

## Segment 23

Father: No, as I said, Betty, James will always be your son and my son. He wants you as a mother and you are a good mother to him. I have no intention of letting anyone else be his mother.
M1:
Mother: I wish I knew that for sure. It seems that with all the time the

|  | three of you spend together that she will take over my role. That could really happen if James lived with you full time. |
|---|---|
| M2: Father: | Lucy might spend time with James right now, but that doesn't necessarily mean she'll always do that, or that she intends on replacing you. |
| M3: Mother: | Ted, she has been with you for a long time. How can you say that she won't want to take over and use James to strengthen your relationship with her. I think it is much more serious than you think. |
| M4: Father: | Betty, be reasonable, here. |

M5:
Suggested Intervention: M4
Content: Ask the father if he has solidified any relational plans with Lucy.
Rationale: Because the father seems unsure about the role of the other woman in James' life, and the issue will figure prominently in any agreement, it is important to integrate these plans into the discussion. The father's final comment in the segment is an unnecessary stab at the mother and could only serve to incite her because it is an insensitive comment made at a critical time.

## Segment 24

| Father: | Well, I really don't have any plans with Lucy right now. My relationship with Lucy is not very clearly defined right now. We have no plans to get married after the divorce. |
|---|---|
| M1: Mother: | But with only her influence in James' life... |
| M2: Father: | Look, Betty, I suppose I shouldn't say this but there have been other women in my life other than Lucy. I mean, it's my business, but Lucy and I aren't really that serious right now. |
| M3: Mother: | This is just hard for me, losing my son like this. I want him to be a part of my life. |
| M4: Father: | Betty, you aren't losing your son. Look, just tell me what you want and I'll be reasonable about letting you see James. |

M5:
Suggested Intervention: M4
Content: Summarize the father's position and reassure the mother that

the father is not interested in replacing her as a mother. Ask the mother what specific steps the father can take to reassure her that she will not be replaced as a mother.

Rationale: The father's position on this issue needs to be quickly reinforced as a means of pulling the couple closer together. To ask the mother for proposals to deal with this issue is probably useful at this point, as a means of setting the foundation for proposals on the flexibility issue. The last utterance in the segment gets off the track with the father presenting a proposal that is really not appropriate at this delicate time. Also, notice that the intervention points are beginning to move later in the segments. The couple is beginning to communicate well together so the mediator can begin stepping away from the situation a bit.

## Segment 25

Mother: Well, I don't know exactly what he can do. I just want my son to be part of my life so I can be there when he needs me. Maybe if James spent less time with Lucy that would help. I just don't know.

M1:

Father: I'm not sure I can regulate exactly how much time Lucy spends with James. Anyway, the actual amount of time they spend in one another's presence isn't the real problem here.

M2:

Father: The real problem is how close James is with his mother and with Lucy. I think James is old enough right now that he can be close with his parents and with other adults that aren't his parents. He understands these things. Do you see him pulling away from you, Betty?

M3:

Mother: Not really, I guess. Maybe if you just talked to him about my concerns that would help.

M4:

Father: You could talk to him, too, you know. You could tell him how you feel about it and get his reaction. Have you ever talked to him about your concerns?

M5:

Suggested Intervention: No intervention is necessary here.

Rationale: The couple is communicating quite productively here. Some very important information is being shared, and the mediator can relax control here because things are moving ahead positively.

## Segment 26

Mother: No, I guess I haven't talked to him about it. I've just been so upset about this custody dispute.
M1:
Father: Well, why don't you do that and let me know if there is anything I can do to make sure his relationship with his mother is OK.
M2:
Mother: One thing you can do right now is drop your suit to be James' only parent. I don't think that's fair.
M3:
Father: I am trying to help you here. What are you talking about?
M4:
Mother: I am talking about dropping your suit.
M5:
Suggested Intervention: M3
Content: Restate the father's offer to help out with the problem of assuring the mother that she is not being replaced. Indicate that some closure on this issue is necessary before moving back to the flexibility issue discussed previously. Ask the mother if she will keep the father informed about her discussion with James.
Rationale: Because the mother has moved off the topic somewhat, she needs some redirection to gain closure on the replacement problem. Once the closure is achieved, there can be movement back to the flexibility issue, which will serve as the foundation to an agreement. The reason for disallowing the final two is that the couple risks backsliding a bit, with the mother making a rather bold, confrontive proposal in her second utterance. Keeping the couple on track about the replacement and flexibility issues is important to keep momentum building.

## Segment 27:

Mother: I guess that's all we can do now. I will let Ted know about our talk. James and I really haven't talked like that in a while. I guess it will be good for us.
M1:
Father: I think it will be good for both of you, too. We had a talk like that recently and it helped us a lot.
M2:
Mother: What did James tell you?
M3:
Father: I don't think I can really talk about that, because it would be breaking a confidence. It was just "boy" talk.

# MEDIATION OF TED AND BETTY JOHNSON 207

M4:
Mother: You can tell me. Come on, Ted, I'm his mother.
M5:
Suggested Intervention: M2
Content: Compliment couple on working well together and on their desire to continue communicating about James. Return to flexibility issue and provide summary of issue as it was discussed. Father wants greater access during the week, mother wants son for weekend time. Ask if this is an accurate summary.
Rationale: Given the significant progress made by the couple, they can return to the flexibility issue, upon which the entire dispute now hinges. Getting into what James said at this point is moving away from the subject of flexibility and not in a direction that exposes critical issues or reveals important information.

## Segment 28

Father: That's basically how I see it. My son is growing and I want us to grow together. I don't think being a weekend father will do that.
M1:
Mother: OK, I'm not really that happy with the arrangement either because of the weekend problem we talked about before, you know, not being able to have James with me one full weekend a month.
M2:
Father: I'm just afraid that if I don't get things nailed down legally that I'm not going to be able to gain more flexibility in the current arrangement.
M3:
Mother: What is with this legal thing all the time?
M4:
Father: I've just found that when possible, it is best to make sure that the legal holes are covered.
M5:
Mother: Yes, but the strictly legal approach doesn't take into account individual choices.
Suggested Intervention: M3
Content: Summarize agreement on the lack of satisfaction with the current arrangement. Indicate to the father that the legality of the agreement should be put aside for the moment. Instead, it's important to talk about the kind of time you want to spend with James. Ask father to detail what kind of time he would like to spend with James.

Rationale: Summarizing agreement brings the issue into clear focus again. Taking the focus off the legal issues places the topic back on the best interests of the child. The last three utterances accomplish the same objective the mediator is trying to achieve, but they digress away from the parenting issue that needs developing here.

## Segment 29

Father: All right, I guess you're right. It is important to talk about what's best for James and me. Well, as I said, I would like more flexibility during the week. I would like to see James during a weekday evening. I could pick him up at school and we could spend the evening at my house. I could have him back at Betty's at 9:00, in plenty of time for bed at 10:00.

M1:
Mother: What about weekends? Do you still want to see James one overnight every weekend? Because I need some time here too.

M2:
Father: No, I think you could have one weekend per month with James entirely to yourselves. That would be fine with me.

M3:
Mother: I would really like that, but I want that day of the week that you are going to take James nailed down so I know when to expect you.

M4:
Father: Well, I would really like some flexibility there. I would like to take him on different days, depending on what was going on.

M5:
Mother: On different days? You know, Ted, sometimes in the past you haven't been 100% reliable in picking up James. I don't know if I like this flexibility stuff. I am willing to nail down my weekend with James.

M6:
Suggested Intervention: M6
Content: Ask the father how the flexibility would work, and what kind of assurances he could provide to the mother about being on time.
Rationale: The custody issue appears fairly resolved, and the flexibility issue needs only a boost to get it moving to a final agreement. Because the couple is communicating effectively, there is no need to interrupt them before the segment is completed.

## Segment 30

Father: Well, I guess we could plan on my taking James every Wednesday. And, if something special is going on that week, I could

| | |
|---|---|
| M1:<br>Mother: | call you [to mother] and tell you what night I would want to work out an arrangement to pick up James.<br>That would be fine, as long as you call first. I would appreciate knowing as much in advance as possible. What about my weekend? I might want some flexibility too? |
| M2:<br>Father: | Well, you could take James on the last weekend of every month. If you want to change that, let me know several days in advance. |
| M3:<br>Mother: | That would be fine. I guess it would be best to just work together to solve these problems. Do you still want to see James on the other three Saturdays? |
| M4:<br>Father: | Yes, I think it would be best to maintain that arrangement too. |
| M5:<br>Suggested Intervention: M5 | |
| Content: | Summarize the points of agreement. Indicate that the couple appears to have selected joint legal custody with the child living primarily at the mother's house, with a specified amount of time with the father. Congratulate the couple for learning how to work together productively. Indicate that the agreement is not written in stone and that they can change it if necessary. Offer to write up the agreement. End of mediation. |

## CONCLUSIONS

The simulation certainly represents an easy case in the sense that the couple entered mediation to resolve a key predivorce problem. As indicated in the research, these mediations may be easier to manage because couples have had less time to build animosities toward one another. Also, the case was easy because there were only two main issues to be resolved: flexibility for the father and maternal replacement for the mother. The mediations used for research in this book presented many complex issues that pose significant challenges for the mediators.

The simulation also illustrates the interactive management model in a variety of ways. First, the intervention points were selected to avoid the person-focused, unnecessary escalation of language intensity, double-bind immediacy, and attack–defend verbal aggression cycles. The points were also selected to keep the couple focused on the task, instead of allowing them to explore relational issues that digressed significantly from the topic at hand, and were largely expressions of fear that could unnecessarily anger both parties.

Second, understanding these communication patterns was critical for mediators in setting up their intervention strategies. In the early going, the mediator stuck with the phase organization to orient the couple properly to the process, gain background information, and pull out key issues. Because the research reported in this book so strongly recommends securing and reinforcing a strong mediation structure, these mediator-intervention decisions seem justified. The mediator also reframed frequently to pull out key issues that ultimately served to provide insight into the dispute for both parties.

Finally, the mediation simulation should illustrate the need to slow down the mediation and to prevent it from becoming a runaway train that crashes because it was out of control. The mediator intervened frequently during the early part of the mediation because it was in danger of running away. However, as it progressed, the couple seemed more skilled at sharing productive information. So, the mediator backed off a bit. The mediator slowed the train by adhering to the structure and by providing disputants with insights about their concerns. As a result, they ended the mediation with a productive direction and a solid agreement.

# Appendix A: Coding Procedures for Chapter 5 Analyses

## VERBAL IMMEDIACY

### Coding Procedures

To begin the verbal immediacy coding, each talking turn was numbered in each of the 20 transcripts. Talking turns that overlapped other speech were also counted in the analysis. To code verbal immediacy–nonimmediacy, the transcripts were unitized and then categorized using the two immediacy categories of spatial and implicit. In unitizing the transcripts, the point of division was a verb used structurally as action related to an agent. Thus, all simple sentences and simple independent and dependent clauses were units. Noun clauses were considered separate units, but infinitives and participial phrases were not. This pattern is equivalent to that suggested by Wiener and Meharabian. Any talking turn that lacked a verb was also treated as a unit.

Both immediacy–nonimmediacy categories were coded, using a "1" to "3" scale with "3" indicating the presence of a high level of immediacy for that particular dimension in that particular unit, and "1" indicating nonimmediacy on that dimension in that unit. A "2" indicated mixed levels of immediacy. Mean levels of immediacy for each utterance were then calculated. Difference scores, computed by subtracting one disputant's score from the other disputant's score, were necessary for testing the extent to which participants used similar levels of immediacy throughout the course of the mediation.

The reliability for each item using eight coders for the summed scale $a = .90$. The reliability for spatial immediacy was .90, and .93 for implicit immediacy. Unitizing reliability (Guetzkow, 1950) was .07, indicating that the maximum error in unitizing was about 7%.

## LANGUAGE INTENSITY

### Coding Procedures

Each talking turn for each disputant and the mediator was examined for the presence of the six categories of intensity just listed. The unit of analysis was the word or phrase in a particular utterance containing some intense language. If a word or phrase was judged as fitting into more than one category, a decision rule was used in which the item was coded into the category most highly correlated with intensity (Bowers, 1964). Also, the speaker and the length of each utterance were recorded, as well.

Although the specific markers of intensity provide a detailed view of intense language behavior, Bowers (1964) and Bradac et al. (1979) suggested that language intensity should be examined as a global variable that impacts receiver response. Thus, a composite intensity factor was defined as an additive function of the six marker categories weighted by their correlations with perceptions of intensity provided by the Bowers (1964) research. The intensity factor value of each utterance was then calculated by multiplying the weight times the frequency of occurrence of each type of marker and summing across the six categories. The weights are as follows: obscurity = .59; metaphor = .83; qualifiers = .89; profanity, sex, and death metaphors = 1.0.

This weighting procedure has some very positive features for coding and analyzing the data. First, the weighting scheme essentially lumps the six categories into four by adjusting them for their theoretical impact on the intensity of the encounter. This has the advantage of reducing coding ambiguity in some tricky judgments. For example, if a person said, "You really screwed me over," it might be difficult to decide if this is an instance of profanity or a sex metaphor. The definitions listed earlier would probably place this as an act of profanity. However, the weighting scheme takes away the effects of any such coding errors because the weighting of the two categories is the same. Also, the errors are reduced between categories that are likely to produce the greatest coding confusion (i.e., between profanity, sex, and death metaphors). The weighting scheme also reduces ambiguity as indicated here by serving as a coding rule. Specifically, if any ambiguity arose between one category or another, the rule mandates adjusting the word to the category with the higher weighting.

The extent to which the weighting scheme reduced errors is evidenced by the relatively high reliability estimates. Interrater reliabilities for the intensity marker coding indicates consistent estimates across raters. Specifically, alphas for the individual indicators were as follows: obscurity = .90, qualifiers = .89, metaphors = .79, profanity = 1.0, death metaphors = 1.0, and sex metaphors = 1.0. Average interrater reliability was .93 for the entire coding scheme. Clearly, these language features can be reliably identified and categorized by trained coders.

Second, the weighting procedure allowed the data to be analyzed using parametric statistics because the weighting allows the categories to be arrayed on an interval scale of least intense to most intense. Parametric statistics are more powerful in assessing the relationship between variables because the distribution of the variables is taken into account in the calculations. This increased information yields a greater potential of detecting important differences in the data.

To obtain a metric that would allow intensity comparisons between interactions of differing lengths, the composite score for each utterance was divided by the total number of words in the encounter. In this way, each utterance is viewed as contributing a zero or greater proportion to the total intensity of the encounter. In calculating the intensity of a subset of the utterances in a transcript, it is necessary to include in the denominator only the total number of words in each cell of the breakdown. This avoids bias by weighting each utterance's intensity proportionate to verbal productivity. Thus, the longer the session, the less weight is given to any particular instance of intense language.

## DATA ANALYSIS ISSUES: VERBAL IMMEDIACY AND LANGUAGE INTENSITY

The analysis of these data pose some very significant challenges that should be reported. The first challenge relates to the reliability of individual utterances as the unit of analysis. According to Hamilton and Hunter (1985), data should be collapsed across utterances and analyzed at the subject level to avoid the inherently unreliable nature of coding each unit into only one category. To avoid this problem, means were created for each husband, wife, and mediator across all the variables in the analyses. All the analyses reported here were conducted on these mean scores.

Another challenge facing the analysis of these data relates to the number and involvement of the mediators. Because only 8 mediators participated in the study, and they were not evenly balanced between agreement conditions, it is statistically improper to analyze the data as if all mediations were conducted by a different mediator. Unfortunately, there is no really good way of taking this problem into account statistically. Options such as deleting mediations conducted by the same mediator in different conditions to give a totally balanced design would significantly reduce the sample size and the power of the analysis to detect small effect sizes. As a result, the decision was made to treat each mediator as different across all 20 sessions. Because the problems and couples in each session were very different, this decision does not seem unreasonable.

A third data-analysis issue relates to analyzing these transcripts across time. Ideally, some substantive criteria would be available to divide the transcripts into phases of interaction. For example, it would be convenient if the mediators announced when one phase was completed and another begun. However, mediators regard the phase structure as an informal tool and not something that is announced. This leaves the researchers with precious few substantive criteria to use in dividing the transcripts into chunks. Thus, time will be examined by simply dividing each transcript into three equal parts, based on the total number of utterances in that transcript. Thirds was selected over some greater number of divisions because some transcripts were relatively short, with only 150 utterances each. As a result, obtaining a stable estimate of the mean level of immediacy and intensity in a phase requires some reasonable number of utterances per phase. Of course, selecting fewer than three phases would not reveal any curvilinear effects.

Fourth, the use of three time periods and three subjects per transcript creates a data-dependency problem. Specifically, interactants are likely to affect one another's immediacy and intensity, both from utterance to utterance and over time. To resolve this dependency problem, both time and speaker (husband, wife, mediator) will become within-subject factors in repeated-measures ANOVAs with immediacy and intensity as the dependent variables and outcome as the independent variable. Also, the models will be effects coded based on the expected relationships presented above between the dependent and independent variables.

## THE ISSUES ANALYSIS

### Coding Procedures

The unit of analysis used in the issues analysis is the uninterrupted talking turn. To begin coding, the authors identified and numbered each utterance in all 20 transcripts. Each utterance was coded using the set of issue categories identified earlier: factual, interest, value, and nonrealistic or relational issues. Each code was given a numerical value of 1 to 4, respectively. A fifth category, "other," was added when no issue was apparent in an utterance. This fifth category was given a numerical value of zero. For example, when a speaker simply agreed with the prior utterance, asked the other to repeat a statement, or simply provided some information supporting his or her own position, the coders were instructed to apply an "other" code to these utterances.

Coders were instructed to follow a specific set of procedures in applying these issue codes. First, they were trained to code both the mediator's and the disputants' utterances. For the mediator, the coders were instructed to identify the type of issue the mediator directed the disputants to discuss. For example, the mediator might interrupt and comment on a relational issue that disputants brought up and attempted to refocus their attention on some interests associated with that relational issue. In that case, the mediator's comment would be coded as an "interest"-directed issue. This problem arose very infrequently because most mediator interventions were very brief. Finally, if the mediator did not direct the conversation toward a particular type of issue, then the utterance was coded as an "other."

Second, the coders were instructed to select the "dominant" issue code in each utterance. The dominant code, based on the issue hierarchy described earlier, was judged to be that code reflecting those issues most difficult to manage by mediators. As indicated previously, relational issues represent the most difficult challenges for mediators because these issues often access problems that caused the dissolution of the marriage. The next most-difficult issues were judged to focus on individual values which access disputants' perceptions of right and wrong, and therefore access individual core beliefs and values about the world. Interest issues were considered third most dominant or difficult for mediators to manage because articulated positions can be negotiated when they are not based on deep-seated emotional/relational problems or value concerns. Finally, factual issues were judged as least-difficult to manage by the mediators because most of the factual issues (e.g., how much money each parent makes) can be easily resolved by examining the case record. Although coders were instructed to use this procedure when multiple issues were discussed, the problem arose very infrequently, probably because most comments in mediation are relatively brief. Only when the mediator specifically asks for complex information does a disputant begin to bring up complex, interrelated issues.

Using Guetzkow's (1950) reliability formula, the categorizing reliability for this coding procedure using two coders over five categories was .91. This reliability estimate was considered sufficiently high to proceed with data analysis.

The 20 transcripts revealed 2,486 issue comments by the husband, 2,377 by the wife, and 1,927 issue directives by the mediator. Approximately 2,400 utterances were coded in the "other" category because no issues were disclosed in these utterances.

## Data Analysis Issues

Consistent with the analyses associated with verbal immediacy and language intensity, these analyses posed some additional challenges. Specifically, the same four problems identified for the immediacy and intensity data apply to the issues data. As a result, the data were collapsed across utterances and analyzed at the subject level. Also, the data were analyzed across the same three time periods, and repeated-measures ANOVAs were used with time and speaker as the within-subjects factors and the issue variable used as the dependent variable. To assess the effects of immediacy, each of the immediacy variables were covaried with the dependent variable: issue.

In addition to these challenges, one other unique problem arose in these data. The problem involves the large percentage of "other" codes in these data. Approximately 38% of the participants' utterances did not involve any issue statements. To deal with this problem in the analysis, two options were available. First, the "other" data could be omitted with the analysis focusing only on the utterances containing some issue value. Second, the "other" data could be included in the study. This second option would add one interesting bit of information to this study; that is, it would indicate how much of that person's contribution was focused on issues in dispute during each of the three time periods. For example, if one person's mean issue level for a given time period was below 1.0, it would indicate that that person spent a great deal of time doing something other than bringing up one of the four issues examined in this study. This is important information, particularly for mediators, because the focus of mediation is on managing issues, for the most part. Given these two options, this study decided the second was more desirable because of the potential of learning more about what participants are and, in some cases, *are not* doing to further issue discussions.

## POSITION-ADJUSTMENT STRATEGIES

### Coding Procedures

The unit of analysis in this study is the uninterrupted talking turn. To begin coding, each utterance in all 20 transcripts was identified and numbered. Each utterance was coded using the set of position adjustment strategies identified earlier: attacking, defending, bolstering, and integrating. Coders were not asked to specify which tactic within each category disputants were using. The tactics only served to exemplify the various position-adjustment strategies. A fifth category, "other," was added when the utterance could not be interpreted as having position adjustment information associated with it. Each code was given a numerical value one to four: attacking = 1, defending = 2, bolstering = 3, integrating = 4, and other = 0.

Coders were instructed to follow a specific set of procedures in applying these position adjustment codes. First, they were trained to code only the disputants' utterances because they were the parties negotiating. Second, they were instructed to code the strategies as they were directed toward one another or to the mediator. For example, a husband might bolster his own position in response to a mediator question. Or, a wife might attack a mediator for not allowing her to tell her side of the story.

Third, consistent with the issue analysis, coders were instructed to select the most competitive positioning strategy in each utterance. For example, if an utterance contained both an attacking and a defending strategy, then it was coded as an attack. This coding rule was selected because the competitive strategies tend to limit the other's behavioral options by demanding a specific kind of response to save face. Because their constraining power is greater, their influence over the direction of the interaction is likely to be greater. As a result, the coding scheme should be biased in favor of detecting the more competitive strategies. As revealed in chapter 6, this problem occurred infrequently because the talking turns in these transcripts tend to be quite brief. Also, it is highly unlikely that a disputant would combine an attack with an integrative strategy, thereby accentuating the coding errors. Most of the upcoding occurred when disputants would respond to the other defensively and then attack with the latter part of the utterance, or they would provide a defensive comment backed up by some bolstering mechanism. Because the coding scheme will be analyzed as an ordinal scale, the differences between these coding choices should not unnecessarily influence the outcome of the analysis.

Using Guetzkow's (1950) reliability formula, the categorizing reliability for this coding procedure using two coders over five categories was .95. This reliability was considered acceptable to proceed with the data analysis.

The 20 transcripts revealed 2,965 position-adjustment strategies by the husband and 2,959 by the wife. Only 318 utterances were coded in the "other" category. Because only 5% of the data were coded in the "other" category, it appears that the coding scheme was effective in providing an estimate of the position-adjustment strategies disputants were using in the mediations.

## Data Analysis Issues

These analyses also pose some special data-analysis problems. To compensate for four problems discussed with respect to the immediacy and intensity data, these position-adjustment data were collapsed across utterances and analyzed at the subject level. Also, the data were analyzed across the same three time periods,

# CHAPTER 5 CODING PROCEDURES

and repeated-measures ANOVAs were used with time and speaker as the within-subjects factors. The position adjustment coding was the dependent variable. To assess the effects of issue type, immediacy, and language intensity, each of the variables associated with these constructs were covaried with the dependent variable.

The following are tables associated with chapter 5.

### Table 1
### Issue Type Frequencies by Outcome and Speaker

| Outcome | Speaker | Fact | Interest | Value | Relational |
|---|---|---|---|---|---|
| Agree | Husband | 549 (.37)* | 526 (.36) | 21 (.01) | 388 (.26) |
| | Wife | 574 (.38) | 539 (.36) | 50 (.03) | 355 (.23) |
| | Mediator | 398 (.32) | 778 (.62) | 5 (.003) | 80 (.06) |
| No Agreement | Husband | 372 (.36) | 177 (.17) | 39 (.04) | 433 (.42) |
| | Wife | 294 (.34) | 171 (.20) | 21 (.02) | 388 (.44) |
| | Mediator | 297 (.43) | 291 (.43) | 24 (.04) | 72 (.10) |

* raw percentages in parentheses

### Table 2*
### Issue-Type Cell Means

| | Agreement | | | No Agreement | | |
|---|---|---|---|---|---|---|
| | Time 1 | Time 2 | Time 3 | Time 1 | Time 2 | Time 3 |
| Husband | 1.86 | 1.94 | 1.90 | 1.66 | 2.64 | 2.44 |
| Wife | 1.76 | 1.86 | 1.75 | 1.61 | 2.44 | 2.31 |
| Mediator | 1.16 | 1.23 | 1.27 | 1.11 | 1.12 | .95 |

* Means are derived from a three-way, repeated-measures ANOVA with three speakers, two outcomes, and three time periods. After the appropriate effects coding, the results revealed a highly significant three-way interaction, $F(1,72) = 629.47, p < .001, \eta^2 = .75$.

## Table 3*
### Language Intensity Means by Time Across Agreement Sessions

| | Agreement Session | |
| --- | --- | --- |
| | Agreement Reached | No Agreement Reached |
| Time 1 | .89 | 1.13 |
| Time 2 | .57 | 1.26 |
| Time 3 | .48 | 1.12 |

*The overall analysis identified a significant outcome by time interaction $F(1,16) = 44.94, p < .01, \eta^2 = .07$.
Language intensity also covaried significantly with both outcome $F(1,17) = 4.97, p\ .03, \eta^2 = .07, \beta = .48$, and speaker, $F(1,35) = 7.89, p < .01, \eta^2 = .11, \beta = .49$ at Time 1.

## Table 4
### Verbal Immediacy Covariates with Issue Type

1. Spatial Immediacy: Significant interaction of issue use and speaker at Time 3, $F(1,35) = 9.15, p < .01, \eta^2 = .09, \beta = -.31$.

2. Implicit Immediacy: Significant interaction of issue use and speaker at Time 1, $F(1,35) = 2.74, p < .10, \eta^2 = .05, \beta = .34$.

Significant interaction of issue use and outcome at Time 3, $F(1,17) = 3.45, p < .08, \eta^2 = .16, \beta = .41$.

## Table 5*
### Position-Adjustment Cell Means by Time Across Agreement Sessions

| | Agreement Session | |
| --- | --- | --- |
| | Agreement Reached | No Agreement Reached |
| Time 1 | 2.11** | 2.11 |
| Time 2 | 2.20 | 1.78 |
| Time 3 | 2.29 | 1.80 |

* The three-way, repeated measures ANOVA results found a significant outcome by time interaction, $F(1,36) = 34.08, p\ \eta^2 = .23$.
** As means increase, movement toward integrative strategies increases.

## Table 6
### Verbal Immediacy Covariates with Position Adjustment Strategies

Implicit Immediacy: Significant interaction of position adjustment strategies and speaker at Time 1, $F(1,17) = 4.00$, $p < .06$, $\eta^2 = .18$, $\beta = -.43$). The means reveal that the husbands were more direct than the wives at time one (1.81 vs. 1.78) as disputants engaged in more competitive strategies.

## Table 7
### Issue Type and Position Adjustment Covariates

1. At Time 1, issue type covaried significantly with outcome, $F(1,17) = 16.06$, $p < .001$, $\eta^2 = .05$, $\beta = -.69$, with the agreement disputants discussing more interest issues ($M = 1.80$) and the no-agreement disputants discussing factual issues ($M = 1.65$).

2. At Time 2, issue type covaried significantly with speaker, $F(1,17) = 5.07$, $p < .04$, $\eta^2 = .23$, $\beta = -.48$. The husbands ($M = 2.29$) mixed in more relational issues than the wives ($M = 2.15$), as the conflict intensified.

3. At Time 3, issue type covaried with outcome $F(1,17) = 6.16$, $p < .03$, $\eta^2 = .03$, $\beta = -.51$, but does not appear to affect the significant difference in position adjustment between the agreement conditions.

# Appendix B: Coding Procedures for Chapter 6 Analyses

## MEDIATOR-INTERVENTIONS STUDY

### Coding Procedures

The unit of analysis used in this study was the uninterrupted talking turn. Each speaking turn attempted by the mediator was defined as an intervention. Each of these interventions was coded using the set of categories identified in the first part of this chapter. Coders were instructed to determine first whether the intervention was a structuring, reframing, or expanding strategy, and then they were asked to determine which of the five tactics the mediator was using. In the event that multiple tactics were identified, coders were instructed to identify the first tactic used. Multiple tactic coding was rarely a problem because nearly all interventions exhibited only one tactic. The coding procedures for the position adjustment and issue development strategies are discussed in Appendix A.

Using these procedures, the 20 transcripts revealed 2,920 mediator interventions. In the agreement condition the following strategy frequencies were observed: 660 structuring, 630 reframing, and 494 information-expanding strategies; in the no-agreement condition: 369 structuring, 415 reframing, and 352 information-expanding strategies.

The reliabilities for the coding schemes were computed using Cronbach's alpha. For the intervention coding scheme, the reliabilities for each of the three categories was .71, .71, and .69, respectively. The reliabilities for coding the disputant utterances was attack: .78, bolster: .80, and integration: .79. These estimates were calculated across six coders and 400 units (200 disputant utterances and 200 mediator interventions). We are confident that these low reliabilities did not significantly impact the quality of the coding because we continued to monitor coding throughout the study and were quite confident that reliabilities improved considerably as the study progressed.

## THE PHASE ANALYSIS

### Coding Procedures

The unit of analysis used in this study was the uninterrupted talking turn. To begin the coding, the authors identified and numbered each mediator, husband, and wife utterance in each of the 20 sessions. Each of the mediator utterances was coded using the entire set of categories listed in chapter 6. The husband and wife utterances were also coded using this category scheme. This coding reflects the extent to which the disputants discussed those topics as directed by the mediator. For example, when a husband made a comment about what kind of relationship he had with his daughter, it was coded as a background/history comment.

Coders were instructed to determine first whether the utterance topic related to the process of mediation, the background/history of the dispute, the issues/problems of the current dispute, or the proposals to resolve the current dispute. Following this judgment, they were asked to determine which of the four tactics listed here the mediator used in his or her utterance. In the event that multiple tactics and topics were identified, coders were instructed to identify the first topic and the first tactic used. Multiple coding was rarely a problem because nearly all interventions were very terse.

Using these procedures, the 20 sessions revealed the following frequencies: agree husbands: 1,785, agree wives: 1,913, agree mediators: 1,999, no-agree husbands: 1,176, no-agree wives: 1042, and no-agree mediators: 1,236. For the agreement disputants, 56% of their utterances were included in the background-information category; 15% in the orientation category; 20% were in the issues category; the remaining 9% were in the proposal development category. For the no-agreement disputants, 30% of their utterances were in the orientation category; 49% were in the background information category, 12% were in the issues category, and 9% were in the proposal category. The mediator intervention totals are displayed in the results section.

The reliabilities for each of the four main strategies using Guetzkow's (1950) procedure were .81, .83, .84, and .83, respectively. These reliabilities provide some confidence that the categories were being accurately applied to the data.

## Data-Analysis Procedures

*Number of Phases.* This chapter searches for four mediation phases. None of the mediators in the transcripts were trained to use the four phases presented in this chapter by announcing when they were moving from one phase to the next. Thus, there were no specific markers to determine when disputants progressed from one phase to another one. Perhaps the only way to solve this problem from an interaction analysis perspective is to divide the interaction into some number of equal parts and to observe the development of the interaction patterns between disputants and mediators at these various points.

The only question is, into how many parts should the interaction be divided? Poole (1981) suggested dividing the interaction into at least twice the number of hypothesized phases. For this chapter, each mediation session would be divided into eight equal parts. The rationale for this division formula is that more parts than phases makes it possible to detect deviations from an hypothesized phase structure. For example, this chapter hypothesizes a general decrease in process issues from the first to the second phase. However, process interventions might need to increase after the first phase if the mediator has not successfully addressed the process issues in the first phase. Looking at only four points instead of eight would obscure the magnitude of such an increase.

To accomplish this division, the total number of utterances in each transcript was divided into eight equal parts. The data are plotted against these eight divisions to track the disputants' behaviors and the mediators' intervention choices.

***Statistical Issues.*** Because the data reflect the same analysis challenges as described in the prior chapters, a repeated-measures multiple analysis of variance (MANOVA) is used to analyze the data. The two repeated measures will include the eight time periods and the three types of subjects. The rationale for this repeated-measures design is also contained in Appendix A.

The following are tables associated with chapter 6.

Table 1
Position-Adjustment and Issue Development Mean Scores Regarding Structuring Interventions

|  | Position Adjustment* | | | |
|---|---|---|---|---|
|  | Agreement | | No Agreement | |
|  | Prior | Subsequent | Prior | Subsequent |
| Time 1 | 2.39 | 2.57 | 2.49 | 2.66 |
| Time 2 | 2.43 | 2.52 | 2.17 | 2.17 |
| Time 3 | 2.71 | 2.77 | 2.24 | 2.22 |

|  | Issue Development** | |
|---|---|---|
|  | Prior | Subsequent |
| Time 1 | 1.31 | 1.20 |
| Time 2 | 1.88 | 1.82 |
| Time 3 | 1.64 | 1.48 |

\* These data revealed a significant three-way interaction between outcome, time, and location with respect to disputants' position adjustment strategies, $F(1,38) = 22.58$, $p < .001$, $\eta^2 = .13$.
\*\* A significant time-by-location interaction was observed regarding disputants' issue development $F(1,19) = 20.58$, $p < .001$, $\eta^2 = .11$.

Table 2
Structuring Intervention Tactics at Time 1

| Tactic | Agreement | No Agreement |
|---|---|---|
| 1. Listening marker | 67 (32%) | 45 (31%) |
| 2. Identify role/ Process of mediation | 30 (14%) | 14 (10%) |
| 3. Identify/Enforce agenda | 9 ( 4%) | 9 ( 6%) |
| 4. Terminate/Initiate discussion | 31 (15%) | 23 (16%) |
| 5. Identify/Enforce interaction rules | 74 (35%) | 53 (37%) |

## Table 3
### Structuring Intervention Tactics at Time 2

| Tactic | Agreement | No Agreement |
|---|---|---|
| 1. Listening marker | 86 (40%) | 42 (39%) |
| 2. Identify role/ Process of mediation | 28 (13%) | 23 (21%) |
| 3. Identify/Enforce agenda | 6 ( 3%) | 7 ( 6%) |
| 4. Terminate/Initiate discussion | 24 (11%) | 7 ( 6%) |
| 5. Identify/Enforce interaction rules | 69 (32%) | 30 (27%) |

## Table 4
### Structuring Intervention Tactics at Time 3

| Tactic | Agreement | No Agreement |
|---|---|---|
| 1. Listening marker | 49 (20%) | 35 (30%) |
| 2. Identify role/ Process of mediation | 33 (14%) | 8 ( 7%) |
| 3. Identify/Enforce agenda | 17 ( 7%) | 16 (14%) |
| 4. Terminate/Initiate discussion | 30 (13%) | 7 ( 6%) |
| 5. Identify/Enforce interaction | 107 (45%) | 50 (43%) |

## Table 5
### Reframing Intervention Tactics

| Tactic | Agreement | No Agreement |
|---|---|---|
| 1. Provide orientation information | 36 ( 6%) | 14 ( 3%) |
| 2. Identify/Reinforce points of agreement | 154 (24%) | 87 (21%) |
| 3. Reframe utterances as proposals | 124 (20%) | 47 (11%) |
| 4. Negatively evaluate disputant's position | 81 (13%) | 87 (21%) |
| 5. Create alternative proposals | 235 (37%) | 180 (43%) |

## Table 6
### Position Adjustment Mean Scores Regarding Requesting Interventions

| | Agreement | | No Agreement | |
|---|---|---|---|---|
| | Prior | Subsequent | Prior | Subsequent |
| Time 1 | 2.30 | 2.28 | 2.33 | 2.47 |
| Time 2 | 2.75 | 2.48 | 2.23 | 1.89 |
| Time 3 | 2.71 | 2.80 | 1.96 | 1.98 |

* A significant three-way interaction between time, outcome and location was observed for the position adjustment strategy, $F (2,32) = 5.35, p < .01, \eta^2 = .34$. For the issue development variable, the three-way interaction was also significant $F (2,32) = 3.18, p < .05, \eta^2 = .22$.

## Table 7
## Requesting Intervention Tactics

| Tactic | Time 1 | Time 2 | Time 3 |
|---|---|---|---|
| 1. Request clarification of prior utterance | 96 (24%) | 54 (26%) | 69 (29%) |
| 2. Request relational or feeling information | 26 ( 7%) | 22 (11%) | 35 (15%) |
| 3. Request clarification of a proposal or topic | 93 (23%) | 54 (26%) | 35 (15%) |
| 4. Request proposals | 168 (42%) | 63 (30%) | 76 (32%) |
| 5. Request opinion of the other's proposal | 18 ( 5%) | 15 ( 7%) | 22 ( 9%) |

# References

Allen, N. (1984). Joint custody: A long awaited solution or mere promise? *Conciliation Courts Review, 22,* 39-48.
Beer, J., & Stief, E. (1985). Mediation and feminism. *Conflict Resolution Notes, 2,* 27-28.
Bienenfeld, F. (1983). *Child custody mediation.* Los Angeles: Science and Behavior Books.
Bernard, S., Folger, S., Weingarten, H., & Zumeta, Z. (1984). The neutral mediator: Value dilemmas in divorce mediation. *Mediation Quarterly, 4,* 61-74.
Black, M., & Joffee, W. (1978). A lawyer/therapist team approach to divorce. *Conciliation Courts Review, 16,* 1-5.
Blush, G.J., & Ross, M.A. (1987). Sexual allegations in divorce: The Said Syndrome. *Conciliation Courts Review, 25,* 1-12.
Boster, F.J., & Stiff, J.B. (1984). Compliance-gaining message selection behavior. *Human Communication Research, 10,* 539-556.
Bowers, J.W. (1963). Language intensity, social introversion, and attitude change. *Speech Monographs, 30,* 345-352.
Bowers, J.W. (1964). Some correlates of language intensity. *Quarterly Journal of Speech, 50,* 415-420.
Bradac, J.C., Bowers, J.W., & Courtright, J.A. (1979). Three language variables in communication research: Intensity, immediacy, and diversity. *Human Communication Research, 5,* 257-269.
Brown, P., & Fraser, C. (1979). Speech as a marker of situation. In K.Scherer & H. Giles (Eds.), *Social markers in speech* (pp.33-62). Cambridge: Cambridge University Press.
Brown, P. & Levinson, S. (1978). Universals in language usage: Politeness phenomena. In E. Goody (Ed.), *Questions and politeness: Strategies in social interaction* (pp. 56-288). Cambridge, MA: Cambridge University Press.
Burggraf, C.S., & Sillars, A.L. (1987). A critical examination of sex differences in

marital communication. *Communication Monographs, 54,* 276–294.
Burrell, N. (1987). *Divorce mediation.* Unpublished doctoral dissertation, Department of Communication, Michigan State University, East Lansing, MI.
Carnevale, P.J.D., & Leatherwood, M.L. (1985). *Mediation and the "chilling effect" of med–arb.* Paper presented at the annual convention of the American Psychological Association, Los Angeles, CA.
Coogler, O. J. (1978). *Structured mediation in divorce settlement: A handbook for marital mediators.* Lexington, MA: Lexington Books.
Coser, L. (1956). *The functions of social conflict.* New York: The Free Press.
Courtright, J.A., Millar, F.E., & Rogers-Millar, L.E. (1979). Domineeringness and dominance: Replication and extension. *Communication Monographs, 46,* 179–192.
Deutsch, M. (1973). *The resolution of conflict.* New Haven, CT: Yale University Press.
Diez, M. E., (1983). *Negotiation competence: A conceptualization of the constitutive rules of negotiation interaction.* Paper presented at the Annual Meeting of the International Communication Association, Dallas, TX.
Dillard, J.P., & Burgoon, M. (1985). Situational influences on the selection of compliance-gaining messages: Two tests of the predictive utility of the Cody–McLaughlin typology. *Communication Monographs, 52,* 289–304.
Dillard, J.P., & Fitzpatrick, M.A. (1985). Compliance-gaining in marital interaction. *Personality and Social Psychology Bulletin, 11,* 419–433.
Donohue, W.A. (1981a). Analyzing negotiation tactics: Development of a negotiation interact system. *Human Communication Research, 7,* 273–287.
Donohue, W.A. (1981b). Development of a model of rule use in negotiation interaction. *Communication Monographs, 52,* 305–318.
Donohue, W.A., Allen, M., & Burrell, N. (1985). Mediator communicative competence. *Mediation Quarterly, 10,* 22–32.
Donohue, W.A., Allen, M., & Burrell, N. (1986). *A lag sequential analysis of mediator intervention strategies.* Paper presented to the Speech Communication Association, Chicago, IL.
Donohue, W.A., Allen, M., & Burrell, N. (1989). Models of divorce mediation. *Family and Conciliation Courts Review, 27,* 37–46.
Donohue, W.A., & Diez, M.E. (1985). Directive use in negotiation interaction. *Communication Monographs, 52,* 305–318.
Donohue, W.A., Diez, M.E., Stahle, R., & Burgoon, J. (1983). *The effects of nonverbal immediacy violations on verbal immediacy.* Unpublished manuscript, Michigan State University, East Lansing, MI.
Donohue, W.A., & Weider-Hatfield, D. (1988). Communication strategies in mediation. In J. Folberg and A. Milne (Eds.), *Divorce mediation* (pp. 297–315). New York: Guilford Press.
Donohue, W.A., Weider-Hatfield, D., Hamilton, M., & Diez, M.E. (1985). Relational distance in managing conflict. *Human Communication Research, 11,* 387–406.
Elkin, M. (1985). Defining the interprofessional boundaries between the law and the behavioral sciences in the practice of divorce mediation. *Conciliation Courts Review, 23,* v–viii.
Erickson B., Holmes J. G., Frey, R., Walker, L., & Thibaut, J. (1974). Functions of a third party in the resolution of conflict: The role of a judge in pretrial conferences. *Journal of Personality and Social Psychology, 30,* 293–306.
Felson, R.B. (1978). Aggression as impression management. *Social Psychology Quarterly, 41,* 205–213.
Felson, R.B. (1981). An interactionist approach to aggression. In J. Tedeschi (Ed.),

*Impression management theory and social psychological research* (pp. 181-199). New York: Academic Press.

Felson, R.B. (1982). Impression management and the escalation of aggression and violence. *Social Psychology Quarterly, 45*, 245-254.

Felson, R.B. (1984). Patterns of aggressive social interaction. In A. Mummendey (Ed.), *Social psychology of aggression* (pp. 107-126). Berlin: Springer-Verlag.

Felson, R.B., Ribner, S.A., & Siegel, M.S. (1985). Age and the effect of third parties during criminal violence. *Social Psychology and Research, 68*, 452-462.

Ferrick, G. (1986). Three crucial questions. *Mediation Quarterly, 13*, 61-68.

Fisher, R., & Ury, W. (1981). *Getting to yes: Negotiating agreement without giving in.* Boston: Houghton Mifflin.

Fitzpatrick, M.A. (1984). A topological approach to marital itneraction: Recent theory and research. In L. Berkowitz (Ed.), *Advances in experimental social psychology* (Vol.18, pp. 1-47). Orlando, FL: Academic Press.

Fitzpatrick, M.A. (1987). Marriage and verbal intimacy. In V. Derlegg & J. Berg (Eds.), *Self disclosure: Theory, research and therapy* (pp. 131-154). New York: Plenum.

Fitzpatrick, M.A. (1988). Marital interaction. In C. Berger, & S. Chaffee (Ed's.), *The handbook of communication science* (pp. 564-618). Beverly Hills, CA: Sage.

Fitzpatrick, M.A., & Winke, J. (1979). "You always hurt the one you love": Strategies and tactics in interpersonal conflicts. *Communciation Quarterly, 47*, 3-11.

Folberg, J., & Taylor, A. (1984). *Mediation: A comprehensive guide to resolving conflicts without litigation.* San Francisco: Jossey-Bass.

Folger, J., & Bernard, S. (1985). Divorce mediation: When mediators challenge the divorcing parties. *Mediation Quarterly, 10*, 5-24.

Folger, J., & Poole, M.S. (1984). *Working through conflict: A communication perspective.* Glenview, IL: Scott, Foresman.

Gottman, J. (1979). *Marital interaction.* New York: Academic Press.

Gottman, J. (1982). Emotional responsiveness in marital conversation. *Journal of Communication, 32*, 108-120.

Gottman, J., Markman, H. & Notarius, C. (1977). The topography of marital conflict: A sequantial analysis of verbal and nonverbal behavior. *Journal of Marriage and the Family, 39*, 461-477.

Grossman, C., & Burton, R. (1978). *The effects of father absence on imitative aggressive behavior in boys.* Paper presented at the Eastern Psychological Association, Philadelphia, PA.

Guetzkow, H. (1950). Unitizing and categorizing problems in coding qualitative data. *Journal of Clinical Psychology, 6*, 47-58.

Hamilton M., & Hunter J.F. (1985). Analyzing utterances as the observational unit. *Human Communication Research, 12*, 285-294.

Haynes, J. (1981). *Divorce mediation.* New York: Springer.

Herek, G.M., Janis, I.L., & Huth, P. (1987). Decision making during international crises: Is quality of process related to outcome? *Journal of Conflict Resolution, 31*, 203-226.

Hetherington, E.M., Cox, M., & Cox, R. (1982). Effects of divorce on parents and children. In M. Lamb (Ed.)., *Non-traditional families* (pp. 233-288). Hillsdale, NJ: Lawrence Erlbaum Associates.

Hocker, J.L., & Wilmot, W.W. (1985). *Interpersonal conflict.* Dubuque, IA: W.C. Brown.

Infante, D.A. (1987). Aggressiveness. In J. McCroskey & J. Daly (Ed's.), *Personality and interpersonal communication* (pp. 157-192). Newbury Park, CA: Sage.

Infante, D.A., Trebing, J.D., Shepherd, R.E., & Seeds, D.E. (1984). The relationship of argumentativeness to verbal aggression. *The Southern Speech Communication Journal, 50*, 67–77.

Infante, D.A., & Wigley, C.J. (1986). Verbal aggressiveness: An interpersonal model and measure. *Communication Monographs, 53*, 60–69.

Janis, I. (1989). *Crucial decisions: Leadership in policy making and crisis management.* New York: Free Press.

Johnson, B. (1985). Gender identification among fathers with custody. *Conciliation Courts Review, 23*, 75–78.

Johnson, D. W. (1971). Role reversal: A summary and review of the research. *International Journal of Group Tensions, 1*, 318–334.

Jones, T.S. (1987). *A test of the conceptual and empirical adequacy of the mediation process analysis instrument.* Paper presented to the International Conference on Conflict, George Mason University, Fairfax, VA.

Jones, T.S. (1988). An analysis of phase structures in successful and unsuccessful child-custory divorce mediation. *Communication Research, 15*, 470–495.

Jones, T.S. (1989). Lag sequential analyses of mediator-spouse and husband-wife interaction in successful and unsuccessful divorce mediation. In M. Rahim (Ed.), *Managing conflict* (pp. 93–108). New York: Praeger.

Keenan, E.O. (1978). Unplanned and planned discourse. [Pragmatics Microfiche 3.1, A3–D2]. Department of Linguistics, University of Cambridge, Cambridge, England.

Kelly, J.B. (1980). Myths and realities for children of divorce. *Educational Horizons*, 34–39.

Kelly, J.B. (1981). The visiting relationship after divorce: Research findings and clinical implications. In J. Abt and B. Stuart (Eds.), *Children of separation and divorce* (pp. 338–361). New York: Van Nostrand Reinhold.

Kelly, J.B. (in press). Longer-term adjustment in children of divorce: Converging findings and implications for practice. *Journal of Family Psychology.*

Kelly, J.B., & Wallerstein, J.S. (1977). Part-time parent, part-time child: Visiting after divorce. *Journal of Clinical Child Psychology, 6*, 51–54.

Kelly, J.B., & Wallerstein, J.S. (1979). Children of divorce: The school setting. *National Elementary Principal, 59*, 51–58.

Keltner, J.S. (1987). *Mediation: Toward a civilized system of dispute resolution.* Annandale, VA: Speech Communication Association.

Kessler, S. (1972). Counselor as mediator. *Personnel and Guidance Journal, 58*, 94–106.

Kessler, S. (1978). *Creative conflict resolution: Mediation.* Atlanta, GA: Society of Professionals.

Kiely, L.S., & Crary, D.R. (1986). Effective mediation: A communication approach to consubstantiality. *Mediation Quarterly, 12*, 37–50.

Kitson, G.C., & Raschke, H.J. (1981). Divorce research: What we know; what we need to know. *Journal of Divorce, 4*, 1–38.

Kolb, D. (1983). Strategy and the tactics of mediation. *Human Relations, 36*, 247–268.

Kressel, K. (1985). *The process of divorce.* New York: Basic Books.

Kressel, K., & Pruitt, D. (1985). Themes in the mediation of social conflict. *Journal of Social Issues, 41*, 11–26.

Krueger, D.L. (1983). Pragmatics of dyadic decision making: A sequential analysis of communication patterns. *The Western Journal of Speech, 47*, 99–117.

Krueger, D.L., & Smith, P. (1982). Decision-making patterns of couples: A sequen-

tial analysis. *Journal of Communication, 32,* 121-134.
Labov, W. (1972). *Sociolinguistic patterns.* Philadelphia: University of Pennsylvania Press.
Lederer, W.J., & Jackson, D.D. (1968). *The mirages of marriage.* New York: Norton.
Leitch, M.L. (1986). The politics of compromise: A feminist perspective on mediation. *Mediation Quarterly, 14/15,* 163-176.
Linneweber, V., Mummendy, A., Bornewasser, M., & Loschper, G. (1984). Classification of situations specific to field and behaviour: The context of aggressive interactions in schools. *European Journal of Social Psychology, 14,* 281-295.
Little, M., Thoennes, N., Pearson, J., & Appleford, R. (1985). A case study: The custody mediation services of the Los Angeles Conciliation Court. *Conciliation Courts Review, 23,* 1-14.
Littlejohn, S., & Shailor, J. (1986). *The deep structure of conflict in mediation: A case study.* Paper presented to the Speech Communication Association Convention, Chicago, IL.
Luepnitz, D.A. (1978). Children of divorce: A review of the psychological literature. *Law and Human Behavior, 2,* 167-179.
Markowitz, J.R., & Engram, P.S. (1983). Mediation in labor disputes and divorces: A comparative analysis. *Mediation quarterly, 1,* 67-78.
McGillicuddy, N.B., Welton, G.L., & Pruitt, D.G. (1987). Third-party intervention: A field experiment comparing three different models. *Journal of Personality and Social Psychology, 53,* 104-112.
McIsaac, H. (1981). Mandatory conciliation in custody/visitation matters: California's bold stroke. *Conciliation Courts Review, 19.*
McIsaac, H. (1983). Court-connected mediation. *Conciliation Courts Review, 21,* 1-16.
McIsaac, H. (1985). Confidentiality: An exploration of issues. *Conciliation Courts Review, 23,* 61-68.McIsaac, H. (1986). Toward a classification of child custody disputes: An application of family systems theory. *Mediation Quarterly, 14-15,* 39-50.
McIsaac, H. (1987). *Report of the advisory panel on the child oriented divorce act of 1987.* Special report submitted to senator Alan Robbins.
McLaughlin, M., Cody, M., & Robey, C. (1980). Situational influences on the selection of strategies to resist compliance gaining attempts. *Human Communication Research, 7,* 14-36.
Mehrabian, A. (1966a). Immediacy: An indicator of attitudes in linguistic communication. *Journal of Personality, 34,* 26-34.
Mehrabian, A. (1966b). Attitudes in relation to the forms of communicator-object relationship in spoken communication. *Journal of Personality, 34,* 80-93.
Mehrabian, A. (1967). Attitudes inferred by non-immediacy of verbal communications. *Journal of Verbal Learning and Verbal Behavior, 6,* 294-305.
Mehabrian, A. (1971). *Silent messages.* Belmont, CA: Wadsworth.
Mehrabian, A., & Wiener, M. (1966). Non-immediacy between communicator and object of communication in a verbal message: Application to the inference of attitudes. *Journal of Counseling Psychology, 30,* 420-425.
Mettetal, G., & Gottman, J.M. (1980). Reciprocity and dominance in marital interaction. In J. Vincent (Ed.), *Advances in family intervention, assessment and theory* (Vol 1, pp. 181-228). Greenwich, CT: JAI Press.
Miller, G.R., Boster, F., Roloff, M., & Siebold, D. (1977). Compliance-gaining message strategies: A typology and some findings concerning effects of situational differences. *Communication Monographs, 44,* 37-51.

Moore, C.W. (1986). *The mediation process*. San Francisco: Jossey-Bass.
Moore, C.W. (1987). The caucus: Private meetings that promote settlement. *Mediation Quarterly, 16*, 87–101.
Mummendey, A., Linneweber, V. & Loschper, G. (1984). Actor or victim of aggression: Divergent perspectives-divergent evaluations. *European Journal of Social Psychology, 14*, 297–311.
Noller, P. (1988). Overview and implications. In P. Noller & M.A. Fitzpatrick (Eds.), *Perspectives on marital interaction* (pp. 323–344). Clevedon: Multilingual Matters LTD.
Notarius, C.I., & Johnson, J.S. (1982). Emotional expression in husbands and wives. *Journal of Marriage and the Family, 44*, 483–489.
Osgood, C.E. (1962). *An alternative to war or surrender*. Urbana, IL: University of Illinois Press.
Payne, J.D. (1986). Future prospects for family conflict resolution in Canada. *Conciliation Courts Review, 24*, 51–70.
Pearson, J., Ring, M., Milne, A. (1983). A portrait of divorce mediation services in the public and private sector. *Conciliation Courts Review, 21*, 1–24.
Pearson, J., & Thoennes, N. (1985). The preliminary portrait of client reactions to three court mediation programs. *Conciliation Courts Review, 23*, 1–15.
Pesikoff, R.B., & Pesikoff, B.S. (1985). Child custody in the 80s: The effects of divorce on childhood and teenagers and the concept of joint custody. *Conciliation Courts Review, 23*, 53–55.
Poole, M.S. (1981). Decision development in small groups I: A comparison of two models. *Communication Monographs, 48*, 1–20.
Pruitt, D.G. (1981). *Negotiation behavior*. New York: Academic Press.
Pruitt, D.G., & Rubin, J.Z. (1986). *Social conflict: Escalation, stalemate and settlement*. New York: Random House.
Pruitt, D.G., Welton, G.L., Fry, W.R., McGillicuddy, N.B., Castrianno, L., Zubek, J.M., & Ippolito, C. (1987). *The process of mediation: Caucusing, control and problem solving*. Paper presented to the first conference of the International Association for Conflict Management, Fairfax, VA.
Putnam, L.L., & Jones, T.S. (1982) Reciprocity in negotiations: An analysis of bargaining interaction, *Communication Monographs. 49*, 171–191.
Putnam, L.L. & Poole, M.S. (1987). Conflict and negotiation. In F. Jablin, L. Putnam, K. Roberts, & L. Porter (Eds.), *Handbook of organizational communication: An interdisciplinary perspective* (pp. 549–599). Newbury Park, CA: Sage.
Raush, H., Barry, R., Hertel, R., & Swain, M. (1974). *Communication, conflict and marriage*. San Francisco: Jossey-Bass.
Ricci, I. (1980). *Mom's house, dad's house*. New York: Collier Books.
Roloff, M. (1987). Communication and conflict. In C. Berger & S. Chaffee (Eds.), *Handbook of communication science* (pp. 484–534). Beverly Hills, CA: Sage.
Roth, W.T. (1982). The meaning of stress. In F. Ochberg & D. Soskis (Eds.), *Victims of terrorism* (pp. 37–58). Boulder, CO: Westview.
Rubin, J.Z. (1981). *Dynamics of third party intervention*. New York: Praeger.
Saposnek, D. (1983). Strategies in child custody mediation: A family systems approach. *Mediation Quarterly, 2*, 29–54.
Saposnek, D.T., Hamburg, J., Delano, C.D., & Michaelsen, H. (1984). How has mandatory mediation fared?: Research findings of the first year's follow-up. *Conciliation Courts Review, 22*, 7–20.
Schenkein, J. (1978). *Studies in the organization of conversational interaction*. New York: Academic Press.

Shaw, M.L., & Phear, W.P. (1987). New perspectives on the options generation process. *Mediation Quarterly, 16,* 65–74.

Sillars, A.L. (1980). *Communication and attributions in interpersonal conflict.* Unpublished doctoral dissertation, University of Wisconsin, Madison, WI.

Sillars, A.L., Pike, G.R., Jones, T.S., & Murphy, M.A. (1984). Communication and understanding in marriage. *Human Communication Research, 10,* 317–350.

Sillars, A.L., Weisberg, J., Burggraf, C.S., & Wilson, E.A. (1987). Content themes in marital conversations. *Human Communication Research, 13,* 495–528.

Simkin, W. (1971). *Mediation and the dynamics of collective bargaining.* Washington, DC: Bureau of National Affairs.

Snyder, G.H., & Diesing, P. (1977). *Conflict among nations: Bargaining, decision making and system structure international crises.* Princeton, NJ: Princeton University Press.

Staffeld, W. (1987). *Mediation vs. conciliation: A model for Michigan's circuit courts.* Unpublished manuscript.

Stahl, P.M. (1986). Attitudes and beliefs about joint custody: Findings of a study. *Conciliation Courts Review, 24,* 41–46.

Strouse, J.S. & McPhee, J.T. (1985). Joint custody in Michigan: A survey of the Friends of the Court. *Conciliation Courts Review, 23,* 47–52.

Susskind, L., & Cruikshank, J. (1987). *Breaking the impasse.* New York: Basic Books.

Thoennes, N., & Pearson, J. (1985). Predicting outcomes in divorce mediation: The invluence of people and process. *Journal of Social Issues, 41,* 115–126.

Ting-Toomey, S. (1982). *Coding conversation between intimates: A validation study of intimate negotiation coding system (INCS).* Paper presented at the annual convention of the Eastern Communication Association, Hartford, CT.

Wallerstein, J.S. (1986). Psychodynamic perspectives on family mediation. *Mediation Quarterly. 14–15,* 7–21.

Wallerstein, J.S., & Kelly, J. (1980). *Surviving the breakup: How children and parents cope with divorce.* New York: Basic Boods.

Walton, R.E. (1969). *Interpersonal peacemaking: Confrontations and third-party consultation.* Reading, MA: Addison-Wesley.

Walton, R., & McKersie, R. (1965). *A behavioral theory of labor negotiations.* New York: McGraw-Hill.

Watzlawick, P., Beavin, J.H., & D.D. Jackson (1967). *Pragmatics of human communication.* New York: Norton.

Weaver, J. (1986). Therapeutic implications of divorce mediation. *Mediation quarterly, 12,* 75–90.

Wehr, P. (1979). *Conflict regulation.* Boulder, CO: Westview Press.

Weiner, M., & Mehrabian, A. (1968). *Language within language: Immediacy, a channel in verbal communication.* New York: Appleton-Century-Crofts.

Weitzman, L.J. (1985). *The divorce revolution.* New York: The Free Press.

Welton, G.L., & Pruitt, D.G. (1987) The mediation process: The effects of mediator bias and disputant power. *Personality and Social Psychology Bulletin, 13,* 123–133.

Williamson, R.N., & Fitzpatrick, M.A. (1985). Two approaches to marital interaction: Relational control patterns in marital types. *Communication Monographs, 52,* 236–252.

Wilson, S.R. & Putnam, L.L. (1990). Interaction goals in negotiation. In J. Anderson (Ed.), *Communication yearbook 13* (pp. 374–406). Newbury Park, CA: Sage.

Witteman, H., & Fitzpatrick, M.A. (1986). Compliance-gaining in marital interaction: Power bases, power processes, and outcomes. *Communication Monographs, 53*, 130–143.

Yelsma, P. (1981). Conflict predispositions: Differences between happy and clinical couples. *The American Journal of Family Therapy, 9*, 57–63.

Zappa, J., Manusov, V., Cody, M.J., & Donohue, W.A. (1990). *The communication and evaluation of accounts during child custody mediations.* Paper presented to the Eastern States Communication Association Convention, Philadelphia, PA.

# Author Index

**A**

Allen, M., 16, 22
Allen, M., 114
Allen, W., 35, 36
Appleford, R., 7

**B**

Barry, R., 52
Beavin, J.H., 70
Beer, J., 31
Bernard, S., 6, 21
Bienenfeld, F., 144, 145
Black, M., 144, 145
Blush, G.J., 38
Boster, F.J., 78
Bowers, J.W., 121, 122, 212
Bradac, J.C., 122
Bradac, J.L., 212
Brown, P., 70, 73, 74
Burggrat, C.S., 51, 52, 53, 54
Burgoon, J., 120
Burgoon, M., 79, 80
Burrell, N., 16, 22, 102, 103, 114
Burton, R., 15

**C**

Carnevale, P.J.D., 17, 18
Castrianno, L., 46, 47
Cody, M.J., 78, 128, 139
Coogler, O.J., 5
Coser, L., 110
Courtright, J.A., 89, 122, 212
Cox, M., 14
Cox, R., 14
Crary, D.R., 20
Cruikshank, J., 4

**D**

Delano, C. D., 11
Deutsch, M., 26
Diesing, P., 168, 169, 170, 172, 173
Diez, M.E., 72, 81, 82, 84, 119, 120, 146
Dillard, J.P., 56, 79, 80
Donohue, W.A., 16, 22, 84, 86, 112, 114, 119, 120, 128, 139, 146

# AUTHOR INDEX

**E**

Elkin, M., 34
Engram, P.S., 46
Erickson, B., 47

**F**

Felson, R.B., 57, 58, 59, 178
Ferrick, G., 21
Fisher, R., 143
Fitzpatrick, M.A., 13, 51, 53, 54, 55, 56, 78
Folberg, J., 2, 3, 5, 34, 38, 40, 44, 45, 47, 143, 144
Folger, J., 6, 21, 173
Folger, S., 21
Fraser, C., 73, 74
Frey, R., 41
Fry, W.R., 46, 47

**G**

Giles, H., 70
Gottman, J., 13, 48, 49, 50, 53, 71
Grossman, L., 15
Guetzkow, H., 100, 212, 216, 218, 224

**H**

Hamburg, J., 11
Hamilton, M., 119, 214
Haynes, J., 5, 143, 144
Herek, G.M., 171, 174
Hertel, R., 52
Hetherington, E.M., 14
Hocker, J.L., 90, 137
Holmes, J.G., 47
Hunter, J.F., 214
Huth, P., 171, 174

**I**

Infante, D.A., 60, 61
Ippolito, C., 46, 47

**J**

Jackson, D.D., 12, 70
Janis, I.L., 169, 171, 174

Joffee, W., 144, 145
Johnson, B., 30
Johnson, D.W., 44
Johnson, J.S., 50
Jones, T.S., 21, 22, 51, 53, 62, 63, 65, 66, 112, 140,

**K**

Keenan, E.O., 73
Kelly, J. B., 5, 14
Keltner, J.S., 1, 3, 10
Kessler, S., 40, 45, 109, 143
Kiely, L.S., 20
Kitson, G.L., 14
Kolb, D., 43, 47, 81, 82
Kressel, K., 2, 3, 5, 11, 26, 27, 29, 30, 31
Krueger, D.L., 52, 53

**L**

Labov, W., 73
Leatherwood, M.L., 17, 18
Lederer, W.J., 12
Leitch, M.L., 30
Levinson, S., 70
Linneweber, V., 59
Little, M., 7
Littlejohn, S., 39
Loschper, G., 59
Luepnitz, D.A., 12, 14, 15

**M**

Manusov, V., 128, 139
Markman, H., 49
Markowitz, J.R., 46
McGillicuddy, N.B., 4, 17, 46, 47
McIsaac, H., 11, 12, 15, 16, 18, 19, 24, 25, 26, 27, 94, 173
McKersie, R., 112
McLaughlin, M., 78
McPhee, J.T., 36
Mehrabian, A., 72, 118
Mettetal, G., 49, 50
Michaelsen, H., 11
Miller, F.E., 89

Miller, G.R., 78
Milne, A., 5, 16
Moore, C.W., 3, 40, 41, 42, 43, 44, 45, 46, 47, 80
Mummendy, A., 59
Murphy, M.A., 51, 53

**N**

Noller, P., 50, 51
Notarius, C.I., 49, 50

**O**

Osgood, C.E., 45

**P**

Payne, J.D., 7
Pearson, J., 5, 7, 8, 10, 11, 16, 35, 94, 95, 96, 138, 141
Pesikoff, B.S., 37
Pesikoff, R.B., 37
Phear, 47
Pike, G.R., 51, 53
Poole, M.S., 112, 113, 169, 173, 224
Pruitt, D., 2, 4, 17, 18, 46, 47, 113, 138, 139, 143, 170, 179
Putnam, L.L., 112, 113, 169

**R**

Raschke, H.J., 13, 14
Raush, H., 52
Ribner, S.A., 58
Ricci, I., 40
Ring, M., 5, 16
Robey, C., 78
Rogers-Millar, L.E., 89
Roloff, M., 43, 78
Ross, M.A., 38
Roth, W.T., 172
Rubin, J.Z., 17, 46, 47

**S**

Saposnek, D., 44, 45, 47, 137, 144
Schenkein, J., 98

Scherer, K.R., 70
Seeds, D.E., 60
Shailor, J., 39
Shaw, 47
Shepherd, R.E., 60
Siebold, D., 78
Sieyel, M.S., 58
Sillars, A.L., 51, 52, 53, 54
Simkin, W., 43
Smith, P., 52
Snyder, G.H., 168, 169, 170, 172, 173
Stable, R., 120
Staffield, W., 9
Stahl, P.M., 9
Stief, E., 31
Stiff, J.B., 78
Strouse, J.S., 36
Suposnek, D., 5, 11
Susskind, L., 4
Swain, N., 52

**T**

Taylor, A., 2, 3, 5, 34, 38, 40, 44, 45, 47, 143, 144
Thibaut, J., 47
Thoennes, N., 2, 8, 10, 11, 35, 94, 95, 96, 138, 141
Ting-Toomey, S., 52
Trebing, J.D., 60

**U**

Ury, W., 143

**W**

Walker, L., 47
Wallerstein, J.S., 5, 14
Walton, R.E., 44, 45, 69, 90, 112
Waltzlawick, P., 70
Weaver, J., 20
Wehr, P., 45, 110
Weider-Hatfield, D., 8, 119
Weiner, M., 72, 118
Weingarten, H., 21
Weisberg, J., 52, 53, 54

Weitzman, L.J., 15, 30
Welton, G.L., 4, 17, 18, 46, 47
Wigley, C.J., 61
Williamson, R.N., 56
Wilmot, W.W., 90, 137
Wilson, E.A., 52, 53, 54
Wilson, S.R., 112
Winke, J., 78
Witteman, H., 55, 56

**Y**

Yelsma, P., 52

**Z**

Zappa, J., 128, 139
Zubek, J.M., 46, 47
Zumenta, Z., 21

# Subject Index

**A**

Attorneys
  role in mediation, 27–30

**C**

Cacusing, 4, 102
Child custody
  criteria for determining, 36–38
  types, 35–36
Conflict interaction, 166–167
Crisis bargaining
  in divorce mediation, 175–182
  principles, 168–174

**D**

Disputants
  communication patterns
    content patterns, 75–76, 109
    issue development, 123, 215–217
    issues discussed in transcripts, 109–111
    relationship development, 70–75, 117

    research overview, 69–70
    strategic patterns 76–81, 217–219
  factors influencing, 24–27
  psychological orientations, 39–42
Divorce
  causes, 13
  criteria for successful settlement, 30–31
  levels, 12–13
  nature, 11–12

**G**

Goals, 112

**I**

Interaction management
  crisis bargaining context, 179–182
  definition, 68
  research results, 163–166

**L**

Language intensity
  coding procedures, 212–213

# SUBJECT INDEX 241

data analysis issues, 213–215
functions, 122–123
markers, 121, 129–130, 131–132
Los Angeles Conciliation Court
  mediator orientations, 95–97
  overview, 93–95

## M

Marital interaction
  research overview, 53
  communication patterns, 53–55
  compliance gaining, 55–57
Mediation
  communication research overview,
    61–63
  community, 4
  definition, 1
  divorce
    overview, 4
    features, 7–10
    effectiveness, 10–11, 161–163
  labor, 3
  phases of divorce mediation,
    140–145, 153–159, 223–225
  type of issues, 33–35, 126–127
Mediators
  intervention skills
    coding procedures, 222–223
    evaluating, 146
    framing, 146–147, 150–151
    issue management, 111–112
    listening, 145–146
    requesting, 146, 151–152
    timing, 139–140
    to manage parties' relationships,
      87–91
    to promote issue coherence,
      82–84, 138–139
    to structure process, 84–87, 137,
      148–150
  models, 17–24
  neutrality, 3
  relational messages communicated,
    129–130
  role in mediation, 16–17
  strategies
    professional, 43–48

## P

Position adjustment strategies
  attacking, 114–115
  defending, 115–116
  integrating, 116–117
  issue development, 123–124
  types used in transcripts, 127–129

## T

Transcript features, 97–103

## V

Verbal aggression
  interaction patterns, 57–60
  psychological predispositions, 60–61
Verbal immediacy
  coding procedures, 211–212
  data analysis issues, 213–215
  definition, 118
  functions, 119
  types, 118–119, 129, 131